Failure to Hold

Failure to Hold

The Politics of School Violence

Julie A. Webber

ROWMAN & LITTLEFIELD PUBLISHERS, INC.
Lanham • Boulder • New York • Oxford

ROWMAN & LITTLEFIELD PUBLISHERS, INC.

Published in the United States of America
by Rowman & Littlefield Publishers, Inc.
A Member of the Rowman & Littlefield Publishing Group
4720 Boston Way, Lanham, Maryland 20706
www.rowmanlittlefield.com

PO Box 317
Oxford OX2 9RU, UK

British Library Cataloguing in Publication Information Available

Library of Congress Cataloging-in-Publication Data

Webber, Julie A., 1972–
  Failure to hold : the politics of school violence / Julie A. Webber.
    p. cm.
  Includes bibliographical references and index.
  ISBN 0-7425-1983-X (cloth : alk. paper) — ISBN 0-7425-1984-8 (pbk. : alk. paper)
    1. School violence—Social aspects—United States. 2. School shootings—Social
  aspects—United States. 3. Youth and violence—United States. I. Title.
  LB3013.3 .W43 2003
  371.7'82—dc21

                                                                    2002010603

Printed in the United States of America

♾™ The paper used in this publication meets the minimum requirements of American
National Standard for Information Sciences—Permanence of Paper for Printed Library
Materials, ANSI/NISO Z39.48-1992.

This book is for my parents.
It is also for Katie, for surviving adolescence with me.

Don't bother trying to understand. Don't lose any sleep over it.

—Charlie Decker while "getting it on" in Richard Bachman's (a.k.a. Stephen King) 1971 school shooting classic, "Rage"

Contents

Acknowledgments

I am pleased to acknowledge the intellectual mentoring and companionship of both Michael A. Weinstein and Diane S. Rubenstein. Michael encouraged me to take the "theory odyssey," as he calls it, and I am proud to say it was (and is) a worthwhile trip, filled with many important experiences that I am sure will inform my life and work in the years to come. Michael has also shown me the importance of knowing how to write and think as an autonomous scholar, a gift that he freely and joyfully bestowed on me. Diane has been a source of intellectual inspiration throughout the writing of this book. Her support carried it through some rough spots and I am forever grateful for her phone call to Detroit in the spring of 1998, which helped to turn unformulated inspirations into a coherent thesis worthy of defense, as well as this book. She has taught me many things—more than I can acknowledge here—about the importance of enjoying life (and work) through her example. She is a true scholar and friend.

I also wish to thank William M. Reynolds for introducing me to the educational field. Over the years, Bill has also taken a keen interest in my work and career aspirations by directing me to conferences, introducing me to scholars, and helping me navigate the literature of curriculum studies. Bill has been a friend and a mentor and I am grateful for his encouragement and support, as well as his movie reviews, throughout the last few years.

I would like to thank Robert F. Melson, Rosalee Clawson, Cynthia Weber, Nicholas Burburles, and Gert J. J. Biesta for their supportive and helpful comments.

This book has had a lot of support from members of my graduate cohort at Purdue University. Especially important has been my friendship and conversation with Deems D. Morrione. Deems is a great friend and his commentary on this work has been invaluable. Our projects are so similar that I hope they point to our collaboration at some point in the future on another project of like content. Also at Purdue University, Lars K. Hallstrom, Martyn DeBruyn, Viviana Abreu-Hernandez, Nic Guehlstorf, Tim Seul, Andaluna Borcila, Elizabeth Frombgen, and Timothy Yetman were supportive and mulled over ideas, and when not reading chapters, they gave me ideas and helped me work through the project.

I am grateful to Stephen Eric Bronner and Manfred B. Steger who carefully read and commented on the manuscript. Several of my colleagues at Illinois State read the manuscript and gave me critical feedback. Among them are: Jamal Nassar, Austin Lane Crothers, and Janie Leatherman. I am especially indebted to Janie for suggesting important revisions that I could have never seen. Finally, Tania Pantoja read the draft through the critical eyes of a public school teacher, and I am grateful for her help. I also wish to thank my graduate assistants Dana Grawey and Maher Bages, both of whom helped me a great deal while getting the book to print.

Thanks, as well, to Gretchen Hanisch and Dean Birkenkamp at Rowman & Littlefield for their support in bringing this book to completion.

I also thank my parents, Tom and Jenny Webber, for their gracious support and love over the course of my life.

Introduction

Fantasy, Compliance, and Rage in a Postauthority World

> Power is established on death's borders.
>
> —Jean Baudrillard, *Symbolic Exchange and Death*[1]

"Columbine." So many inexplicable ideas and emotions are trapped in that word. This book does not explain Columbine, the event, but traces a series of shootings that led to that media event on April 20, 1999. By looking at West Paducah, Jonesboro, and Springfield, we can see the impact of and the specific way in which a single detached motive threads these events together, leading to the disaster in Littleton, Colorado. Following Columbine, the series continues albeit never attaining the public momentum or traumatic impact of that afternoon in Littleton. On the Canadian-U.S. border, in Taber, Alberta, Canada, just one week later, a high school dropout opens fire on demilitarized Canadian students. Violence, as a bodily form of communication, is infectious. One month later, on May 20, 1999, a student opens fire in the lunchroom at a school in Conyers, Georgia; amazingly, there are no fatalities. The gun is now pointing downward; the motive is the same but the intent has changed. Homicide is not the ultimate aim of all school shooters. We skip to 2001, where Santee and El Cajon, California, mark the latest episodes in the series. One shooter aiming from the bathroom into the hallway, the other walking confidently through the hallway shooting along the way.

Avoiding the typical urban myth that students will express anger at a hated authority figure, like a principal or teacher, student shooters aim for their peers. What ties the events together is their random nature: Students are not targeted as individuals, but as students. As one student interviewed for *20/20* is claimed to have remarked, the student "forgot what he was doing and hit a teacher."[2]

The motive is public—meaning free and open to anyone who wishes to use it—and is detached from intent. It is expressly linked to the body and practice, to "doing." Helen Morrison perhaps best captures the cause of this phenomenon when she notes that our society does not so much help kids to form a conscience as abuse it. This insight has several pedagogical assumptions buried in it. First, it intimates that kids, no matter what age, have developed some form of conscience, no matter how weak or contradictory it may appear to outsiders. A conscience is the repository of one's life experiences and the conclusions drawn from them that will serve to animate future practice and interaction with others. The history of this conscience and all the events contained in it are not immediately accessible to anyone, and adults are no exception to this existential rule. That we are all dependent, in some way—on others or ideals—is a mark of experience that does not discriminate between the adult and the child. It is only the object, fantasy, or person of choice that varies by level of maturity. Second, this implies that we cannot always choose our experiences; some will have to be tolerated, examined, and scrutinized as to their value in life. In an increasingly "mediated" environment, by which I mean that the media and technology come to script and mold our experience for us, as does the increased efficiency of public policy through technologies of surveillance and control, we have little control over how the media may abuse our conscience by filling it with images and ideas that often have nothing to do with us as psychological individuals, but only as a viewer making up part of a mass society. In democracies, the political organization of power and control is such that we have to be dependent on one another and learn to tolerate one another as best we can, whether we like it or not. Students in public schools are protocitizens. In public educational institutions and in the large public culture in democracies they are "learning" and there is so much wrapped up in that word left unattended to by this society.[3]

The reader looking for a simple answer will find only a meditation on citizenship as it relates to educational experience in the wake of traumatic events in public schools in the following pages. Taking as my object of reflection the most publicized school shootings that have taken place between 1997–1999, I examine them with a view to understanding the dynamics of sociopsychological conflict in schools, especially in their extracurricular spaces. Theoretical interventions into the culture of conflict in public schools are lacking.[4] Moreover, the research that has been completed contributes to an unacknowledged policy of containment in schools, where social interaction between students is bracketed by the security measures placed there to protect students from further acts of school violence.

My argument is that containment of school "violence," a broad-reaching term for "conflict," is detrimental to students' development of the necessary skills that will enable them to function in a democratic society.

I also argue that this containment intensifies the most negative effects of the hidden curriculum of schooling. Michael W. Apple describes the hidden curriculum this way,

> The hidden curriculum of schools serves to reinforce basic rules surrounding the nature of conflict and its uses. It posits a network of assumptions that, when internalized by students, establishes the boundaries of legitimacy. This process is accomplished not so much by explicit instances showing the negative value of conflict, but by nearly the total absences showing the importance of conflict in subject areas. The fact is that these assumptions are obligatory for students, since at no time are the assumptions articulated or questioned.[5]

Thus, from the formal curriculum students learn that conflict or disagreement over the subject matter in class is invalid and, needing to express the disagreement they experience, they channel this frustration into the spaces where the teacher is no longer in control: the hallways, the cafeteria, or the library. These same contradictions operate in society, not just in the formal curriculum. They are acute for adolescents who are in a transitional space in their lives: on the brink between adulthood and childhood, wanting freedom but getting desperately mixed messages about how to attain it or act it out. These are spaces (both in school and in society) that research has rightly concluded have a lack of formal ownership. The dearth of freedom or control that students experience in school has spread to these spaces as administrators and policymakers react to the trauma of a few random and highly publicized school shootings.

In this response, one finds the tyranny of the outlier, holding democratic schooling hostage to the fear and misinformation of an alarmed public. The hidden curriculum of the school is detected in the sociopsychological dynamics that operate in order to validate the unwritten school policies that favor certain students over others, limit student freedom, and hinder positive social interaction. These policies contribute to the alienation of students from each other and the larger society surrounding the school environment, creating an environment that shapes students' orientations to community building in negative ways. These policies also highlight the differences between students, faculty, and the surrounding society, making citizenship formation a difficult task for educators.

The hidden curriculum is an abstract term that describes the real conditions of acting and thinking in consumerist culture and democratic society. One thing that students do have to hold onto is "things" and practices that stand in for relations between people (a mode of interaction that goes deeper, emotionally, than interpersonal communication, which is always incomplete and flawed). Marxism termed this replacement of social relations with things and abstract relations "commodity fetishism," which is the process where accumulation (of "stuff," "ideas," and compulsive behaviors) comes to make up for our lack of a true and meaningful form of relating to other humans.

Slavoj Zizek's discussion of fetishism is instructive if the reader is to understand my use of the term "hidden curriculum" throughout the book. If my interpretation is plausible, the concept of hidden curriculum tries to capture Karl Marx's depiction of commodity fetishism at the school, where the curriculum (broadly speaking) is what represents relations between students; rather than them forging their own relationships with each other, the curriculum mediates their relations for them.

Why does it do this? Schools are reproductive institutions; that is, they reproduce the dominant relations of production in a given society (of goods and services) and arbitrate the concerns of the state's citizenry. Students are poor, rich, middle class, of color, white, gay, and so on. They also have personalities and characters developed at home and in the larger society in which they live. At school, they learn to mediate their subjectivities. They learn to manage their personalities and identities in more or less meaningful ways. In short, they learn how to see themselves as part of a larger whole and their place within it. I have neither the space nor the time to outline the varieties of experience with which students in any given school in the United States at 10 o'clock on a Tuesday morning might enact this very important event of identity formation, but it is crucial that they are able to do this and that they are provided with a meaningful and relevant curriculum, along with the time to converse and interact with one another.

At present, schools' objectives (educational, instructional, social, or otherwise) are dictated by the demands of unrestrained consumerist culture. This is not a myth, and the problem this poses for educators and students is a sad fact. When students are required to study a certain curricular content in order to pass an examination, and that examination and the process of preparing for it mean cutting time for social interaction, classroom commentary, and dialogue, and do not respond to the reality of the students' lives, it is not only pointless, but harmful. This argument comes thirty years after Ivan Illich, who argued that we need to deschool society (he was right). But my argument in this book points to the specific ways in which the hidden curriculum— the unwritten message transmitted in what is not said to students, in the contradictions of school policies, in the aleatory nature of discipline and lack of a uniform code of conduct that rests on purposeful action, in saying one thing then doing quite the opposite and in the lack of realization on the part of an entire society as to what constitutes humane treatment or personalized attention within a mass setting—is harmful. We need to be facilitating students to develop what John Dewey calls practical experience, which is quite the opposite of the formal knowledge required to pass an objective examination. Practical experience developed throughout the entire life of the human being is important because it teaches students how to deal with disappointment, difference of opinion, and human emotion.

The schools, by contrast, reproduce bureaucratic and disciplinary norms. They teach students that getting a job (and doing whatever you have to do to get one) is the only purpose of education. That might be appropriate if we witnessed the rest of the society following a moral code of civility or even reasoned conduct, but instead we see insider trading rewarded with shortened penalties while poverty statistics both within this country and without are reported as collateral damage on television.

In his book *Blowback*, political scientist Chalmers Johnson rehearses all the potential unintended consequences that the United States will face because of exploitative military presence and actions in Asia during the Cold War and in its aftermath. I might read this book as an analysis of domestic blowback with the hidden curriculum representing the unintended consequences of heightened competitiveness, consumerism, and militarization as it reproduces itself and its own rationale in schools.

In a democratic society, leaders have to justify the use of force. One way to avoid having to rationalize imperialist behavior is to mobilize the population by inciting it into a violent and competitive disposition. As if war were inevitable, as if someone like a fellow citizen causes harm, or as if someone undeserving or unqualified might get the job or college degree at the expense of someone else. In short, as if there were no alternative to this zero-sum view, and as if there is no other way to deal with it, save for intense competitive behavior.[6] We witness this behavior in schools in the form of "cliques" that became an object of scrutiny following the Columbine disaster. They represent this herd mentality at the level of the school and how students ban(d) together out of a perceived need for personal security at school.

Another example may get at the heart of what this book demonstrates. Children often mimic adult speech, and many adults are embarrassed after their child says something inappropriate or rude in front of strangers or, while playing with other children, rehearses the fight they had with each other the night before. At this point, the secret is out: Adults are not perfectly responsible or mature in their behavior either. Americans should feel the same shame over school violence, but we do not—en masse—because we cannot face the consequences or accept the responsibility for changing our culture. We might actually have to give up our "stuff" (excessive consumerism) and share, be more consistent, and feel compassion and empathy for others rather than secret joy at their misery; we might actually have to imagine discipline in a new way, as something other than punishment, humiliation, or indifference combined with bribery.[7]

Obviously, there are students who experience the hidden curriculum in much more harsh fashion and yet do not attempt to blow up the school or randomly shoot other students. In chapter 6, I discuss the concept of "relative deprivation" as a way of understanding this distinction in behavior among students. Students who react violently toward the school experience the hidden curriculum to the point of saturation. What they are expected to bear and what they are used to bearing do not match up; they are pushed to the brink. Some students who get there commit suicide; they do not think they have the right to take others with them, and they do not identify with the power brokers of this culture who successfully have their way despite law, opinion, and evidence to the contrary. Some students are already so deprived by American society that they really do not expect much from school and they are, unfortunately, never disappointed. Some are complimentary to the hidden curriculum (they supplement it) because they are told by the hidden curriculum that they are not real contenders (they are also the subjects of many studies that reveal how little they are called on in class or supported academically, especially in math and science) so they tend not to identify with it as well and are no threat to schools.[8] The ones that do reach saturation do not live up to the demands of the hidden curriculum. They experience total deprivation and lack in relation to its ideals while they are being told to act up lest they be "less a man" (man equals power broker in competitive society).

FANTASY

Students may, however, take revenge in fantasy. The objects that aid them in sublimating their revenge are termed "secondary gains," a term I have borrowed from D. W. Winnicott. Secondary gains allow students to sublimate the desire for revenge (against their parents, the school, and the society). The secondary gains are specific objects that supply fantasies through which the student can "play" (Winnicott's term) safely with reality, especially a traumatic one. Examples of these secondary gains might include films, novels, the Internet, personal journals, television situational comedies, comedy itself (our school violence perpetrators are especially keen on *South Park,* but so are people of all ages and generations), fetishes like gun collecting, sports, hobbies such as modeling, and so on.

Many social psychologists are interested in promoting role "modeling" as a way of therapeutically mediating alienated young men back into the productive, civil fold of society. This theory has been deployed in the media on several different registers (from enhanced paternal responsibility schemes to heroes in the media and popular culture), but it fails to take into consideration that one of the reasons why this violence happens is because of the failure of modeling and its identificatory specificity. Youth cannot identify with role models because of the real contradiction between the ones in their everyday lives and the ones in fantasy. The ones in their everyday lives are a product of American culture with its need to make life more efficient, to take practical experience out of the equation in parenting and social life generally. The ones in fantasy (read: popular culture) are much more satisfying because they never die and they always appear consistent, no matter what their beliefs. These role models are not the only ones that capture our collective democratic consumerist attention though, as even objects and technology supply the much needed other to believe in our place, to believe for us.

Zizek acutely analyzes the postmodern fascination with letting technology (a broad term used here to signify tools for making life more efficient, for cutting out the time and, unfortunately, quality of experience and sensation in contemporary life) believe or perform functions in our place. Throughout his work, Zizek refers to the "Big Other." I am particularly interested in his reading of the Big Other in *The Plague of Fantasies,* where he reads the importance of the Big Other in fantasy through his concept of "interpassivity."[9] Briefly stated, interpassivity is when we gradually allow others and objects to do things in our place because we no longer have the time or the inclination to make the time to experience them for ourselves. Zizek's example is of the VCR that tapes films or television programs for us while we do other things, like work. The other aspect to this "having another do in our place" is that we collect more information (films, books, articles, and so on) than we can possibly ever find the time to view much less absorb. He writes, "The paradox of interpassivity, of believing or enjoying through the other, also opens up a new approach to aggressivity: aggressivity is provoked in a subject when the other subject, through which the first subject believed or enjoyed, does something that disturbs the functioning of this transference."[10]

This new approach to aggressivity is applied to school shootings in this book. We find students "triggered" into aggressivity when the technology that they have used to "believe" for them lets them down. Technology is broadly conceived as any tool (it could be a relation to another person that is mediated by a particular conception of friendship as in instrumentalization, a video game, a hero or role model, gun collecting, or Internet surfing). These objects believe in our place, and it is more comforting to know that others believe than it is to imagine what it might take to maintain our own beliefs while living amid nihilism.

To understand how this works, we need to understand three concepts: knowing, doing, and believing. Knowing is our cognitive relation to the world. People know that smoking causes lung cancer, but they believe that it cannot happen to them as long as they see smokers in the world who are not dying of lung cancer. This allows them to continue smoking. They *know* better, but they *keep doing* it.

For, as Zizek writes over and over again in his work, "they know very well, but all the same" (*Je sais bien, mais quand meme*). They (students) "know" that this society is contradictory (for a recent example, see Enron's fallout and the shuffling of blame) but they believe otherwise (fantasy, or in literal examples, especially those indicated by Winnicott's work with children, hope), and, while "held," they do in accordance with belief, not knowledge. As long as the fantasy holds them, they will continue to do in line with the hidden curriculum, where relations between ideas and things have to stand in for relations between people. Indeed, as Zizek writes, "it cannot be otherwise." But once they are deprived of fantasy and give way to the realization that expectations set by the hidden curriculum will not be met, or even compromised partially, another mode of existence takes hold of them. Unfortunately, the disappointment that follows deprivation of this sort is not followed by a compromise formation; that is, that explanation or action that allows one to continue to believe despite the letdown. They are then led to the space (conjuncture or rupture) between the Real and Fantasy. That nothing holds them means that nothing sustains them, except an automatic reversion to type, an enhanced or hypermove to practice. Knowing is now on the side of doing. The ethical gap maintained by fantasy has closed. And, as Jean Baudrillard states, "We have passed from the Other to the Same, from alienation to identification."[11]

As we will see in chapter 6, once this gap closes between reality and the mediating fantasy, once, as Winnicott would say, the let down has taken place, students revert to a form of interpassivity where the environment writes practice directly. Confronted with the choice of realization (i.e., properly speaking the introduction of the reality principle without an adult or even a mature culture to hold them in place), they perceive their only option to be destruction. As the opening quote in chapter 6 will direct the reader to understand, "In the unconscious fantasy these are matters of life and death" to them, even if the larger society around them does not see it that way.

Michael Carneal's act appears "inexplicable" unless we accept the thesis of radical evil.[12] Carneal seemingly mimicked the shooting scene in the film *The Basketball Diaries*, as if he were an automaton (the media reproduce this characterization and it is the one that I use in chapter 2). His defense attorney also argued this point, but, for us, as spectators, the thesis is impossible to accept because it does not reveal the human side of Carneal (i.e., as repentant, guilty, flawed, and in need of redemption). Our only conclusion, as spectators, can be to ban the violent film and locate the standards for detecting violence in the media that take the place of resolution, of a public ritual of coming-to-terms with Carneal's horrific act and our culture's role in it.

I would like to stress that the move from alienation to identification does not imply an increase in alienation, as if it ran along a temporal continuum, but a radical break and instantiation of identification, direct, literal identification with the hidden curriculum. The secondary gains are gone: The student has indicated stress by some form of antisocial behavior (although we may want to question what "antisocial" means in a culture where television is the social outlet most of the time) and the response is to withhold the secondary gains, to contain the student from them (the last objects holding the fantasy together), which allow him to sublimate or play with his rage in an imaginary setting. Now, however, at the moment of identification, instead of looking up (as does the proletariat in revolution, the feminist who locates the source of her oppression in patriarchy, the racial/ethnic minority who locates it in the framework of racist policies and institutions, or the youth who identifies it in generic authority structures), the subject looks over, to the side, to his equals.

This is a historical point that concerns the relations between generations in societies. The key question here is: Why do they take their rage to school and direct it at students, not teachers, not administrators, but random students? The student body represents their version of society, just as for workplace offenders their offices stand in for their abstract disappointment with society (even though these are adults, who should "know" better). This is a democratic problem: the targets are equals, not superiors. Its "patterns in rage" vary only by the shift from the Law of the Father to what Juliet Flower-MacCannell calls the "regime of the brother."[13]

Both Flower-MacCannell and Michael Rogin note the ongoing passage from hierarchical relations between generations (from World War II to the present) to the gradual erosion of boundaries on several different levels: psychologically, the Atomic Age and the Holocaust (indeed many experiences of World War II) destroyed the widespread belief that parents could protect children from harm; materially, the decline of postwar prosperity has cinched the economic bottom line (as the rich get richer and the poor poorer)—without a decline in the pubic perception of prosperity—thereby increasing the rate of competition for scarce goods; and politically, representation is shifty and people can no longer claim that their identity marker is an indication of their fantasy frame (i.e., what they want and how they want to be addressed and recognized), even though their political apparatuses, bureaucratic institutions, and media continue to allocate power (tangible and intangible) along these axes. Finally, I will add one more: The perception that the white male identity category has lost its purpose in the post–Cold War United States, and furthermore, the myth that this category ever had one to lose. This is the so-called zero-sum game logic of this story.

To some, this may seem to reiterate the Hobbesian explanation for conflict that springs from "equality of hope in attaining a thing," since that is what I have seemingly argued the hidden curriculum produces, at least up to this point. The difference is twofold: first, students are held in place not by the brute force or threat of brute force of the sovereign, but by fantasy; second, the equality of hope that they hold stems less from their natural equality (of mind and body) than from the formal equality and ideology of American democracy. This is a far cry from the empiricism of Thomas Hobbes. We are a long way past modern narratives of discipline in relation to contemporary political power.[14] Moreover, when the fantasy fails to hold, and the society and the school fails to hold, the student, deprived of belief, unable to acknowledge the reality principle, falls into pure practice. This is a kind of doing that would have horrified Dewey.

What is even more specific than the choice of school and fellow students is the choice of spaces of exchange within the school (the commons area, hallways, sidewalks, front entrance, rest rooms, and cafeteria) that provide them with one of the important hallmarks of democracy: freedom of assembly. That this violence occurs in these "free" spaces and not in the classroom should alert us to the idea that it is directed against publicity itself. In chapter 7, I outline the uses of publicity that can be imagined under democracy by both Friedrich Nietzsche and John Dewey. While Dewey believes in a free public space of experimentation for the social good, the hidden curriculum's effect has been to undermine this idea in the schools, if not in the rest of the society as well. These are also the areas where the cliques exercise their greatest power, and students who do not find a group identity in them, much less a positive one, are doomed to play the role of outcast. The fantasy spaces of students are at their strongest here in this space where the school curriculum does not retain formal control. Also, it is in these spaces where traditional resistance should take place—these are the "streets" of the school. And, it is here where we witness the best examples of power struggles, between secularism and religion, the Jocks and the "Abercrombie and Fitch Army," the Goths and the drama kids. All of these groups were examined by the media in a critical way following Columbine, not before.

This book does not completely reject any of the mediated explanations for school violence. It does, however, reject the notion that the perpetrators are motivated by any one of these explanations alone, and further that these explanations "motivate." As I have argued throughout this introduction, they are not motivated in a positive sense. A form of autopilot sets in and these acts are influenced by violent culture, the availability of weapons, and psychological strain (perhaps even in some cases, privation).

Nevertheless, none of these explain how the acts are meaningful in the context of this culture and why they commit acts against fellow students, as if they were, literally, infrastructure. Masculinity surely also plays a strong role and I do not in any way claim to have furthered knowledge about that aspect of this problem.[15]

What did become apparent following Columbine was the fact that these episodes of violence are precipitated by power struggles within the school that are influenced by factors in popular culture and the media. This led me to the conclusion that a return to the hidden curriculum might be an appropriate way to analyze this problem, coupled with insights about history, generations, fantasy, and popular culture. Indeed, this book is a mishmash of theories pulled together to explain a very complex social problem. The starting point is Dewey's claim that the school cannot be separated from the society and that the child cannot be separated from the curriculum, if we are to understand either of them. Taking this insight under consideration, I also propose that one cannot understand reproduction without resistance, and one cannot understand the hidden curriculum without fantasy and popular culture.[16]

REPRODUCTION VERSUS RESISTANCE

Part I opens with a quote from Peter McLaren, whose popular book *Critical Pedagogy and Predatory Culture* marks the break in his work and is emblematic of what is happening in the field of educational studies.[17] It indicates that theoretical attempts to understand the breakdown of public schooling are politically untenable. However, his original text for an American audience, *Life in Schools,* embodies the tradition that I attempt to continue in this text.[18] I mention McLaren's work because it performs the tension in critical pedagogy in the most obvious way.[19] According to William F. Pinar et al., the drama of critical pedagogy was born in reproduction theory and died in resistance theory. As a first-year graduate student, I was disappointed to learn that the hidden curriculum as an important educational concept did not survive university discourse's need to produce new theories instead of reworking old ones. McLaren's and Henry Giroux's resistance theory was deemed "normative" and unable to respond to the problem of educational reproduction in a convincing fashion. I guess I was confused by this use of the term "normative," for this book is all about normativity and its consequences and the hidden curriculum's production of nihilistic norms. Those who labeled postmodernism as such confused the time period with the theorists who were willing to look at it. Critical educational theory was at a crossroads, and I think it took the wrong road, but not because of any conscious effort to do so. As Pinar et al. explain,

> We are not suggesting that the problem is McLaren's; it cannot, for example, be simply understood as his inconsistency. Rather, it is the problem—indeed the crisis—of contemporary political curriculum theory: how to reconcile a view of politics that, finally,

has strikes and street barricades in mind, with a more complex view in which what we think and what we do, i.e. the realm of the symbolic, in a semiotic society, represent the location of political action, not the streets.[20]

Another contribution of this book is to further knowledge in this area. We do not have critical concepts to apprehend school violence—or even resistance—on the part of students as long as our philosophies concerning education are thoroughly modern. A concrete analysis of the material factors involved in school violence are no less important because we live in a semiotic society; in fact, they become even more important. Why would resistance take place in the streets when a long time ago critical protestors were proclaiming that any resistance must take place in institutions, specifically in the "long march through the institutions?" That this resistance is mediated by fantasy, and that these fantasy frames are increasingly choreographed by technology is what accounts for our myopia concerning school violence. It takes place in the material realm, but it is instantiated in the chasm between knowing, doing, and believing.

CONTAINMENT

As for the policy of containment, I outline the narrative pattern that serves as a response to each shooting event at a public school site: after the initial shock and trauma of the "unclaimed experience" comes the all-too-familiar litany of already stated (and to date ineffective) explanations and remedies, primarily organized around deterrence, surveillance, and curricular reform.[21] These explanations have been woefully inadequate in anticipating future outbreaks of school violence and, even more importantly, in imagining social policy except in relation to a Hobbesian model of politics as conflict management or as a complete denial of the nature and uses of conflict in democratic societies.

This book differs from previous explanatory studies that reduce both the hidden curriculum (the spaces where violence takes place, the policies that allow for it, and the messages sent to students by it) and the means of expression of the shooters to a dependent variable. The theoretical contention of this work is that although sometimes unintelligible to their authors and seemingly "unmotivated" to their observers, these acts are expressive and would be better understood by textual methodologies (e.g., discourse analysis of actors' nonverbal messages, psychoanalytics of practices, hermeneutic interpretation of experiences, and theoretical interpretation of policy formation). The supposed senselessness of the act inheres not in how meaningful the act is, but in the viewer's lack of a conceptual field to apprehend expressive acts that cannot be located in the author's objective intent. Moreover, it is through the denial of conflict—especially as attributed to youth—that researchers have missed the opportunity to explain school violence through categories that describe them as participants in the human condition.

In my attempt to locate meaning in these seemingly senseless and random acts of violence, I privilege violence as a form of communication and the site where violence takes place as a negative holding pattern capable of arousing more violence in the future.[22] In their efforts to make schools "safe," policymakers and school workers have rationalized an atmosphere of fear and mistrust among students by subjecting them to routine forms of monitoring and discipline, such as metal detectors, locker searches, dress codes, censorship of virtually any suspect media and popular culture, profiling, expulsion, and incarceration. This containment empowers the hidden curriculum to control students in ways that limit their educational freedom and their right to express frustration and disagreement in positive ways, especially through nonviolent means. It is anticipated that they will come to view learning and social interaction as impossible unless provided by a negative form of freedom, a "freedom from" rather than a "freedom to."[23]

I also examine how policy responses and contemporary research have ignored the messages communicated in this violence, preferring to locate interpretive meaning in the epiphenomenal aspects of the shootings. In these responses, we witness another pattern: Media pundits and experts spoon-feed the public rationalizations for the shootings that focus in on the behavioral influences that provoke school violence. Preferring to view the problem as one of lack of rote discipline on the part of students and as the result of negative influences in the form of cultural artifacts (video games, musical lyrics, and violent film and Internet resources), experts have further alienated nonviolent students from school and the curriculum. This alienation and the culture of fear that is bred within it exposes students to a negative developmental model of education, breeding an entire generation of citizens whose potential for positive societal contributions are lacking and whose fear of freedom will be reflected in a negative form of citizenship, possibly one that is inimical to democratic life.

I begin by "reading" three cases (West Paducah, Kentucky; Jonesboro, Arkansas; and Springfield, Oregon) to show how the most pronounced examples of school violence appearing in the media have articulated the educational environment of all schools. Themes related to each shooting have emerged that focus on the previously mentioned epiphenomenal variables used to explain school violence. The highlighted themes are "predatory culture," gun control, psychiatric profiling, and violent video games and popular culture. In examining the arguments made by the experts in the media, I demonstrate some of the fallacious reasoning that is behind the formulation of school policy in the last few years. Most of the arguments are generated by the public's willingness to believe that popular culture and armaments are directly correlated with school violence. The reasoning presupposes that the objects themselves motivate students to use them in improper and harmful ways. All the explanations leave out two key features mediating the relationship between popular culture and students: student subjectivity and the hidden curriculum's inability to acknowledge student subjectivity.

Specifically, this means that subjectivity mediates the experiences had by students both with popular culture and the hidden curriculum, but school policy only recognizes the objectivity of its curriculum, and these contradictions force students to conform to rote discipline in unrealistic ways. There is an overwhelming emphasis on "knowing" in the cognitive sense, but not "believing," so that "doing" becomes a worthless, repetitive gesture on the part of students who can see nothing in education that speaks to them as people. Furthermore, because public school students are not viewed as citizens, their subjectivity is omitted from the curriculum, ostensibly in order to protect them from harm, but this excessive protection keeps them in the negative holding pattern of routine practice animated by hypercognition. Thus, students have experiences but cannot express them and, at present, their only means of expression is contained by security measures implemented for their own good. This holding pattern has the potential to curb their orientation to citizenship in a regressive direction. Without the necessary experience of freedom, students will be unable to function in American society without the false sense of security provided by the school's reaction to violence. Like prisoners, they will develop nonfunctional habits and become dependent on authorities to mediate their subjectivity for them, if it has not happened already.

Chapter 4 follows the discourse of a school prayer movement that has gained members and popularity through the last four years by linking its mission—God in school—to the trauma inflicted by school shootings. By looking at the movement's major sponsor, See You at the Pole, the chapter gleans from its activities several interesting observations concerning citizenship formation and student subjectivity following each shooting event. Finally, the chapter ends with an example of the way in which "witnessing" works to bring the Christian God back into schools as a protector of students from the harm associated with certain aspects of the hidden curriculum foreshadowed by early educational debates between secular humanist proponents and those who favor school prayer. Indeed, the presentation of shootings alone is traumatic enough to provoke many parents to pull their children from public schooling and into the home or the charter option. Even more upsetting to many parents is the way their children are treated at school following shootings, as potential criminals or worse, as criminals simply because of the way they dress, their choice of music or literature, or their psychiatric evaluations.

Chapter 5 provides a theoretical model by which the school shootings can be understood throughout the book. Beginning with a theoretical excursion into the moral writings of Nietzsche, juxtaposed to the ethical and psychological writings of Dewey, the focus is chiefly on whether or not democracy and the experiences it fosters, in difference, can be reconciled to a pedagogy that seeks to foster a sense of community within the schools. Nietzsche claims that most of the conflict circulating in modern society is a function of democracy and the rights and freedoms it promises. Dewey, on the other hand, claims that democracy is the only political answer to fostering community; however, he holds that community cannot be forged until citizens begin to respect and communicate their experiences with one another in intelligent ways. For Dewey, the problem is not democracy, but the ways in which it has not been implemented out of fear of the unknown and the unanticipated consequences of freedom and experimentation. For Nietzsche, democracy can only provide negative freedom that breeds mistrust and fear in its citizenry. For Dewey, democracy has not been interpreted and practiced to the full extent of its potential; we are afraid to be free. This chapter has the potential to demonstrate to researchers the possible citizen models that could be incorporated into the curriculum of schools, showing how containment policy is simply a further expression of the underlying fear communicated by the hidden curriculum. This research may also provide alternative responses to traumatic events such as school shootings.

Chapter 6 constructs a theory of school violence based on the psychoanalytic reflections of child psychiatrist Winnicott and using the generational-historical method introduced by José Ortega y Gasset in his book *Man and Crisis*.[24] Another factor uncovered in the research was aided by Winnicott's work. Through his work with children who were orphaned during World War II, Winnicott developed several concepts and paradigmatic insights that explain youth violence. The chapter extrapolates a few of these insights to explain how the public's reaction to school violence has only encouraged it to continue. Through an extended analysis of the reaction to school violence, the chapter concludes that the problem of school violence is systemic; specifically, that it is located in a generational and environmental problematic caused by democratic culture.

Chapter 7 attends to specific pedagogical problems associated with and encountered in schools as they respond to the fears and concerns generated by school violence. The work of Dewey and Roland Barthes is of primary importance here. The chapter highlights an educational paradox: how to promote freedom in classroom dialogue by referencing popular culture in ways that disarm the negative effects of the hidden curriculum. It examines how to funnel that freedom into an environment already fraught with tension and mistrust. The security necessary to prevent school violence is thus not located in physical control or visual omnipotence for the administration, but in nonphysical security. Students can feel safe without metal detectors and video cameras.

Without these acknowledgments, American citizenship, with its links to freedom, expression, and the right to privacy, is threatened with transformation in unpredictable ways.

NOTES

1. Jean Baudrillard, *Symbolic Exchange and Death,* trans. Ian Hamilton Grant (London: Sage, 1993), 130.

2. Chris Wallace, "Boy on the Brink," *20/20,* 9 February 2000.

3. Culpability, however, is another matter and it is best left to the realm of juvenile justice. The students who commit these horrible acts are still young—too young to know the precise intent with which their bodies and bullets wrote their mind's content. Guilt and responsibility for these acts are best left to the demos: American citizens must atone for these acts as well. As Hannah Arendt argues in *Eichmann in Jerusalem: A Report on the Banality of Evil* (New York: Penguin, 1963), as did D. W. Winnicott in *Deprivation and Delinquency* (London: Tavi-

stock, 1984). before her, we should look to adjudication as a means for repairing a broken civic space, not for satisfying an immediate impulse to revenge. I do not want it to be misunderstood that I am condoning school violence, or the individuals who perpetrate it; rather, I examine this violence from one angle (by no means comprehensive or all knowing, as an "ego of apperception," if you will) from the perspective of a theorist who seeks to understand what students are fatally trying to communicate to the public.

4. Ron Avi Astor, Heather Ann Meyer, and William J. Behre, "Unowned Places and Times: Maps and Interviews about Violence in High Schools," *American Educational Research Journal* 36, no. 1 (1999): 30–42.

5. Michael W. Apple, "The Hidden Curriculum and the Nature of Conflict," in *Curriculum Theorizing: The Reconceptualists,* ed. William Pinar (Berkeley, Calif.: McCutchan, 1975), 95–119.

6. Slavoj Zizek, *The Sublime Object of Ideology* (London: Verso, 1989), 36. My mimicry of Zizek's explanation for how social reality works as an ethical construct is performative, and I am thoroughly indebted to his use of this phrase to demonstrate how this contradictory belief system works.

7. See Nancy Lesko, *Act Your Age!: The Cultural Construction of Adolescence* (New York: Routledge and Falmer, 2001), 149–87.

8. With the exception of Elizabeth Bush, a young woman who brought a gun to school to shoot another girl who teased her and ended up harming not only the other girl, but herself, accidentally—this is quite an irony.

9. Slavoj Zizek, *The Plague of Fantasies* (London: Verso, 1997), 95–117. See also Zizek's original treatment of the problem of fetishism in Zizek, *Sublime Object of Ideology,* 11–55.

10. Zizek, *Plague of Fantasies,* 113.

11. Jean Baudrillard, *Impossible Exchange,* trans. Chris Turner (New York: Verso, 2001), 52.

12. For a cultural exploration of evil, see C. Fred Alford, *What Evil Means to Us* (Ithaca, N.Y.: Cornell University Press, 1997).

13. Juliet Flower-MacCannell, *The Regime of the Brother* (New York: Routledge, 1993).

14. Examples include police in schools, fathers acting as police in schools, role modeling, and hero worship. These are weak attempts at restoring a modern fantasy that can never compete with popular culture and its icons.

15. See R. W. Connell, *The Men and the Boys* (Berkeley: University of California Press, 2000), 212–26.

16. John Dewey, *The School and Society and the Child and the Curriculum,* ed. Philip W. Jackson (1900; reprint, Chicago: University of Chicago Press, 1990), 193.

17. Peter McLaren, *Critical Pedagogy and Predatory Culture* (New York: Routledge, 1995).

18. Peter McLaren, *Life in Schools: An Introduction to Critical Pedagogy in the Foundations of Education* (New York: Longman, 1989).

19. For a discussion of this debate, see chapter 5 of William F. Pinar et al., *Understanding Curriculum* (New York: Lang, 1995).

20. Pinar et al., *Understanding Curriculum,* 310.

21. Cathy Caruth, ed., *Trauma: Explorations in Memory* (Baltimore, Md.: Johns Hopkins University Press, 1995), introduction.

22. D. W. Winnicott, *Psycho-Analytic Explorations,* ed. Clare Winnicott, Ray Shepherd, and Madeleine Davis (Cambridge, Mass.: Harvard University Press, 1989).

23. Maxine Greene, *Dialectic of Freedom* (New York: Teacher's College Press, 1988).

24. José Ortega y Gasset, *Man and Crisis,* trans. Mildred Adams (New York: Norton, 1958).

PART I

TRIGGERING RAGE

Cases of Motivation As Determined by Public Reaction to School Shootings

The future looks empty and intense. Oliver Stone's film, *Natural Born Killers*, gives us a glimpse of the "fun" Citizen Golem that capitalist culture is producing, and the fab time that awaits us in predatory culture. Prepare yourselves, teachers, for curriculum agitado. It's going to be real.

—Peter McLaren, *Critical Pedagogy and Predatory Culture*[1]

Published at the end of 1995, Peter McLaren's book *Critical Pedagogy and Predatory Culture* launched him into fame and sovereign status as the educational theorist of popular culture. This book's prophetic claim seemed to ring true in the following year, 1996, with the onset of film-related copycat killings taking place in the small, rural town of Moses Lake, Washington. Barry Loukaitis's particular form of "curriculum agitado" consisted in his choice of place for the shooting: algebra class. His purported intention was to shoot a boy who had teased him, although when he arrived at the classroom he just kept shooting his semiautomatic weapon until three others went down. Eerily, at Loukaitis's trial, the prosecuting attorney argued that "clearly" he had been profoundly influenced by Oliver Stone's film *Natural Born Killers,* despite the fact that "there are hundreds of thousands of kids who watch these things and don't blow away their schoolmates."[2]

Several cultural arguments are at play in the media's accounting for the school shootings, especially in the early phases of the "pattern" that the *New York Times* so convincingly condensed into one main theme: the violent culture of film, or in a more generic sense, McLaren's "predatory culture," which in the aftermath of the shootings appears to be the argument of the pro–National Rifle Association right wing. Left and Right will converge as the shootings erupt, switching positions, abandoning traditional ideological concerns, and adopting those of their former adversaries, but one thing remains clear: Neither side wants to admit that school shootings are a problem whose roots lie far beyond any simple causality related to cultural artifacts, that rather they are embedded in social practices and the environment of the school and the society.

In the following chapters, my aim is to assess the arguments that attempt to convince readerships and the public terrorized by school violence that these incidents are the inevitable result of youth's engagement with predatory culture, weapons, or of some privation peculiar to the individual shooter related to mental illness. Chapter 1 examines the shooting in West Paducah, Kentucky, and focuses on how that shooting was cathected to "predatory culture" in the mediascape. Chapter 2 reads the shooting at Jonesboro, Arkansas, through the media's focus on the age of the perpetrators and the availability of firearms to children. Chapter 3 looks at the shooting in Springfield, Oregon, through narratives of mental illness and schizophrenia. The shootings are attached by their referents in the media, as well as by the ideas that link them in a series of shootings.

"Predatory culture" is a term that describes culture not in terms of specific symptoms or manifestations, but strictly according to its prey (youth usually, but sometimes even adults) and motivational factors that are located in privations of individuals (weakness, insecurity, and consumer desire circulating in the public sphere) *delinked* from societal processes or structures. All of the shooting incidents, especially those covered in detail in the next three chapters, were tagged with a motive that provided a convenient disavowal of direct responsibility on the part of the media, parents, and the public or community. The motives gave the public an outside target onto which it could transfer its distress.

Loukaitis's rampage in an algebra class was connected to a copy of the Stephen King story "Rage" that was later found in Loukaitis's bedroom. Charlie Decker, the central character and shooter in the story, kills two teachers and holds his algebra class hostage in order to, in his words throughout the story, "get it on." Decker, allegedly similar to Loukaitis, is primarily angry at his father for treating him like "the birdshit on his windshield" because, as he says, his motto is "Keep It Tight and Keep It Right. And if a bird shits on your windshield, you wipe it off before it can dry there. That was Dad's life and I was the birdshit on his windshield."[3] Decker is obsessed with his father's disaffection with him and his inability to live up to his father's masculine expectations for him (enjoying male bonding in the woods and mistreating his mother, while identifying with her makes him a "sissy"). The media reported that Loukaitis's father had just left him and his mother to live with another woman.

In the story, Decker is mad at his father for some vile things he said to some other men about his mother on a camping trip; specifically that if he caught her with another man, he would give her a "Cherokee nose job," apparently a punishment the Cherokee Indians used to apply when a woman committed adultery. "The Cherokees used to slit their noses. The idea was to put a cunt right up on their faces so everyone in the tribe could see what part of them got into trouble."[4]

King writes of his own story, written under the pseudonym Richard Bachman, "I was not quite young enough when these stories were written to be able to discuss them as juvenilia. On the other hand, I was still callow enough to believe in oversimple motivations (many of them painfully Freudian) and unhappy endings."[5] But, like Decker, Loukaitis opened fire on his algebra class and targeted a student who had teased him, and unlike Decker, ended up shooting until he ran out of ammunition. Loukaitis, like the other shooters examined in the next three chapters, intended to do one thing, and ended up unable to control himself and the scene. Decker held the room hostage and none of the students were afraid of him, except for the one he hated from the start. While in the room for two hours, he forced them to listen to his unhappy stories only to finally release them in exchange for a trip to the mental hospital.

In the Bachman story, unlike the other shootings analyzed in this book, the students appear to be united against only one other student (staged as Decker's competitor for the affections of another girl in the room) and by their shared predicament as teenagers in a rural Maine town full of social contradictions. By the end of the story, students are urging Decker to murder the hated classmate (and bully) and cooperate with him even when he no longer poses a threat to them. Most importantly, Decker is in control of the shooting situation and while all the students discussed in the following chapters carefully planned their crimes, they lost control at the scene. The media would, without explanation, come to call this aspect of school shootings random because it is inevitably what disrupts the carefully laid plan each student has made.

Wearing the signature uniform of school shooters, Loukaitis donned a black trench coat and boots to start off the movement, having carefully chosen the outfit on a shopping trip with his mother weeks before the shooting. Later, these stylizations would come to mark the school shootings in a significant way, as shooters planned their outfits for the event. Some might believe that students wearing these uniforms would inevitably shoot up a school; they are wrong. King is correct. It is a mistake to believe in "oversimple motivations" and the point of this book is to outline all the oversimple motives attributed to school shooters throughout the 1997–1999 school years and attempt to corner the common element that "triggers" the "rage" of contemporary youth—that is, what motivates them to go to school and engage in "curriculum agitado." While most of the national discourse surrounding school shootings would have them connected through the logic of mimicry, by contrast, chapter 1 demonstrates that, while they all do appear to believe that fellow classmates are the appropriate target for their rage, the rage itself is fomented by the hidden curriculum of schooling. More to the point, the alienation and repression that students experience within the physical spaces of the school contradict and exacerbate the parallel alienation and repression coming at them from the rest of the society.

An oversimple reading of the hidden curriculum would have all its effects located at school, but there is ample evidence in these cases that they are more likely situated somewhere in between the school, the public, the home, and the generation. It is located in the public culture that tolerates the contradictory and cruel treatment of youth in the United States outlined in the introduction (and later in chapter 5). The public always misreads the Nietzschean logic that "God is dead" to imply an empirical claim that God does not exist at all, when in fact what Friedrich Nietzsche means by this claim is that because Western moderns have stopped believing in him en masse and in a structural way (fearing him and respecting others out of fear of his wrath), they have effectively banished him from importance in human life. Nietzsche's claim is symbolic, not metaphysical. Over and over again in shooting accounts, one finds the claim that it is those who find comfort in his writings who are the nihilists, whereas it is clear, at least to me, that students are targeted in the public sphere as subjects of a cruelty that Nietzsche diagnosed properly as a democratic problem.

As will be shown, the "adolescent" in contemporary society is slowly becoming obsolete as a viable subject-position and students in schools are experiencing the repressive effects of this unconscious policy directed at them by all the aforementioned agencies of the state and the public that supports it. Many educational scholars bemoan the category of adolescent because it is a "fake" developmental distinction, having been created after the arbitrary imposition of grades and school levels by curriculum specialists at the close of the nineteenth century. However, just because it is socially constructed does not mean that it is not a useful term that can bargain for some "relative autonomy" for students.[6] Furthermore, John Dewey is often criticized for writing about the child and the curriculum as a continuum, as two boundaries of a lifelong learning experience, but this logic dispenses with the contradictions that are themselves products of the policing of developmental categories and one would think that progressives would support the continuum thesis.

Recently, pundits have been arguing for the abolition of the high school, claiming that students in those grades are already adults and that therefore they should be made responsible for their actions. This is all coming on the heels of school shootings and increasingly high incarceration rates for adolescents. As fourteen-year-olds are tried as adults, the logic goes, students should be shoved off the dole of public education. But there is no discussion of the corresponding rights and material means they would be supplied with in order to assume the responsibilities of adulthood. This normative debate shows only that students are the ones getting bashed around while the public tries to figure out what it wants for them.

School shootings add justification to arguments for abolishing high school in favor of charter schools, vouchers, and standardized testing. None of these options would contribute to citizenship education or the development of individuals capable of acting in public, tolerating others, and understanding how to live the common life. In fact, in its reaction to school shootings the public demonstrates its own bad conscience, ressentiment, and cruelty. Some will argue that the public's reaction is simply akin to Alexis de Tocqueville's observation that in United States it is the "pulpits aflame with righteousness" that make it exceptional, but this normativity detached from an idea of public welfare attuned to the realities of contemporary life, one that is plural, diverse, and commodified, is part of the problem, not the solution. As the next three chapters move from shooting to shooting, the only "patterns in the rage" appear in the reactions to them, and they reveal less about the shooters' intentions than they do the beliefs of the public that consumes them.

NOT MIMICRY, SERIALITY

I opened this chapter with Moses Lake and "Rage" because it was one of the first shootings and yet it was the least covered in the media. It, like Pearl, Mississippi, would be recuperated later, following the shootings in Paducah, Jonesboro, and Springfield, as the origin of what would become the serial crime of school shootings. Similarly, the Pearl case went relatively unnoticed, except by *People* magazine, and was at the time interpreted and contained by religious arguments that were relatively uninteresting to the media, except as a cult-intrigue case.

When the news came that Luke Woodham had added another shooting to the list, the media let local interpretations lie unchallenged. At sixteen, Woodham was said to be acting under the influence of another eighteen- or nineteen-year-old, also later tried for conspiracy in the case. The Pearl public accused both boys of satanic worship. In fact, six teens were tried in connection with the killing of Woodham's former girlfriend and another female student. It was alleged that the cult, known as Kroth and led by Grant Boyette, the older boy, had encouraged Woodham to commit the shooting. Woodham was tried separately for the stabbing murder of his mother the morning before the shooting. Again, wearing a black trench coat, Woodham entered the commons area at the school to find his former girlfriend and kill her. He passed a note to another student just before the shooting that read, "Throughout my life I was ridiculed. Always beaten, always hated. Can you, society, truly blame me for what I do? No, you can't. Yes, you will, the ratings wouldn't be high enough if you didn't, and it wouldn't make good gossip for all the old ladies."[7]

But the ratings simply were not high enough yet. It took West Paducah and Michael Carneal to make school shootings into a serial movement linked by shared experiences with violent popular culture. These cultural experiences are common in most students (even nonviolent ones); what links them is the "memory of the will."

No one mentioned the words of the shooters themselves, their notes, or their comments made to friends as ample evidence that they were undergoing serious strain at school. Even if they had not believed them, the persecution fantasies found in the notes should have at least made them of interest to the school and parents. Instead, the public chose to pin the motive for shootings on a blank form of violent culture that is not tied to any specific generative source or responsible party. Culture somehow "gets violent," sometimes with the help of Hollywood, but usually all by itself.

Similarly, guns jump into the hands of youngsters, drive them to school, dress them up in their uniforms, aim, and pull their own triggers. Like McLaren, the public assumed that culture was predatory and that it needed to protect students from these negative influences, unwittingly exposing them to even more harmful influences in the form of monitoring, surveillance, and a generalized diffidence in relation to them.

Central to understanding this argument concerning the "predatoriness" of culture will be a theoretical reading of the concept and its use-value for reading the accounts given to describe the shooting at West Paducah that came after Moses Lake. I have chosen the West Paducah case because it is the last case before Columbine blew all these interpretations into circulation together, in which violent media are assumed as motivating factors in the shooting series. The case following it, Jonesboro, drew specific attention to the culture of and access to firearms, and was quickly followed up by the Springfield shooting by Kip Kinkel, which drew attention to the "deviant individual," or loner incapable of being subdued by psychiatric treatments. Finally, the events at Columbine High School in Littleton, Colorado, brought the violent culture filtered through the film and video thesis so "close to home" for many Americans that President Bill Clinton was compelled to call together a summit with major players in the film and television industry. In short, Littleton escalated "media violence" into a national problem; therefore, it is important to understand the theoretical justifications at work in national and academic discussions of school violence.

My engagement with the shooting at Paducah will take on an environmental tone in order to shape the case according to the arguments concerning culture, especially the notion of predatory culture and its relationship to this case. I argue that instead of emphasizing culture's predatory nature, analysis might yield clarity if the case were read through the specific social formations that react to the school shootings as traumatic episodes. As traumas, the shootings are not read as the effects of a stable subjectivity that is preyed on by a monolithic cultural force with a hungry mind of its own, but as scenes where subjectivity is always already fractured and refractured with each passing event. In a sense, the culture of violence we witness in the media is anticipated by a population literally jacked into the technological performance of cruelty. The split between mental and manual labor in society causes people to organize their experiences according to the "codes" of media that are spatially and temporally circumscribed. This leads to the increasing reification of practical knowledge; experience that is integrated (having both physical and mental aspects to it) is thrown by the wayside as students (and adults) begin to experience themselves as dependent on the codes for knowledge of how to perform the simplest of acts.

Also important are the reactions to shootings of adult culture in its confrontation with youth culture. In many ways, the motive for the shootings at West Paducah's Heath High School is overdetermined. As the media passes judgment on the shooting spree, the motives pile up in the American cultural consciousness. Did Carneal do it because he was angry with his parents for keeping secrets from him, as the police authorities claimed? Or was it because he was a self-proclaimed atheist, as students claimed, who targeted prayer at school even though he had been confirmed in the Lutheran Church several months before?[8] Was he sick of being teased and treated like a loser at school, as the media claimed? Which Althusserian "ideological state apparatus" is responsible: the family, the church, the media, or the school? As the trauma faded, the list of possible motives continued to accumulate new iterations of motive. But a more interesting question than why such incidents occur is: What is the dominant characteristic of culture that militates against these institutions forming compromises with one another on such a purportedly important issue?

Instead of addressing these arguments as single explanatory variables, I analyze the way they authorize a particular reading of the shootings in relation to the school as a functionary for citizenship. The school is the site where these anxieties accumulate and are played out, specifically in the unofficial spaces where students have some power that approaches relative autonomy—in the lunchroom, lobby, school yard, and hallways—and at the times when they are called on to mediate their subjectivity—before and after school, in the exchanges between classes, and at the meals they share as students in the cafeteria. The role of the school in American society is the most important thematic unearthed in the various interpretations. The reactions to the shooting events have put into question the success of the school in reproducing the fiction "America," which, while nostalgically written and thought of as a transparent reality, is in practice the productive result of many subjective readings. The students have particular understandings of the school's role in reproducing citizenship. Never an innocent concept, citizenship is performed by students in schools everyday, in ways that adults fail to recognize or discount as inauthentic or immature.

NOTES

1. Peter McLaren, *Critical Pedagogy and Predatory Culture* (New York: Routledge, 1995), 25.

2. "From Adolescent Angst to School Shootings: Patterns in the Rage," *New York Times*, 14 July 1998, A1.

3. Richard Bachman, "Rage," in *The Bachman Books: Four Early Novels by Stephen King* (New York: Plume, 1977), 43.

4. Bachman, "Rage," 15.

5. Bachman, "Rage," ix.

6. Louis Althusser, *Lenin and Philosophy*, trans. Ben Brewster (New York: New Left, 1971), 127–86.

7. "Two Teens Charged with Planning School Shooting Rampage," *Associated Press*, 16 October 1997, 1.

8. Jim Abrams, "Kentucky Suspect Is a Churchgoer: Pastor Refutes Claims That Teen Accused in Shootings Was Atheist," *Detroit News*, 3 December 1997, at detnews.com/1997/nation/9712/03/12030132/htm (last viewed February 8, 1999). This statement is a sign that the local community was engaged in an ongoing struggle to redefine the meaning of Carneal's acts through religion. However, Carneal's pastor would have none of the accusations stand, as he boldly said, "It was not the act of an atheist. It was the act of a sinful Christian."

1

West Paducah, Kentucky: *The Basketball Diaries* As Predatory Culture

So what led Michael Carneal to the point of killing? Perhaps he wanted power or control he couldn't have—power he had to earn, but could not wait for. Michael showed impatience for something everybody wants. Should the people of Paducah forgive him? This question is hard to answer. Some see him as an innocent adolescent, caught up in a world of violence. Others see him as a child who wanted attention but got it the wrong way and, in this case, the sick way. Both assumptions are reasonable, but which one is right?

—Elspeth Call, 8th grader from New York[1]

Michael Carneal, a fourteen-year-old student at Heath High School, was found guilty of killing three students and intent to kill five others. He is serving twenty-five years in prison without the option of parole. The son of a "prominent" defense attorney in McCracken County, Kentucky, Carneal's elevated socioeconomic status and moderate religious background (he is Lutheran, one of the most socially and politically liberal Christian denominations) has been contrasted with that of his victims: poor and deeply religious.

The thirty-five students he found praying, as they did every morning before classes began, in front of the school on Monday, December 2, 1997, were assembled in self-proclaimed nondenominational Christian prayer led by Ben Strong, whose father, Bobby Strong, is a minister at the Assembly of God Church. Strong had been Carneal's friend because they both belonged to the brass section of the school band.

25

In fact, the door through which Carneal entered the school that day was the always unlocked band room door that opened into the lobby of the school where the kids were praying. Strong had been warned by Carneal the Friday before in school, "Don't go to the prayer meeting, something big's going to happen," and, in retrospect, Strong remembered the wildly paranoid thoughts he had had all weekend. Nevertheless, by Monday morning he had convinced himself that Carneal would actually do nothing. Strong did say that he had told a friend and his older brother about the ambiguous threat, but he explicitly avoided alerting adults: "I don't want to necessarily tell any adults, because they could do something crazy, [*sic*] and if he was planning on doing something crazy, if they tried to stop it, he'd make it even worse. Because that's just the way it is."[2] Later, in a *New York Times Magazine* article, it was revealed that Strong had spent the night at Carneal's house the Saturday before, so apparently they were close friends.[3]

Eyewitness accounts from persons other than Strong (who was acting in the event rather than watching or reacting) describe Carneal's surreal calm as he walked into the lobby and "calmly stuffed his ears with plugs as if he were preparing to fire at target practice."[4] At this point in recollection, all witnesses (even Strong) said that they thought it was a joke until he began firing and that it was not until they watched fear come over *other* students' faces that they scrambled to find cover inside the nearest classroom.

In an instant, the mood of the entire room changed when Carneal began firing the first three of the ten shots. The principal, Bill Bond, who was on the phone in his office at the time, heard a round of three pops, a pause, and then seven more shots fired in succession before he ran down the hall to see what was happening. Meanwhile, Strong approached Carneal asking, "What are you doing? Why are you doing this?" and pushed him against the wall, forcing Carneal to drop the gun. Carneal, according to Strong, replied, "I can't believe I'd do this." Bond arrived at that moment to kick the gun out of the way and, oddly he has said, "I put my arm around the boy and walked him off to the office." Bond later said that Carneal only said, "I'm sorry," and that he was apparently in a daze from the events, that "[h]e acted just like he had been caught with some minor offense."[5] Bond's interpretation of the event was that only the first three of the shots were aimed (three girls died, though no one knows the order in which they went down so no one can determine if he was singling out individuals) and the rest was random shooting. Carneal is said to have had no anger or hostility toward any particular person in the circle, and the pattern of the shooting seems to confirm this statement. Most of the recent shootings have proceeded in this way, after the first shot several random ones follow until the ammunition is depleted, as if the assailant cannot stop shooting.

DREAMING OF RAGE

Actually, we can never give anything up; we only exchange one thing for another. What appears to be renunciation is really the formation of a surrogate or substitute. In the same way, the growing child, when he stops playing, gives up nothing but the link with real objects; instead of playing, he now phantasies. He builds castles in the air and creates what are called day-dreams.

—Sigmund Freud, "Creative Writers and Day-Dreaming"[6]

Later on at the police station, Carneal was asked where he got the "idea" to shoot up the school. He responded, "I saw it in a movie. I saw it in *The Basketball Diaries.*" The accounts seem to indicate that Carneal was baited into giving an answer like this one, blaming someone or some "idea" for his own motivations. There is, however, a school shooting scene in the film that fits the definition of New York University professor Toby Miller's concept of a "trigger scene."[7]

Leonardo DiCaprio, playing the young, heroin-addicted Jim Carroll, bursts into his same-sex parochial school classroom and shoots every student (except his three friends) and the teacher. Prior to this scene, he is shown sitting in a bathtub, ostensibly writing the *Diaries* and saying of his addiction (you do not know if it is heroin or writing), "You can't stop dreams—they move in crazy pieces, anyway they want, and suddenly, you can't move anything." The camera jumps to a dream sequence. After this, he is shown falling asleep in the tub. In the dream (the sound and visual effects change slightly in this scene, thus, there is a perceptual difference between the "reality" and "fantasy" depicted in the film; the shift is bracketed by muted sounds, so we might ask just how close Carneal was trying to get, by bracketing sound with his earplugs, in re-creating the filmed experience), DiCaprio, wearing a long black leather trench coat and carrying a shotgun, walks through the school and knocks down the door to the classroom; behind him is a picture of Jesus.

While shooting, he deliberately stops and then pivots on the heels of his cowboy boots to get a precise aim at his next victim (this event is not random, though it may be target practice), simultaneously cocking back the chamber to release the previous cartridge. These movements are very cool and collected and the slow motion combined with his elevated height and stature relative to those sitting make DiCaprio look tougher than he does in the rest of the film's scenes. (It makes sense, right? This is his fantasy.) His friends all laugh hysterically (especially Mark Wahlberg) and cheer him on while he takes down every other student in the room, until he turns to the desk at the front of the room and yells some obscenity—in slow motion—right before he kicks over the monsignor's desk and shoots him (earlier in the movie this teacher had paddled him at the front of the class). The camera abruptly jumps to DiCaprio being startled awake by the same teacher—in class and in film reality—slapping his desk.

If this is an example of what has been called a film-related copycat crime, then there is one noticeable difference between the actual event and the movie. Carneal "accidentally" (whatever that means in this context) shot one of his friends (possibly two) and it seems that his remorse in the lobby was because he had just realized his blunder. In the film, all of DiCaprio's friends are there to witness and enjoy the shooting display, and all those who are shot are the ones who laughed or secretly smiled—à la Sigmund Freud's insight about a "child being beaten"—when Di-Caprio, earlier in the film, got paddled at the front of the class. "The punishment for perfection," according to Jean Baudrillard, "is reproduction," and so it seems that if Carneal wanted to reproduce the fictional crime in *The Basketball Diaries*, he failed, which was a great disappointment to him; at least that is what the newspaper accounts indicate he was sorry about.[8]

At his trial, Carneal was described as "detached," a kid whose interests should have lain more with conducting scientific experiments than with "killing his classmates." But everyone failed to see the obvious connection between the detached, objective attitude that science requires in order to realize its objectives and Carneal's demeanor at the shooting. Carneal was doing exactly what they described. Thus, there is no paradox in his behavior. At once endorsing the positive normative aspects of scientific experimentation and also disavowing its undesirable characteristics, the courtroom voyeurs blamed Carneal for throwing their psychological splitting into relief in the aftermath of the shooting. As will be outlined in chapter 5, the public is unable to reconcile traumatic events with reality without the aid of punishment in the form of ressentiment or bad conscience. In the court's reaction to Carneal's crime, one can easily see the beginnings of a bad conscience forming in the community of West Paducah.

While many want to continue to believe the basic premises of liberal education exemplified by John Dewey's cool detachment from the consequences of experimentation, they are unable to take up his dare to self-motivate and to react in a positive manner. Critical intelligence would not be of help in understanding the reactions to this case, but bad conscience might be a decent starting point. The onlookers and the traumatized want to believe in a progressive notion of education, but not if it comes with unintended consequences. A slight deviation from the floating norm of objectivity embedded in the hidden curriculum of education will be punished for not validating the symbolic imaginary of liberal education. Bad conscience is the way in which people who believe in something—that is by its very nature valueless—distance themselves from that particular failure when it does not fall in line with their larger idealist agenda. Outliers omitted, bad conscience allows them to continue believing in progressive ideals.

The disappointment that comes from failing to reproduce (ideas, grades, behaviors, styles, the exact model of citizenship, or the law-abiding subject) may be increasingly interpreted as the worst crime in American society and one noted *copiously* by behaviorist psychologists. In this case, however, if one grants that Carneal was only doing his duty and trying to reproduce, according to the fundamental and structural laws of this society, then he was only disappointed that he failed to be exactly what he was expected to be and failed to do what was shown to him through various mundane practices in school.

Indeed, a *Court TV* report indicates that Carneal "falsely remembered that the character [DiCaprio] shot five students while other students cheered."[9] It is unclear what the youth "falsely remembered" (the number of shots fired? the laughter?), but it seems that his mnemonic capabilities were on trial and that only if he had reproduced the event in the film exactly would he have had a reasonable case for triggering. It was "reproduction with a difference"; the melancholic who "falsely remembers" how to repeat the given order of things is doomed to punishment once that identification is *outed*.[10] Furthermore, even though the practice that is reproduced turns out to be the wrong one, it does not mean that Carneal is a "bad seed," but only that he got the codes for conduct confused and chose the wrong practice to mimic. But there is no way to ensure that Carneal or any other student at school has the "critical intelligence" so valued by both Dewey and Friedrich Nietzsche (without a clear sense of practical knowledge). Education today teaches only abstract knowledge, knowledge that is "detached" from any experience, history, or emotional understanding, detached just like Carneal. Proof of this, if I may use that word, comes from the fact that violent films are not the only ones to have inspired copycat crimes; according to *Investigative Reports*, family films and television programs have provoked their share of copycat violence.[11]

Tim Kaltenbach, the prosecuting attorney, accepts the copycat thesis as a substitute for motive in the shootings. His comments on motive imply that this peculiar type of incident is expected when a society combines easy access to firearms, violent films, and the "normal instability of a 14-year old." Kaltenbach emphatically denies any motive based on revenge or religious intolerance, but does see the plausibility of role-playing or the re-creation of film plots.[12] In a separate interview, prayer circlers indicated that Carneal would stand around with a few of his friends and watch them pray ("He would just stand and watch. . . . I don't ever remember him saying anything"—writing a film script in his head, daydreaming?).[13] Several other students confirmed Carneal's love for movies and explained that one of his hobbies was making home videos in which clay characters acted out the scripts he had written for them.

Perhaps the greatest stumbling block to understanding the relationship between film and violence is that, as one editor of *National Magazine* put it in an Arts and Entertainment interview, "the relationship between cause and effect is very, very complicated." This notion of "complication" does not yet focus on the key issue of mimicry: We constantly fail to repeat correctly even though we try desperately to do so through our practices, specifically the ones we call habits. Complicating the cause-and-effect scenario might mean taking into account certain similarities and differences between the filmed event and the real one, and subtle differences or failures to get the mimicry down to an exact prototype.[14] In the public educational systems of democratic societies, the presumed prototype manufactured is the bare citizen, lacking in qualities save for those measured by numbers (e.g., the test score, the grade point average, the sports score, or the stock quote). It is ironic that democratic citizens are supposed to be capable of autonomous decisions based on their interests when all the while they are produced on the kindergarten-to-twelfth-grade assembly line. They are produced in just such a manner that it is assured they will never make a decision without, as Immanuel Kant once wrote, "referring to the cart to which they are harnessed."[15]

The role that identification with images and objects, or words and nonverbal gestures can play in "triggering" school shootings is perhaps even more important. For example, the Catholic imagery in *The Basketball Diaries* is pervasive and linked up with a major theme in the story of Jim Carroll's life. The memories recounted by Carroll as a student and basketball player at St. Vitus Academy in Manhattan are inextricably bound up with the Roman Catholic Church's emphasis on prayer as a practical prescription for virtually everything that haunts an adolescent life. His relationship with his mother seems clearly to show this pattern of identification, misidentification, and displacement. Over his bed hangs a large picture of Jesus, his mother prays to a little makeshift shrine of Mary in her bedroom, and the lady across the fire escape engages in a kind of worship-oriented repetition-compulsion.

Other relationships in the film also portray this pious aspect, but also point to the frustration of not identifying with the faith (the irony of confession; the hypocrisy of priests, lay teachers, and coaches; and the perversity of corporal punishment). The practice of prayer is supplemented by the images that surround the person performing the practice, and the posture of prayer is juxtaposed to Carroll's obsessive poetry writing. His writing and his heroin addiction may be viewed as reaction-formations to his inability to practice Blaise Pascal's imperative, "Kneel down and move your lips in prayer and you will believe!"[16]

Never able to believe or comply, Carroll uses the writing and the heroin as vehicles for the self, while all the other institutions around him (the school, the church, and the family) collude to contain him so that he occupies a subject position that he knows is false and cannot believe in. One of the articles found in Carneal's bedroom shortly after the shooting was a card congratulating him on his confirmation, the sacrament shared by Catholic and Lutheran Churches that makes one both an adult and citizen within that community. This card, as well as a "Footprints" bookmark (the one that demonstrates the existence of God through footprints in the sand), was found in his ammo box, along with a stockpile of ammunition and supplies. A note was found that was never released to the public, but it was allegedly written in poetic form; well, some say poetry and others say it was unintelligible.[17]

In a deconstructivist vein, the lines between literature and addiction have been examined by Avital Ronell's *Crack Wars,* a reading of Gustav Flaubert's *Madame Bovary.*[18] Ronell insists on the inseparability of addiction and literature, noting that the mania that sutures the two in an indistinguishable way is disavowed by society and its laws, which accuse the binary of a "crime." Untethered from reality through the medium of fiction, this binary is wound pervasively through *The Basketball Diaries* as well as the narrative accounts of West Paducah. Even clinical psychologist Dewey Cornell had to testify banally at Carneal's trial that "while Carneal showed signs of schizophrenia and paranoia, he still was aware of the sentence he was about to receive." He further noted that "Carneal was tormented by his crimes and was ready to receive the maximum punishment because he believes he deserves punishment."[19] Thus, even though Carneal showed signs of mental illness, he had the capacity to accept punishment for the imperfect crime and was tormented by the outcome. It is unclear if his torment was revealed to gain a lesser sentence or for the comfort of the victim's families, but it is clear that Carneal had to be quasi-rational in order to stand as a citizen before the law and be charged, not only as an adult, but also as a competent one.

While bystanders (the nation, the political "community") might want to write off this incident as an extrapolitical event, neither the courts nor police officials wanted to do so and, in order for punishment to be meted out, Carneal had to be signified a rational citizen. According to Dr. Diane Schetky's forensic evaluation, "It is my opinion that Michael Carneal, although mentally ill, did have an appreciation for the criminality of his behavior and the capacity to restrain himself when he killed three students at his school and injured five others."[20] Indeed, according to other forensic psychologists, one of the key behavior problems associated with juvenile crime is linked to a particular form of restraint, usually signaled by the inability to hold urine. Childhood enuresis (persistent and chronic bed-wetting), according to Charles Patrick Ewing, is the most popular symptom used to diagnose and predict adolescent violent behavior.[21] Over and above animal torture and fire setting, bed-wetting is the preferred symptom because it signals that these individuals "cannot hold their tensions, are impatient, and are impelled to act. They feel the urgency of the moment psychologically, as at an earlier date they could not hold their urine."[22] This bodily interpretation of violence assumes that the consciousness of kids is ill formed and is unable to distinguish between emotional tension and physical tension. Perhaps it is the preferred method of diagnosing violence in adolescents because it is the easiest of the symptom-triad to confirm as parents can easily report bed-wetting at home; fire-setting and animal torture are much more difficult patterns of behavior to account for in retrospect.

The most troubling outcome of psychological interpretations that stress the relationship between the body and the mind is that they use these categories to define subjects who are experiencing adolescence, a category used to signify the source of bewilderment that *adults feel* toward children.[23] Adolescence, according to Dr. Spencer Eth, dates back to Greek historian Hesiod in the eighth century B.C., who exclaimed, "[T]he present youth are exceedingly wise and impatient of restraint." This critical category used by adults to describe the children whom they cannot control is by definition characterized by the *child's inability* to practice restraint, not the adult's inability to understand and restrain them. Clinical psychologists, however, dispute this characterization and argue that "psychopathology" (broadly defined as the inability to restrain oneself) is not a "normative feature of adolescence, but may indicate a diagnosable disorder that in the absence of appropriate treatment can disrupt the developmental processes of adolescence and progress to adult disturbance."[24]

In this definition, the categorical specificity of adolescence suddenly drops out of the developmental equation, except where it holds the place of that now ambiguously situated subject confined to an age group with a specific legal status (now ambiguous in light of school shootings and the dismantling of the juvenile justice system). The performative effect of this definition is that it restores belief in a "normal adolescence" where previously the age group was defined by its inability to be either a normal child or adult. When G. Stanley Hall gave adult frustration at uncontrollable children the name "adolescence" in 1904, he did not suggest that it be used to comfort adults who feel disrupted by their children's presence in their daily lives. It is not a coincidence that Hall's coinage of the term followed on the heels of the creation of a separate legal system and corresponding detention centers for youth that were designed to administer "treatment as an alternative to punishment."[25] The first juvenile justice system was created in Illinois in 1899 and was dismantled a hundred years later. Adolescence, as a temporal marker between child and adult in society, is becoming a clinical disorder or disease that must be eradicated. The increasing popularity of psychiatric diagnoses like character disorder and personality disorder are part of the same "clinical gaze" that Michel Foucault describes in *The Birth of the Clinic.*[26]

This is not to say that "adolescence" exists one way or another, as a fictional category that should be maintained or discarded, but to note that it is manipulated by all these cases of school violence and strategies of experts until its only mark is that it needs to be eradicated, like a beast of burden for adult culture. Adolescents are not efficient; they are themselves manipulative (as most people are), confusing, emotionally conflicted, violent, and peaceful. They are more human than human because they embody all the irregularities, carelessness, and indifference that are omitted from the hidden curriculum of schooling and the society's norm of progress. They get in the way. Schools, in their quest to make students more receptive to acceptable norms of success, only devise counseling programs (if they even have them) to therapeutically mediate students back into the fold of the hidden curriculum. When they refuse, as many do, they are labeled, drugged, expelled, or jailed. Now, with the dismantling of the juvenile justice system, they are less inclined to even be given a second chance or to get some time to figure out what they want.

As Mike A. Males argues in his book *The Scapegoat Generation*, adolescents are now targeted as a public health problem. Scare statistics about teenage pregnancy, sexually transmitted diseases, new "drug" problems, and a lack of basic respect for society on the part of youth are easily disarmed by Males's analyses of them. He does this by showing how these problems are disproportionate with the actual cases of such problems, especially with the insinuation that they are the fault of the adolescents alone, without any influence from specific adult elements of the society at large. For example, he shows that teenage pregnancies are not disproportionately the result of teen-teen sex, but are the age-old product of sex between teenage girls and older men. He cites statistics showing that seven out of ten teenage pregnancies are the product of sex between teenage girls and adult men.[27]

An advocate for the juvenile justice system, Steven Drisch, speaking on public radio, argues that the breakdown of the system is detrimental to the development of teenagers. Like D. W. Winnicott's claim that violent kids who lash out at society must be punished according to the laws in place, they do not need to be featured as the object of society's revenge simply because they have committed a crime. The judge is responsible for mediating the public's revenge feelings when teenagers commit crimes. Instead, in Carneal's case, several victims were allowed to vent their anger at Carneal's sentencing hearing, where they were videotaped and spread on the media. Psychiatrists who analyzed Carneal found him "sane" and the courts tried him as an adult (he was fourteen at the time of the shooting), so he was not given any avenue for leniency or understanding because the overriding reason for the trial was to satisfy the revenge of the town and the nation, and the victims' friends and families. These trials and the sentences are one way to use revenge to change the law, thereby changing the prospects for teenagers.

Given this conceptual ambiguity, it is odd that many studies reporting the causes of adolescent violence and recommending preventive measures stress the importance of understanding the rational basis of school violence. And yet it is unclear what rationality has to do with any of the school shooting sprees, unless one can pin a motive to a rationale that the public (adults) is willing to affirm; that is, comforting to *them* in this turbulent time kids are experiencing. Since the studies focus on the justifications that students give for committing a violent act against school, others, or property, they are inevitably led to control for other factors involved in the violent acts (such as the institutional location, the identity characteristics of the actors and their interplay, and the focus of the object of the violence), maintaining that the problem of school violence may be understood through rational perspectives and that because any offense can be given a rational justification, the problem lies with the value-system that underlies the culture and society in which the kids live.

Through this "social interactionist" perspective, there emerges a pattern to violent behavior that is rooted in the negative effects of violent culture such that adolescent behavior will mirror (predictably) cultural symptoms. It is argued that the only way to prevent such behavior is to change the value-system or to look for students who are "at-risk" for violent behavior.[28] Mocking the former option, the researchers suggest integrating the latter into the curriculum of schools in order to prevent the triggering of such events by disturbed individuals. In the same stroke that they discount theoretical interventions into the culture of violence, they argue that these events are not predatory because they have rational justifications. In American culture, they argue, violence is simply an acceptable and rational means of solving conflicts, therefore, the only option available to schools is to implement surveillance measures to scan for deviant behavior among the students.

So far, we have seen that most psychiatric explanations for school shootings are designed to quell adult fears of children. Various anxieties on the part of adults reacting to shootings allow them to ignore the more salient features of the events and at times to discount completely their specificity in order to pretend that they occurred for some other reason that can be prevented "next time." Immediately following the Paducah shooting, parents and the McCracken County School Board members met to discuss school safety to prevent this kind of shooting from happening again, but the solutions they formulated in no way took into account that it would be a student enrolled in school doing the shooting! They discussed metal detectors and agreed to lock down the schools each and every day. It is as if they were unaware what war they were fighting and that they did not know their enemy (or category, if you like). For example, students arriving late would have to be "buzzed in" the automatic front door to the school, no longer free to enter side doors like Carneal had done when he entered through the band room the morning of the shooting.

In a reversal of this reactive logic, short-term policy focused on searching students at the elementary school the following Wednesday when classes resumed. The principal at Farley Elementary School is said to have "had her staff search every student backpack and book bag in the school Wednesday, just to make a point." And she added, "We didn't expect to find anything, but we wanted to get the children used to the idea that we can do that and we will do that. We can search their backpacks as long as we search all of them. The devil was from within at Heath . . . you constantly have to let [students] know we're looking for problems; we can't let our guard down."[29]

Given the extreme cost of such measures, another possible solution is to train teachers to notice the "opening moves" of student violence. The opening moves are the more or less nonverbal or verbally truncated forms of conflict that precede the violence (e.g., throwing off one's jacket, light pushing, or name calling). In the case of West Paducah, these measures would have worked. Carneal did not have any "opening moves" (unless you count sticking the earplugs in). Furthermore, the situation under which the shootings took place fell outside the cognitive mappings of social interactionism because there was no social interaction at the time of the act; there was the very dream-like Carneal and his gun, doing his best to bracket any interaction with reality.

While these measures may be useful for understanding certain types of conflict that have a short past and take place in the present moment—an engaged violence— there is no model for preventing the individual who is determined, with calculated intent, to shoot fellow students at random. Carneal's violence is not so much interesting for its motiveless or senseless qualities as it is for its disengagement with reality and sense data. In order to commit this crime, Carneal had to take the sounds of others out of his cognitive range. This is disengaged violence. For instance, Carneal stole his guns from neighbors on Thanksgiving Day by breaking into their garage and, interestingly, this theft went unreported until after the owners checked their garage to make sure their guns were not the ones used in the shootings. Not only did Carneal steal the guns and ammunition on that day, but authorities also searched his bedroom after the shooting and found another complete stockpile of ammunition and weapons. This collecting is considered evidence of premeditation, but there is another aspect to it as well, since this collecting and stockpiling is a common feature in school shooting incidents. But before discussing the stockpiling it is necessary to rehearse some other arguments concerning the "trigger" in this case.

Carneal's parents revealed that he had been upset by an article in the school newspaper two months prior to the shooting. In fact, after this article he began to "unravel" according to his parents and to the sketch notes later made public by psychiatrist Dewey Cornell who had evaluated him prior to the trial. A section of the school newspaper entitled "Rumor Has It" indicated that Carneal and a friend had "feelings for one another." According to Cornell's notes, Carneal was teased several times daily following the article and called a "faggot" and, while he slowly disintegrated on the inside, his parents were unaware of his problems; he went out of his way to feign normalcy.[30] At this time, he began collecting weapons and writing stories describing the type of deaths his fellow students would suffer from a character, not coincidentally named Michael. So, two years later the public learns that Carneal was suffering from the hidden curriculum of schooling and was no longer able to keep his fantasies of killing classmates from becoming reality. He began to see the merit in making his fantasies real when he was publicly humiliated at school.

STOCKPILING

Stockpiling is a common practice for all the shooters analyzed in these case studies. The students' bedrooms are littered with magazines about guns, true crime stories, and so on, but while this practice is presented by the media as bordering on the obsessive, it is not uncommon within the larger adult male population of the United States and this is something no one, not even gun control advocates, has been willing to admit. Plenty of adolescent and adult males in the United States engage in some form of weapons stockpiling, which is what make the motives for ambushing the "compounds" at Waco or Ruby Ridge, *because of stockpiling,* seem so ludicrous in retrospect.

Even if the parents or authorities had known about the student shooters' stockpiling (Kinkel's parents had bought him guns and taken shooting lessons with him, and the Jonesboro kids were raised with guns all around them: Andrew Golden's grandfather was the town's conservationist and Mitchell Johnson's father and stepfather regularly left handguns lying on the kitchen table), the behavior is not deviant; it is a common (and therefore, normal) adolescent male practice that the newspapers exaggerated to make it seem deviant for the presentation of these cases.

Look at the norm, in 1993 there were nearly 200 million guns in private hands in the United States. Furthermore, according to the National Institute of Justice's National Survey on Private Ownership and Use of Firearms (NSPOF) data, "it has been indicated that the top 20 percent of firearm owners possessed 55 percent of privately owned firearms. Of gun owners in 1994, 10 million individuals owned 105 million guns, while the remaining 87 million guns were dispersed among 34 million other owners." In another study, which has gun owners singled out by type, the National Institute of Justice states that "the total number of privately owned firearms is 192 million: 65 million handguns, 70 million rifles, 49 million shotguns, and 8 million other long guns. . . . Of the handguns, 48 percent were revolvers, 40 percent semi-automatics, and 12 percent were reported as 'some other type of handgun' by respondents." The study notes that "of the millions of guns in civilian hands, they include everything from cheap .22 caliber 'snubbies' to finely made high-powered rifles worth thousands of dollars." And finally, the study finds that gun ownership is "highest among middle-aged, college-educated people of rural small-town America. Whites were substantially more likely to own guns than blacks, and blacks more likely than Hispanics."[31]

Considering that most gun owners are male and possess more firearms than (like Carneal) they could possibly use at one time, it does not seem odd to law enforcement officials that fetishism is practiced by adult male gun owners (and possibly some women too, even though Freud thought it was impossible for women to have fetishes)—it is only odd when adolescents and children practice gun fetishism. This subtle disavowal by law enforcement officials of fetishism as a regular (normal?) practice is only invoked when the offenders happen to be either children or sequestered groups professing a faith other than that allowed in normal American society (e.g., militias or nonaligned religious/political groups). A local Federal Bureau of Investigation agent from Lafayette, Indiana, later confirmed to me that law enforcement agencies generally do not understand stockpiling, because it does not make sense that the shooter would carry more firepower than necessary. He added, obviously, the "masculinity" argument was bankrupt because when men stockpile weapons, it is to increase their sense of power when they *lack* it in comparison to other men!

Sheriff Frank Augustus in West Paducah was convinced that Carneal must have had accomplices, because he carried four weapons into school that morning taped under a blanket (two shotguns and two .22 caliber rifles). He transported all of them (along with several rounds of ammunition) in the car with his older sister Kelly and into the school through the band room door, assuring both the band teacher and his sister that the contents concealed under the blanket were a science project (indeed it was).

Augustus could not understand why Carneal might need all those weapons. On a rational plane, this simply "goes without saying" (Louis Althusser) and this evidential fact must imply that Carneal was bringing the extras for an accomplice: "I don't believe this boy planned this out by himself. . . . I believe there's someone else out there we need to talk to. I believe it's another student." It is interesting that the sheriff needs to believe (he had a "gut feeling") that Carneal had an accomplice(s) to the shooting because of the large number of weapons he carried. The sheriff's reaction to Carneal's fetishistic activity, an intuitive disavowal exemplified by his gut, confirms what Kaja Silverman labels as a "dominant fiction" operating in American culture concerning adolescents: They do not have fetishes, they have "hobbies," "activities," and adult-supervised collecting. Big men have fetishes that are legitimate (and certainly never called such a thing), and only they, especially in the case of school shootings, can fetishize without supervision.[32]

WHO IS THE PREDATOR? WHO IS THE PREY?

It used to be that mediatic spaces were zoned outside of you. When you thought you felt like watching TV or listening to the radio, you would get up and switch the power on. This way you thought you were under the spell of spontaneity, internally combusted, and the external hallucinations would respond to your command. It was bizarre back then, everyone hoping they were autonomous, but in fact more or less hypnotized by these allotechnologies, held off at a distance that was just that much more fascinating.

—Avital Ronell, *Crack Wars*[33]

West Paducah brought the issue of school prayer into the national consciousness in a way not possible before: through the exploitation of trauma. As we shall see in chapter 7, because Carneal opened fire on a prayer circle at the front of the school, the rights of Christians became important nationally and their well-known anger at secular culture and values was given pride of place when discussing school violence initiatives. The radical Right (and to some degree its more tolerant variants) has long criticized this violent and promiscuous culture that preys on the innocent, especially children. Given this feature of the case, Peter McLaren's argument concerning predatory culture is relevant, but who or what is the predator exactly? What is its source? Citizenship—the ability to practice public acts through competing claims of legitimacy and to identify them with a political group or cultural medium—becomes the dominant tactic for fighting a culture war against youth, ostensibly on their behalf. Oh, and by the way, did not the Left used to represent youth against authority?

If this is the theoretical case, then it is necessary to analyze the notion that culture is predatory and what this aspect of culture does to affect the curriculum and students' orientations to it. Curriculum is not just books and lesson plans; it is every conceivable message transmitted to students in schools, either through linguistic or nonlinguistic means. Many in the radical wing of curriculum theory have underscored the importance of understanding the "hidden" or noncognitive aspects of the curriculum that are present in school practices, such as Michael W. Apple's insights discussed in the introduction. For McLaren, however, the hidden curriculum that produces his "Citizen Golem" is an abstracted form of capitalism, a pervasive evil that forces Hollywood to produce films that glorify violence and predatory behavior. The symbolic importance of predatory culture is exemplified through its effects: "Our eyes and ears no longer belong to us. They have been replaced by John Wayne Bobbitt's penis and Tonya Harding's beefy thighs," and this is because in "predatory culture it is virtually impossible to be cotemporal with what one observes and desires."[34] This chasm between desire and identification (as, of course, observation) signals a lapse in the subject's ability to distinguish the real from the ideal, reality from dream, and fact from fiction.

The notion that culture is directly responsible for violence is relevant to Carneal's act. Carneal was not outwardly frustrated or aggressive toward students prior to the shooting. His conduct during the event displays the detachment and disengaged anger of filmed experience (or great acting). Since filmed experience, according to McLaren, is the noncontemporaneity of observation and desire, it is helpful to review the arguments concerning television's impact on youth-desiring mechanisms.[35]

McLaren's reading of predatory culture is authorized by Lawrence Grossberg's reading of television in "The In-Difference of Television," where he argues that television does not care about its viewers' affective reactions to its manipulation of meaning.[36] When we leave the room where the television is housed, it could care less, because television's power lies in its indifference to human desires. Television short-circuits our ability to react to its manipulations of images in much the same way that billboards on the freeways of major cities act as signposts with no deliberate or logical message, but only an affective one that is dependent on our subjective interpretation.

An example (not given by Grossberg) is the poster created and distributed by the Trauma Foundation, a San Francisco–based antigun lobby. It reads: "Lead has been determined to cause pools of blood on school playgrounds by the children of Jonesboro, Arkansas. Other risks include infants being horribly maimed."[37] This poster first appeared in San Francisco schools in September 1998, and then in YMCAs throughout the country. Eventually, the foundation hopes to decorate classrooms nationwide.

The text of the poster attempts a collapsing of affective desire into effective discipline. While manipulating the viewer's affections and (private) anxieties about guns, it transmits a disciplinary lesson. According to Grossberg, television does the same thing, except not in a responsible way, as in the case of the Trauma Foundation, since television is more concerned with a "pose-modernism," that is, television concerns itself with manipulating images and meanings on-screen with no responsible lesson at hand to effect a critical politics of the medium. Television is indifferent to meaning because it does not care if the viewer learns any lessons; it simply transmits these messages without restraint. Television, *like its public,* has no conscience.

There is no weakness in the televisual for a countercultural movement to exploit and foil television's indifference to viewer insecurity. Television is the cruelest analyst because it refuses to calm one's fears concerning its messages and images at the same time that its constant availability caters to one's private life and desires. Television is evil because it does not have a human need to reassure the viewer that the message was taken the wrong way, or that he or she even has the right to be concerned. Grossberg's television, unlike Baudrillard's, while equally indifferent, is a poser. It pretends to be our constant analytic companion when really it just gets off on our masochistic need for it. Baudrillard's television does not even care about the masochism and this bothers Grossberg, for whom television should remain a hostile, yet worthy, enemy. Grossberg criticizes Baudrillard for collapsing reality into ideology: "But Baudrillard confuses the collapse of an ideology of the real (including its various scenes) with the problematising of the link between ideology and reality. Again, it is not the social that has imploded but a particular ideological structuration (public/private) which seems no longer effective."[38]

In an interesting (though very common) disavowal of television, Grossberg nostalgically longs for the public-private bifurcation that allowed for a public sphere in which common problems could be redressed while private desires, narrow self-interest, and personal problems are bracketed. If television implodes this ideological structuration, it is because it is a venue for private desires, narrow self-interest, and personal problems, to which no common solutions are possible. Television simply reverses the ideological structuration that Grossberg describes as imploded. And yet, if television implodes (or reverses) the priority of the ideological structuration on which the social rests (at least in democratic societies that enforce laws that attempt to fix a public-private binary), then the social is also imploded; otherwise, television's permissive venues would not have been filled by the many indifferent messages that Grossberg criticizes.

Both McLaren and Grossberg miss the point of the social in Baudrillard; that is, the social wanted predatory culture because it fulfills its purposes. There is no separate sphere or gap in which a conscience critical of television can be formed from the analytic viewpoint, because television is the social.

While we may think that we walk away from television and understand the critical difference between its ramblings and our own practices, we are wrong, because there are none to discern in a world where all social roles are scripted. Predatory culture is a compelling concept because it allows for a tangible scapegoat: the media. But the media is not separate from the public sphere so much as it is the public sphere. This publicity of the media makes it, ironically, an intangible scapegoat. Thus, a category arises to describe a reality that does not exist and this is how the public disavows responsibility or honesty in the face of school shootings in the first place. Every explanation is a distraction from more obvious features of a shooting. Carneal was conducting a scientific experiment, an activity our society ordinarily rewards with money or status. He was re-creating a movie scene, but this does not mean that the filmmakers are responsible for the attack, because the imperative that Carneal was following was not to get angry and shoot students out of the same anger that Jim Carroll harbored, but to get it exactly right. He wanted to experience the movie (earplugs, random shooting that misses friends, and therefore ends up appearing very skilled) exactly as it unfolded technically, not morally.[39]

As we shall see in chapter 5, engagement with the public sphere, according to Nietzsche, entails entering it to redress some wrong committed against an individual or group that is crystallized in an event. Following Carneal's indictment in December 1998, specifically, three months later, the parents of the slain girls from Heath High School filed a lawsuit. Their suit was not filed against the school district, Carneal or his parents (although there are suits pending against the parents), or the original gun owners, but against three major media providers: film production conglomerates, Internet website providers, and video game companies. After the orgy was temporarily over (the shootings had stopped nationwide, for a bit, anyway) and Carneal was serving his sentence, and the media coverage had exhausted itself and moved on, the families decided to sue the real culprit: the social. A lawsuit was the only way to redress a wrong in the public sphere since the law is what circumscribes those spaces.

McLaren's argument concerning predatory culture is identical to the one that the lawyer for the girls' parents gave at a press conference: "We intend to hurt Hollywood. We intend to hurt the video game industry. We intend to hurt sex porn sites."[40] Hurting a social that pretends to uphold the public-private binary (or the law) means hurting it through the courts, through procedural punishment. The lawsuit, which asks for $100 million in punitive damages and $30 million in compensatory damages, seeks to rectify the public's insatiable hunger for a particular type of social by making it harder for companies to provide such venues for experimentation and expression. These companies are the predators who "influenced" Carneal's behavior by refining his shooting technique (video games), triggering the shooting (*The Basketball Diaries*),[41] and providing him with sexualized images of women and connecting the objectification of women in pornography with the fact that all of Carneal's victims were female students (porn websites).[42]

As for Carneal, shooting the prayer circlers appears to have been an experiment in the social by which he tested his theory of filmed experience in the Real. Ronell depicts a nostalgic past in which people "held off" the social offered to them by television, but one can see how this bracketing is futile when the desire to express the personal is so readily available and encouraged by every other social medium, including the school. Similarly, television makes it possible to experience the social in a detached fashion by disabling the viewer's ability to talk back to the medium or be given reassurances by it. While schools continually disavow the impact of television on students' lives and on interpretations of life in the United States, except in a reactionary or containing way, they contribute to the growing alienation of a generation of students from their parents who wish them to remain stuffed in simulacra that comfort them, to which they give the name childhood.

Dewey might tell them that they cannot have it both ways. When confronted with the generation of parents affectionately given the name Baby Boomers, Dewey would be likely to respond in much the same way he responded to the generation of the 1910s that mirrors their behavior. In *The School and the Society and the Child and the Curriculum*, Dewey deconstructs the adult-child binary and warns those who seek to contain the child in their paradigms and conceptual containers that they will have to confront the fact that the child has a mind of his or her own and that he or she will respond to their attempts at protection sooner or later.[43] For Dewey, one cannot let the boundaries of the social fall and then expect children never to enter into the mire. In fact, preventing the child from entering the social in experimental ways leads to destructive attempts to do so by the kids who are willing to try. Hurting the corporations is the highest form of ressentiment because it does not affect the social in any meaningful way; the social is, like television, indifferent to meaning and this is something that all the lawsuits in the world will not change.

NOTES

1. Elspeth Call, "Who Will Stop the Madness?" City Honors Home Page, at cityhonors.buffalo.k12.ny.us/city/Dims/98Jan/Jan%20LAYOUTS/who.html (accessed February 8, 1999).

2. James Zambowski and Jennifer Wohller, "Thanksgiving Day Fuels Seconds of Horror," *Paducah Sun,* 2 December 1997, A1.

3. Lisa Belkin, "Parents Blaming Parents," *New York Times Magazine,* 31 October 1999, 67.

4. Bill Bartleman, "Confessed Killer Can't Explain Deadly Rampage," *Paducah Sun,* 2 December 1997, 1A.

5. Detroit Free Press, 1997, 1.

6. Sigmund Freud, "Creative Writers and Day-Dreaming," in *The Freud Reader,* ed. Peter Gay (1907; reprint, New York: Norton, 1989), 489.

7. Toby Miller interview for the Arts and Entertainment Channel's *Investigative Reports.*

8. Jean Baudrillard, *The Perfect Crime,* trans. Chris Turner (London: Verso, 1996), preface. The central thesis of his book is this: "Though the crime is never perfect, perfection, true to its name, is always criminal. In the perfect crime it is the perfection itself which is the crime, just as, in the transparence of evil, it is the transparence itself that is the evil. But perfection is always punished: the punishment for perfection is reproduction." This brilliantly cryptic aphorism signifies the irrationality at the heart of reproduction: at once obsessed with perfection qua perfection, but at the same time expecting "values" to be represented in that perfection!

9. "Kentucky v. Michael Carneal: Kentucky School Shooter Sentenced to Life in Prison without Parole," *Court TV,* 16 December 1998.

10. Judith Butler, *The Psychic Life of Power: Theories in Subjection* (Stanford: University of California Press, 1997), 6.

11. Arts and Entertainment's *Investigative Reports.* This particular segment featured Toby Miller mentioned in note 7. Miller gives ample evidence of the connection among right-wing or values-oriented programming of media, culture, and subject-forming practices.

12. Bill Bartleman, "Shooting May Be Tied to Film: Kaltenbach," *Paducah Sun,* 4 December 1997, 1A–15A.

13. Bartleman, "Confessed Killer," 1A.

14. Another example of this is Virginia Cade who tried to remake the bank robbery scene from *Set It Off.* Convincing some boarders at her house to be her accomplices, she not only led an actual bank robbery attempt, she also made them rehearse the scene at home several times to make sure they got it exactly right. When they failed, she is said to have been extremely agitated.

15. Immanuel Kant, *Perpetual Peace and Other Essays,* trans. Ted Humphrey (1784; reprint, Indianapolis, Ind.: Hackett, 1983), 41.

16. Louis Althusser, *Lenin and Philosophy,* trans. Ben Brewster (New York: New Left, 1971), 168.

17. This hearsay is relevant to the intrigue of the case because Carroll is and was a poet as is the main protagonist in *The Basketball Diaries.* He is writing poetry throughout the film; mimicry is key.

18. Avital Ronell, *Crack Wars: Literature, Addiction, Mania* (Lincoln: University of Nebraska Press, 1990).

19. "Kentucky v. Michael Carneal."

20. "Kentucky v. Michael Carneal."

21. Charles Patrick Ewing, *Kids Who Kill: Bad Seeds and Baby Butchers—the Shocking True Stories of Juvenile Murders* (Lexington, Mass.: Lexington, 1990), 11.

22. Joseph Michaels, "Enuresis in Murderous Aggressive Children and Adolescents," *Archives of General Psychiatry* 94 (1961), quoted in Ewing, *Kids Who Kill*, 10–11.

23. This reminds me of President Bill Clinton's press conference following the shootings at Littleton, Colorado, when he said of the National Rifle Association, "[p]eople, categories are not realities!" Apparently, people are not realities unless they are mobilized by groups that oppose psychiatric intervention and monitoring/surveillance in schools.

24. Kathleen Heide, *Young Killers: The Challenge of Juvenile Homicide* (Thousand Oaks, Calif.: Sage, 1999), 8.

25. Lawrence Fitch, "Competency to Stand Trial and Criminal Responsibility in Juvenile Court," in *Juvenile Homicide*, ed. Elissa Benedek and Dewey Cornell (Washington, D.C.: American Psychiatric Press, 1989), 146.

26. Michel Foucault, *The Birth of the Clinic: An Archeology of Medical Perception* (New York: Vintage, 1994), 1–21.

27. Mike A. Males, *The Scapegoat Generation: America's War on Adolescents* (Monroe, Maine: Common Courage, 1996), 48.

28. The category "at-risk" has been criticized as a racist category. The term is arguably a veiled way to discuss minority performance in schools to justify the tracking and negative placement of these individuals in lower venues. Furthermore, most research concerning at-risk students does not focus on improving their academic performance, but providing extracurricular reasons for their failure to score high on achievement exams. See W. Watkins, "Black Curriculum Orientations: A Preliminary Inquiry," *Harvard Educational Review* 63, no. 3 (1998): 321–38.

29. Jennifer Wohller, "School Panel to Examine Safety Options," *Paducah Sun,* 4 December 1997, A18.

30. Belkin, "Parents Blaming Parents," 78.

31. National Institute of Justice, "Guns in America: National Survey on Private Ownership and Use of Firearms" May 1997, at www.ncjrs.org/txtfiles/165476.txt (accessed February 7, 2002).

32. Kaja Silverman, *Male Subjectivity at the Margins* (London: Routledge, 1992), 15–17.

33. Ronell, *Crack Wars,* 67.

34. Peter McLaren, *Critical Pedagogy and Predatory Culture* (New York: Routledge, 1995), 9.

35. Bill Readings, *The University in Ruins* (Cambridge, Mass.: Harvard University Press, 1995), 142. Readings writes, "Alongside national broadcasting (PBS, RAI, CBC, BBC), we have a series of narrowcast channels (like MTV or BET) that aggregate individuals temporarily as demographic statistics rather than as a community or a society."

36. Lawrence Grossberg, "The In-Difference of Television," *Screen* 28, no. 2 (1987): 28–45.

37. "Beware the Smoking Gun," *Creative Review,* 1 September 1998.

38. Grossberg, "In-Difference of Television."

39. This, I think, is the intuitive disavowal of American society that cannot admit that school shootings are the result of students doing exactly what they have been told to do their

whole lives. The messages are not transmitted solely by music, video games, or movies, but also by lesson plans, science classes, stock quotes, and military excursions abroad. In other words, this situation is a total validation of the Milgram study's findings *except* that under technological progress and democracy authority is undermined, thereby creating role disorientation (see Stanley Milgram, *Obedience to Authority: An Experimental View* [New York: Harper and Row, 1974]). Combine this role disorientation with an increasingly militarized culture that fears everything unknown and that locates its power and allegiance in the individual, not the community, hermeneutic interpretation, or humanist praxis, and the result is sporadic episodes of fascistic practice. These episodes are scripted by the technologies and policy procedures that the individual follows without question in a deontologizing culture. It is not a matter of restoring authority in a leader at this point; it is too late and will only result in widespread fascism as only a malevolent leader could command the obedience. The hypothetical leader would only resort to nostalgic portraits of American life that no longer exist, as Grossman naively does, or as leaders in the Balkans have. See chapter 3.

40. Gina Holland, "Two Teens Charged with Planning School Shooting Rampage," *Associated Press*, 16 October 1997, at wire.ap.org/GoToAP.cgi?FRONTID=HOME&SITE=KYELI&enter=Go (accessed August 15, 2002).

41. *The Basketball Diaries*, dir. Scott Kalvert, Island Pictures and New Line Cinema, 1995.

42. James Prichard, "Fighting Back," *Associated Press*, 12 April 1998, at abcnews.go.com:80/sections/us/DailyNews/paducah990412.html (accessed April 14, 1999).

43. John Dewey, *The School and the Society and the Child and the Curriculum*, ed. Philip W. Jackson (1900; reprint, Chicago: University of Chicago Press, 1990).

2

Jonesboro, Arkansas: Guns and Their Seductive Qualities

What makes today's children bring those guns to school when their parents did not? And the answer to that question may be that the important ingredient, the vital, new different ingredient in killing in modern combat and in killing in modern American society, is the systematic process of defeating the normal individual's age-old, psychological inhibition against violent, harmful activity toward one's own species. Are we taking the safety catch off a nation, just as surely and easily as we would take the safety catch off of a gun, and with the same results?

—Lt. Col. Dave Grossman, *On Killing*[1]

Men do become angry; they do act hatefully and explode in rage against others. But not here. Something far more dangerous is revealed: the capacity for man to abandon his humanity, indeed, the inevitability that he does so, as he merges his unique personality into larger institutional structures.

This is a fatal flaw nature has designed into us, and which in the long run gives our species only a modest chance of survival.

It is ironic that the virtues of loyalty, discipline, and self-sacrifice that we value so highly in the individual are the very properties that create destructive organizational engines of war and bind men to malevolent systems of authority.

—Stanley Milgram, *Obedience to Authority*[2]

Theories and studies of war have always drawn on psychological literature that questions the role of the individual in the process of killing. Furthermore, that literature has engaged in questioning an individual's relationship to an authority that may come in the shape of a role model, a law, a bureaucracy, or a technological limitation/innovation. Theories that borrow from the individual's reactions to explain conflict by groups of nonindividuals, namely war (for war is defined as group conflict), are especially prone to ignoring the facts of the individual case, subsuming the rage and its causes under the guise of human weakness, irritability, and societal exacerbation.

One can think of numerous studies whose very titles suggest such relationships: classics, such as Stanley Milgram's *Obedience to Authority,* Robert Jay Lifton's *Nazi Doctors,* and Hannah Arendt's *Eichmann in Jerusalem.* This tension was played out in the recent debate between Daniel Goldhagen, author of *Hitler's Willing Executioners,* and Christopher R. Browning, author of *Ordinary Men.*[3] The debate hinged on the reasons why people kill, under whose direction, and with what degree of malice toward their victims. What all the authors share in common is their concern for understanding why humans kill other humans, under what conditions killing becomes permissible activity, and a dedication to learn the ideas that killers have formed about an enemy, as well as how those ideas are formed.

This chapter delves into that monstrous debate concerning gun control prompted by the school shooting at Jonesboro, Arkansas. In order to accomplish this task with some theoretical consistency, the philosophic thematic that coats the features of this case is drawn from Lt. Col. Dave Grossman's safety catch premise. That is, Grossman shares with other scholars concerned with war and aggression the idea that societies have self-imposed regulations that prevent the Hobbesian war of all against all, or the descent into anarchy that many political realists would equate with war. They believe in the social contract in as much as it is informed and enforced by a sovereign, whether a benevolent dictator or bureaucratic structure, to keep individuals in line, so to speak, from killing each other, thereby ensuring that lines of filial harmony and material reproduction are not disproportionately resting in the hands of weak individuals. They also share a concern for locating these authoritarian structures in a society that either inhibits or permits civil war, ethnic conflict, episodic scapegoating, and even simple prejudice.

The diacritical difference between Milgram's approach and Grossman's is illustrative of the fallacies born out by public scrutiny of gun control as prompted by the Jonesboro shooting (i.e., guns do not kill people, people kill people or its reverse proposition, people do not kill people, guns kill people[4]). For Grossman, the assumption is that humans are instinctively driven to avoid killing one another and that deformed authority structures scrape away at the limiting factor to make killing possible; they enable killing. It is the same for Milgram, except for one subtle difference: He does not begin with the comforting assumption of primordial avoidance, but postulates that humans always need a structure in which to operate and furthermore that some structures appearing neutral are perhaps the most violent and permissive ones. Milgram's study shows us an ironic fact about humanity and technology, while Grossman's analysis of killing gives us a pleasing, yet straightforward, simplistic look at violence from the perspective of the military mind. Say, for example, the command and organizational structure of the armed forces, which Grossman promotes as having positive authority figures. As will be demonstrated later, Grossman has a romantic image of the "old" military before the Pentagon commodified it and sold its techniques to video game companies. Grossman's text is permeated with nostalgia for a lost past of human reconciliation to violence based on noble authority, much like the belief he shares with sexologists that before the Victorian age of sexual repression there was an Edenic sexuality that was "freed" by the revolution instigated, but not finished, by Sigmund Freud. According to Grossman, we are apparently living this sexual "liberation" in the present era. But for now, it is imperative that this theoretical paradox of "killing" is deconstructed because it goes to the heart of the matter concerning the public's reception of the gun control debate as elicited by Jonesboro.

The public, for its part, does not enjoy debating these morbid questions at the level at which they are most precisely defined, at the level Milgram and his colleagues might have discussed them at Yale. Perhaps this is why Milgram's study has received so much criticism from ethicists who view his means of experimentation as exploitative of some intrinsic human faith. Instead, the public prefers debates about killing to be framed in a way that is both simple to understand (reasonable enough) and that does not search the depths of human organization to the degree where understanding killing becomes possible. It wants theorems that are psychologically palpable and that mark a Foucauldian "incitement to discourse." Indeed, it took two prepubescent boys shooting up a middle school to get the public even to begin asking questions about, not cruelty and violence, but guns and the wide-spread obsession with them in the United States. But the debate was immediately framed by Grossman's theories and the National Rifle Association's publicity campaign to strangle Capitol Hill, so that instead of ever exploring the role of guns as transitional objects, mediators of feelings, and accessories to masculinity, those in favor of avoiding the subject begged Hollywood and the video game industry to meet and devise a censorship policy.

As each perspective blames the other for youth violence, the only result is censorship of objects; not even scant attention is paid to addressing the problem of youth violence. It is with these insights in mind that this chapter attempts to outline the perspective of the nation in relation to the Jonesboro's theme: the safety catch is off, and it needs to be locked back, and tight.

A NATION OF ENABLERS

Grossman's theory of violence "enabling" relies on a similar logic to that of the theory of predatory culture. He argues that American television provides negative role models for children and these figures always win their favor because they have the reality effect of television on their side: "There is a direct relationship between realism and degree of violence enabling."[5] The effect of this is that this relationship is amplified in video games and popular culture because mediated entertainment uses technology to hone its degree of realism, while on a moral plane it twists and distorts that reality by setting it in cruel situations and untrue reversals of character (e.g.,the ax murderer is your next door neighbor, the hero who becomes a mass murderer, and the cop who is stupid or ineffectual). Thus, the chances for real violence being provoked by viewing these mediated fantasies is increased because of the particular way in which these media stage the social and contribute to the breakdown of the protective layer of inhibition thereby enabling "violence."

Unlike Thomas Hobbes's argument in *Leviathan,* the protective layer of inhibition is not something that is regulated or managed by governments, law, or the police: "artifice."[6] Instead, according to Grossman, it is a physical component of the brain: the midbrain (it is natural). Missing from Grossman's theory is any explicitly stated concept of civilization or of social regulation modeled and constructed in politics or law that relies on human will or creativity for its maintenance; societies do have structure, but it is authoritarian by nature for Grossman. In fact, this is a reversal of the Hobbesian commonwealth, which is "artificial" and its breakdown is a "natural" condition in Hobbesian parlance, the state of nature. Furthermore, the question of breakdown or holding failure is not one that is dialectically mediated for Grossman—nor can it be simulated, such as one side pretending to the real or natural with the other simulated and fake, continually collapsing into one another with no progressive unity or synthesis between opposition forces such as nature/culture, civilization/discontent, and Eros/Thanatos—but of nature (or the real) getting twisted and distorted beyond recognition by scientific tools devised by the military to defeat an enemy. The "real" is a structure that is authoritarian and given by nature and yet, at the same time, it is vulnerable to value twisting—that is how it enables people to kill each other, by failing to hold them in line with their true natures. A painful combination of technological control and moral education might serve as Grossman's policy prescription for youth violence.

My reading does not problematize holding failure per se, indeed that is the title of this book, but it does problematize a concept of society that is based on a tenuous opposition of psychological forces from material ones. For Grossman's theory implies that our actions are separate from our beliefs, imposed on us from without by technology and the military. That is why his theory must rest on "leaking" technologies from the military to the domestic U.S. population, however, at this point in history, following a summary of monumental events like Hiroshima, World War II, Chernobyl, Three Mile Island, cloning, and so on, it is impossible to decipher the lines between technology and human reality; these spheres cannot be separated because they are mutually reinforcing and have been so for quite some time. They are mediated by our collective ideas about power, language, and authority.

Proverbially speaking, Grossman wants to get back to the Real authority in his reified concept of society. The "leaking" of military technology to the public causes the breakdown of the midbrain (which stands in for society in his theory as synecdoche). He argues that classical and operant conditioning strategies in video games, combined with the immoral storytelling of Hollywood, slowly wear down the midbrain of individuals, eventually enabling them to commit violence against other humans. Traditional authority, he argues, was based in positive social values such as respect for the law, worship of heroes who saved the day, responsible programming, and fiction that refrained from using realism as a stylistic or literary device. This traditional authority was what held the "safety catch" on violence in the nation. However, it is unclear how this safety catch is any more reliable or preferable than those catches on the guns Mitchell Johnson and Andrew Golden stole from a locked gun cabinet the day they killed three students and a teacher in Jonesboro.

In the next section, the details of this shooting will be examined keeping in mind Grossman's theory of the safety catch. My analysis of Grossman's ideas will resume following that section, but I will focus more intensely on Grossman's revisioning of predatory culture in order to argue that his mutation in the national conversation is an endorsement of the Foucauldian "repressive hypothesis."[7]

Grossman argues that American researchers have the same relationship to violence that virgins have to sex. Violent media are like pornography, introducing youth to sex and killing without explaining intimacy and ignoring the "fact" that sex is a procreative act. That is why we need a study of "kilology," much like the nineteenth-century exploration of sex as sexology. (Some students might argue that destruction is a procreative act, similar to anarchists in the late nineteenth century who felt the same way about the destruction of the state[8]). Similarly, the nation compares juvenile violence to juvenile sex when it presumes that the adolescent lacks experience and is innocent. It also demands that two things, guns and sex, should be taught to them by a knowledgeable (not necessarily experienced) adult in order to promote public health and order. Whatever is being said, not done, about sex and violence is politically correct. But it is unclear where systematizing and talking about violence will get a militarized culture that has organized its relationship to violence in such a way as to maximize the power that certain subjects can gain in the social milieu.

The point is that the relationship between sex and violence is far from separate in practice; the two are intimately linked in practice, as they are mediated by death. Recall the Jean Baudrillard quote at the start of the introduction to this book: "Power is established on death's borders." Our psychological relation to death is what motivates the way we organize our relationships to sex (restrictively by limiting it to heterosexual, reproductive intercourse within the confines of marriage) and violence (restricted but transgressed by eruptions in the social sphere that "shock" and "dismay" us as civilized beings). It is a failure of political imagination that has led to our bankrupt knowledge/power of and in relation to sex and death. Violence as both concept and public problem comes to triangulate the relationship between the authorities and the public, the adult and the child in American society. Moreover, it is what keeps the two connected, yet surreptitiously isolated. Violence *is* sexy and that is what makes it predatory. The signifying chain coupling school shootings until it mounts to a "national problem" that explodes at Columbine is motivated by the idea that children are innocent and helpless in relation to objects and artifacts circulating in the public sphere.[9] The commentary on school shootings is as sexed as the lewd acts of the shooters.

TWISTS IN THE SERIALITY OF THE EVENT

On March 25, 1998, two young boys methodically planned the theft of a minivan belonging to the parents of one of them and set off on a ride to steal a few high-powered rifles (equipped with scopes) from the other boy's grandfather's home. Only after they had been unable to obtain weapons from one boy's father's locked gun case did they decide to break into the grandfather's collection. (Reader: please note that the safety catch was on these boys in innumerable ways and they went out of their way to take it off.) At the father's house, they even tried a blowtorch and a saw on the locked gun case. (Incidentally, the father later noted that he had other guns out in the open that they could have easily taken.) After arriving at the grandfather's house, they opened his locked gun case to retrieve their choice of weapons, packed up a heavy load of camping gear and food, and dressed in fashionable hunting gear: camouflage hats, pants, and jackets. They even painted their faces.

Next, the boys drove to a clearing set above and behind Westside Middle School to set up the rifles, carefully measuring the distance and adjusting the scopes attached to the guns for better shot accuracy, as if preparing for target practice at camp or a trip to the shooting range with a positive role model. Once set up, one boy ran over to the school and once inside, pulled the fire alarm, and then quickly ran back to the spot in the clearing.[10] Known as Cole Hill, the clearing was an ideal space for setting up target practice. The boys knew this, as they had staked it out the previous day. It was a prime spot for targeting their prey: students. The students, thinking they were saving their lives by evacuating the school at the alarm's sound, filed out of the building as the doors, as planned, locked them out, barring anyone from returning to a building presumably on fire.

Initially, the shots were recognized by the students as a prank, such as firecrackers, just like West Paducah. Girls were hit first and they did not realize they were shot until blood appeared, believing they were falling prey to a student prank. As the students began to disperse from their ordered single-file lines into a chaos, trying to get out of the line of fire, they realized the shots were coming from Cole Hill and ran to avoid them. As the shooting boys caught on to the students' self-protecting behavior, they began shooting faster, focusing on the challenge of shooting running targets, aware now of their blind advantage (very much like shooting a deer from a blind). Golden was a member of Practical Shooters, a club that teaches both kids and adults how to fire on moving targets with speed and efficiency to hone reflex and co-ordination. As the students began to run, Golden had an opportunity to practice his hobby. Johnson later claimed to have fired over the student's heads, although later ballistics tests confirm that bullets taken from one student's chest and leg match the gun used by him. In all, nine students were shot and four died from their wounds, three girls and English teacher Shannon Wright, who jumped in front of another girl and saved her life.

They fired twenty-seven times then ran into the woods behind the school, away from the police called to the scene.

THE PRISONER'S DILEMMA AT ELEVEN AND THIRTEEN

In the prisoner's dilemma, the game theorem used to predict behavior and make suggestions about human motives, two law breakers are caught in the act by the police, apprehended, and placed in separate interrogation rooms. Isolated from one another, the prisoners cannot get together to work out a common version of the events of the crime in order to alleviate full responsibility. This isolation is supposed to cause them anxiety about the other's story. The game is appropriately called a "mixed motive game" for this very reason: the players cannot anticipate each other's version of the story and can no longer trust one another as the police interrogators pressure them to confess, especially to turn evidence against the other in exchange for a lighter sentence.

To foil this exercise of intangible power by police, each prisoner must maintain a silence about the other's involvement in the crime. The police, through different forms of deception and badgering (such as good cop/bad cop), attempt to extract a confession from at least one of them. Both get a lighter sentence if they stay quiet. Statisticians and game theorists demonstrate that more than likely one will rat on the other before the prisoners can survive the police interrogation and win the game. So, they always argue that the safest way to play the prisoner's dilemma is to give in before the partner can and save oneself. In the worst-case scenario, both prisoners give up the information on each other right away and both get stronger sentencing. Common wisdom suggests that the ultimate lesson of the prisoner's dilemma is to give in to the interrogator or the law in the end. This is because inevitably one of them has to pay back society for the crime and the symbolic importance of this lesson is that, especially when the crime is widely publicized and sensitive, someone will have to be sacrificed to satisfy the people.

At first glance, the parallels between the Jonesboro shooting and this game theorem might not seem obvious. The boys both admitted guilt and everyone knew and saw them committing the crime. They were both taken to jail and, as minors, would be subject to Arkansas law, which had no reliable provision for trying kids so young, eleven and thirteen, as adults.[11] When the police officers apprehended them running through the woods behind Cole Hill, they found them dressed in camouflage outfits with their camping gear dragging behind them, packed for hiding out in the wilderness. The boys had planned the shooting and their getaway. The police already knew the guns were from Golden's grandfather's home and they knew from several students caught in the gunfire that they were Mitchell Johnson and Andrew Golden. When taken into custody, the boys refused to speak to the police until their parents arrived at the police station. The problem with this case is that the public did not want to view children as adults; it needed to see them as children, but their parents were another story, because we "believe" that children are not violent. This is a myth structuring U.S. society and Grossman's analysis of the leaking of violence into the domestic space.

The responsibility for highly publicized crimes is always moral responsibility, an ambiguous penalty demanded by the public to suture the wound opened by the crime. The prisoner's dilemma is played out on a moral plane in school shooting cases, when the parents are called to atone for the sins of their children. Political and legal measures are taken to prevent another incident from occurring, but the heated emotional and psychological "working through" takes place through the battery of the parents and the demonization of their school-shooter kids. The national debate concerning parental responsibility is ridiculous (especially when few parents look after their children's interests in this way). Though they may not be held criminally responsible (many are calling for laws to address this lack), they are always held morally responsible, which is what makes them subject to civil suits later in the name of neglect. To date, there is no law stating that parents are responsible for school shootings, but there will be once the moral revolution being waged in the name of ressentiment has made these laws seem fair and appropriate to the public.

The line between the criminal and the moral is becoming increasingly blurred as states pass laws that hold parents criminally responsible for the minor child's crimes. States, such as Michigan, have passed legislation that makes it possible to send parents to jail in lieu of the children to juvenile detention (we might also ask about this trend given the equally blasé attitude of most people toward the dismantling of the juvenile justice system, which is not a "system" per se, but fifty-one separate adjudicating bodies with their own rules and procedures. The blasé attitude is toward the very idea of juvenile justice as separate from adult justice) just to "make a point" that the state will not tolerate negligent parents. "Making a point" is a morally motivated action, as parents are not serving the time for an equal crime so much as they are being disciplined, in place of the child, to satisfy the society. The law's expressed purpose is to deter parents from thinking of children as individuals (rather than extensions or possessions), subject to the same laws in a democratic society. Furthermore, therapeutic or developmental intervention from a special system, such as that provided by a reform-oriented juvenile justice system, is ignored. Every public policy measure like this is punitive; a penalty will encourage parents to look after their kids' interests and developmental progress. Who needs this law more, the parents, the kids, or the people favoring the law?

As the Golden and Johnson parents began to come under scrutiny, the life histories of the boys were rehearsed to the press by friends and neighbors. Scott Johnson,

Mitchell's father, drove in from Missouri to meet his son at the jail. He was granted a special chat with his son in the corner of the courtroom before the juvenile hearing because he had not had an opportunity to speak with him yet.

Later, Johnson told reporters outside that he knew his son was wrong and that he thought he should be punished, but disagreed that Mitchell should plead sane and guilty. At the trial, he registered his dissent with the court adjudicator, claiming that Mitchell's mother and her lawyer advised Mitchell to do it, but that he was unsure that his son knew what he was doing. Scott Johnson squealed first, by talking to the press and making a plea to the court on his son's behalf.

Meanwhile, Andrew Golden's parents refrained from talking to the press. Andrew was immediately turned into the "bad seed." The parents did not realize they were in the middle of a morality play of the prisoner's dilemma.

Their sons, obviously unable to speak for themselves or to advocate their case, were dependent on their parents' ability to play the game. Both boys would be charged as juveniles because Arkansas law would not allow for them to be prosecuted as adults, even though many officials went to Janet Reno and the Clinton administration in a plea for the federal government to override Arkansas law and try them in a federal court. At the time, commentators were arguing that the arena where the highest penalty would apply be used, but that was apparent lip-service to an angry public, because the federal government has no power over public schools, unless the crime is against someone because of their race, national origin, or status as a police officer.[12] The feelings of public revenge were high in Jonesboro.[13]

Amid all this controversy surrounding guns, the Second Amendment Foundation amplified the political rumor that President Clinton was "embarrassed" by a recent National Center for Education Statistics report (commissioned by Clinton in the wake of Paducah and Jonesboro) that found the "incidence of crime in schools has not grown significantly over the last two decades." In fact, since 1992, the only recorded high incidence year in this decade, "violent deaths in schools have actually declined to less than one-half the rate found in 1992–1994" according to a National School Safety Center report.[14]

TARGETING GIRLS

As coverage of the boys continued, the public learned that Johnson asked for some "scripture stuff" in his jail cell. Johnson also wrote a letter of apology, asking everyone to forgive him and claiming he did not think anyone would die from the shooting. Golden complained about the food and beverage choices.[15] Both boys cried for their mothers and asked their jailers, rather naively, when they were going to get to go home.

Johnson's father continued to plead for leniency for his son, begging that people stop asking for the death penalty and arguing that his absence in his son's life probably explained a part of the event. His mother wanted his lawyer to plead guilty, but his father wanted him to argue for his innocence instead of taking the legal punishment as a child and confinement in a juvenile detention center until the age of twenty-one.

Still, Golden's parents said nothing publicly and in this silence the papers ran stories reporting that they were both postal workers in different offices in the county. They also printed the grandfather's statement made on ABC's *Primetime Live* and quoted in *Time* magazine: "With apparent deliberation, the shooters were aiming high at their targets, at points where bodies are most fragile. The victims were apparently 'selected because of their sex or who they were. It was not random shooting, where you just shoot out there. . . . [I]f that were true, you would have had shot as many boys as girls.'" *Time* notes that only one male was shot of the fifteen, and he was Golden's cousin.[16]

Running stories examined both boys' characters in the *Jonesboro Sun* and *Time*. Johnson, the elder of the two, was portrayed as a confused young man, torn between his divorced parents and stepparents, and jilted by coy, yet cruel young girls at his school. His character was not flat like Golden's. He had many sides that were trying to reconcile with one another. He wanted to be in love with girls who he thought flirted with him at school and he wanted his parents to get back together. He talked about being in a gang at school, but everyone knew he was just lying for attention. He voluntarily went to a friend's church on Sundays, joined a youth group, and called all the adults "sir" and "ma'am." It was implied that the instability of his home life and his parents' divorce were probably responsible for the shooting.

He was apparently reported to be upset by his parents' 1994 divorce; many people argued that his behavior had changed dramatically after their split and that he incorporated their failed marriage as his own and tried to make it right. One of his old friends came forward to talk about Johnson's former suicide threats, saying that he routinely had crushes on girls at school and, when they refused him, he threatened suicide to them and others if they did not "take him back," even though they had never reciprocated. In one incident, he secured a gun and rope he intended to use on himself after one girl "broke up" with him, even though she had no idea he thought that they were going out. The reports insinuate that he was stalking girls at school, but the report does not make much out of this behavior, except to treat it as the normal behavior of a love-sick adolescent whose depression over his parents' divorce probably explains it.

Stalking is a crime in the United States, but it is never addressed when it takes place at schools. Adults are protected by stalking laws while adolescents are not because it is the parents' and schools' responsibility to protect students from stalking, and because parents and school officials do not want to believe that students stalk each other.[17] In this instance, it seems the school is not a public place, even though when other issues are brought forward and scrutinized, like school prayer, it is a very public place where students should be allowed to exercise this right. Studies show that girls are in constant fear for their safety at school, but administrators are reticent to punish this "normal" male behavior, just like lawmakers are slow to punish stalkers. No one wants it to get out that stalking is a routine practice in schools and this silence is just as informative as the literal piles of studies reporting it from anonymous surveys.[18]

At the trial, the prosecuting attorney questioned the fact that Johnson and Golden had only killed women. It was later reasoned that the girls choir had been the first group of students to evacuate the building following the drill. It was all very logical. These innocent young boys are the victims of the guns, too young to be angry with other students at eleven and thirteen, even though Johnson had a problem with another female classmate just days before the shooting. The victims who lived argued that they were targeting students, specifically female students. As proof, one girl said, "This guy was aiming at Emma. . . . He was fixing to shoot her and Mrs. Wright moved in front of her. She got shot. She did. I watched her."[19]

And yet, the focus on the gender aspect is obscured by reports that girls were targeted because they filed out of the building first, or because of Golden's involvement in the Practical Shooters club. The media refused to put the stories together, reporting the "facts" separately as they unfolded from eye-witnesses. Nothing was ever made of Johnson's problem with girlfriends. Nothing was said about Golden. Gun control was the only answer because it is the least common denominator of school shootings; the rest is too messy to attempt to explain.

The disavowal of the gendered aspects of this case far outweighs any others because even as Johnson's awkward girl obsession is revealed, each story is equalized by the media's assertion that it was Golden's idea because he had a bad reputation in town already, whereas Johnson had just moved there and appeared to be very sweet to everyone who knew him. He had even warned a girl at school the day before the shooting that she would find out about a big surprise the next day, after he had told everyone he was in a gang. Much like Luke Woodham's murder of his mother and then his former girlfriend and another girl in the hallway at Pearl High School, this case was marked by a lack of commentary concerning the problems these boys had with girls, especially the ones they murdered.

This omission is mirrored in the expert literature. William Pollack, a Harvard psychologist, made regular appearances on the news throughout the school shooting coverage of Columbine, featuring his book *Real Boys*. To this point, his discussion of the ill-fated socialization of boys in American society is more exacting than any others covered in the news. While he links the problem of rage and violence to boys, he also reifies the "boy" from the rest of the society, claiming they are "crying with bullets, not tears."[20]

He separates the boy from the societal problem of masculinity, even while he links the lack of tears to the "boy code," which, like masculinity, is changed to project a child's problem, not one that carries over to men and boys through the construction of masculinity in society. In Pollack's book, the socialization problem is contained to youth and, though he admits in indirect ways that there are problems with masculinity in American culture, the problem is primarily a developmental one.

The problem with Pollack's thesis is that masculinity, as it crosses over into public culture or even how it relates to women and nonnormative men, remains unquestioned. Instead, he cites Mary Bray Pipher's *Reviving Ophelia* as the female analogue to his book that deals with the problems of girls.[21] Separating the two socialization problems by sex is important because there are different experiences and problems associated with those experiences from the perspective of those subject positions, being a boy or a girl. However, the overall effect of this separation is to heteronormalize the discussion of masculinity and gender, ignoring the way the two positions are not so much really separate as analytically separate. In this way, questions of violence and masculinity associated with modern warfare, police brutality, public shootings by adult males, junk bondsmen, and domestic violence are obscured.

Johnson's behavior, everyone decided, was to be viewed as crying out for help when no one was there to really detect it, especially his parents. Boys are more a product of their environment, according to Pollack, and they should be given more room to deviate from the boy code, something that he spends four hundred pages describing in his book. All of the talk surrounding Johnson centered on his relationship to girls, his polite and gallant demeanor at church meetings, and his tendency to make up stories, such as being a member of the famed Bloods, a gang that did not exist in rural Jonesboro. This contradictory behavior of Johnson's makes him a candidate for the true-false self-dichotomy discussed in chapter 6, having projected one compliant self to adults and letting out signs of conflict in small ways. As one Jonesboro resident commented, "I thought when they were talking about the camouflage clothes, he must have more camouflaged on the inside than we could see on the outside. He seemed like such a neat young man."[22]

Golden, on the other hand, was a "bad seed." He constantly wore camouflage clothes, carried a hunting knife, and rode his bike all over the neighborhood, posing a threat to all the littler boys and girls. As suggested by the *Time* title, he played the "hunter" to Johnson's "choirboy."

As noted earlier in this chapter, gun control became the theme through which the media presented this case. Golden was the representation of everything that is wrong with kids and guns, as every picture of him showed him pointing a gun and aiming at the camera or wearing hunting gear. Johnson is presented as a polite young man who was approached by Golden on the bus the day before the shooting with the idea. Apparently, the two boys had not been seen together before that day and the event came as a total shock to anyone who knew Johnson. By contrast, all of Golden's neighbors (one of whom lost their daughter in the shooting) told reporters that they would not allow their kids to play with Golden because he was a bad influence.

As the media drew the links between his postal-working parents, conservationist father, and hunting and gun training, they marked Golden, the youngest of the two shooters at eleven, as the poster child for gun control. Quotes from friends have him receiving his first gun the second his eyes were open after birth. The neighbors would not let their kids play with him because he was "evil acting" and it was alleged that he constantly threatened other kids.[23] But the overwhelming portrait of Golden was for the benefit of gun control advocates.

Consider this depiction, "Santa gave Drew a shotgun when he was six. The home video of Drew as a tot, rushing to the backyard shooting range, has been played again and again, serving as metaphor and explanation, the macho little-boy equivalent of the dolled-up kindergarten beauty queen."[24]

While Golden is queered in this passage, he is also cast as the male equivalent to JonBenet Ramsey, another victim of predatory culture. The papers are quick to point out the decorations in Golden's grandfather's home: deer antlers and gun racks. Still, Golden's parents remain relatively quiet as the press uses his pictures as screens for the public's projected anxieties and desires, until they find out that Scott Johnson had not been as forthcoming in his confession as was previously believed. A woman in Minnesota reports to the media that Mitchell Johnson molested a two-year-old girl the summer before the shooting.[25] Scott Johnson hires an attorney who specializes in father's rights to their children to spin a new story: Mitchell was also sexually abused when he was six and seven.[26]

RAGE IS AS RAGE DOES

Hi. My name is Mitchell. My thoughts and prayers are with those people who were killed, or shot, and their families. I am really sad inside about everything. My thoughts and prayers are with those kids that I go to school with. I really want people to know the real Mitchell someday.

Sincerely, Mitchell Johnson

—Letter read by Scott Johnson[27]

Mitchell Johnson's father appeared on the *Montel Williams Show* with his lawyer Tom Furst. The subject of the show (following the Littleton, Colorado, and Conyers, Georgia, shootings) was teen rage. Jonesboro had previously been tagged by the media as a case concerning gun control, with the town supporting such logic and adding to the story; after Littleton, the shooting could be rewritten as having been prompted by a special form of teen rage, an uncontrollable anger experienced by boys during their teens that cannot be reasoned with by any peer or adult around them. Rage becomes a disease or dysfunction that boys feel. (Or is it because only *now* that boys may be viewed as feeling, sentient beings that it can be called rage?) Appropriately, two boys who are raging come on the show to talk about how they envy Johnson because "he is not a hero or a criminal; he's a human being who wants his respect." The possessive inflection is interesting. A target of bullying at school, this young man (who said he wanted to grow up to become a musician like Jim Morrison so he could teach the world like Morrison did) felt that respect was something owed to all like-minded students from others, probably those in power. Here, one meets up with a contradiction in the Hobbesian element of the hidden curriculum.

The hidden curriculum is produced by nonregulated practices of students, that is, in the absence of adult supervision or ideas, but within the boundaries and system of privileges set down by the adults running the school. In common parlance, the schoolyard bully is usually discussed with Hobbesian verbiage or, as D. W. Winnicott so eloquently puts it, "I'm the king of the castle! You're the dirty rascal!" is the mantra chanted by students in school, who compete with each other for intangible elements of power.[28] The intangibles are things like fame and "respect" and they are found and won in competition that takes place in the less regulated spaces of the school such as the lobby, commons, lunchroom, and library—places that find their adult analogue in the public sphere of democracies. Yet, the hierarchy is already established in these spaces by students who conform to societal standards of conduct, knowing they have the favor of the school's authorities on their side. The bully or group of bullies is just this group of students and they are the ones that others will inevitably have to face.

However, the difference in schools is that the bully is no Leviathan, at least not the way that Hobbes conceived of the Leviathan as common power to "awe" them all. Normally, parents or onlookers would assume that the people in charge—the administrators and teachers—would be able to serve this function, but as we shall have seen by the end, students must learn how to conduct themselves in these spaces without adult regulation if they are to ever learn how to become peaceful citizens in a democratic community. When students can no longer practice this self-regulation in the absence of the power, they are experiencing a reversal of the "state of nature" because it is the pseudopower of the bully that stands in for the benevolent leader so longed for by conservatives. The bully abuses the position of leader and "turns dictator," venting his own frustration and rage on those who are unlike himself and represent identity characteristics that question his authority. The pretense of democratic equality and the equalization of all social values give students the impression that they deserve prestige and power at school.

The boys who were raging on the *Montel Williams Show,* like school shooters, want one of two things: the respect of the leading "cliques" or to take their place. The brothers are fighting. The public does not give them a chance to see how they might unite against the society in order to change it in constructive ways and how they turn their frustration onto each other and anything resembling the feminine especially, because they are convenient scapegoats and because the bullies have used them as shields. (Why is the murder of the feminine an end goal in all of this masculine rage? Floating effeminacy?)

This interpellation is intended to shame and it hits its mark every time. Like Charlie Decker, the character in Stephen King's story "Rage," these school shooters are triggered by embarrassments or refusals from girls and public humiliation associated with being gay or judged as being effeminate. Fathers become the central figures in the coverage of school shootings. Scott Johnson was heavily invested in clearing Mitchell (and himself of responsibility) of the molestation charges. He began to argue publicly that father's rights should become a prominent political issue because if he had some control over Mitchell's life, instead of the state, he would have been able to get him help and perhaps prevented the shooting. This is a campaign to clean up the image of deadbeat dads and the *Montel Williams Show* is the perfect avenue for this topic. Eventually, the conversation on the show turned to this topic.

When the conversation focused on the role of fathers and sons in American society, especially the rights of divorced fathers lacking custody, Scott Johnson became very animated, arguing that he could not help his son and felt powerless in relation to the bureaucracies upholding custody agreements. Much has been made of the fact that Mitchell had molestation charges filed against him in Minnesota the summer before the shooting by the mother of a two-year-old girl living nearby in his father's trailer park. Mitchell's father claimed that both states (Minnesota and Arkansas) denied him any role in Mitchell's rehabilitation and, caught up in red tape, Mitchell never received psychiatric counseling. He was denied the right to assert a parental role in Mitchell's life.

Williams became very active in the conversation at this point, jumping in and saying, "I myself am a divorced father who pays an inordinate amount of child support and, if I want to go over to that state she's living in, *yank her up by the hair*, and take an active role in her life—making decisions about what she does—the state says I can't."[29]

It is interesting to note that when the discussion centers on boys and their fathers, that relationship is discussed as critical to the emotional development of a "nonviolent" boy, but when the discussion turns to that between a father and daughter, it falls into a possessive, abusive, economic relationship where the man's power is limited only by the state; the state is limiting access to the father's possessions.

The discussion is inextricably gendered and tied to the family. When fathers have their backs against the wall because of public discussions about any range of topics from school shootings to gangs, the paternal relationship is economized and questioned only to the extent that the fathers are unable to exert the magical presence in their sons' lives that would make them docile and respectable, but to whom? Charlie Decker understands very clearly that he will never have an amicable relationship with his father and even though he is publicly humiliated in front of a love interest, he does not take his anger up with his father; instead, he takes it up with a popular boy at school who later dated her.

By contrast, mothers are made to look ineffectual and weak by default. Since they cannot apparently "get by" (as they apparently should) without the financial assistance of the father, they are presumed weak in every other sense. Women cannot socialize boys to become heroic men, so again, they are weak. Both parental figures become the losers (and victims) as the kids get battered in the process. They learn what it is like to be men and women all right, just like their angry, resentful parents.

The whole discussion reinforces the age-old assumption that men are lazy and women are weak, but the assertion made by fathers' rights organizations does not lead forward to nonviolent social relations, but backward to Oedipal politics. Jonesboro, while sparking the gun control debate in Congress, also questioned the role of the father in the life of the son. The loss of the father was mourned in the coverage of Jonesboro, even while people neglected the role of Golden's parents in his life, probably because they lost the symbolic war for a leaner public sentence.

These two concerns—for the reproduction of real, implicitly paternal authority, harkening back to the law of the father as it figures in contemporary discussions of the family and boy socialization, and for the reproduction of patrimony in public and politics—are echoed in Grossman's theory that features the "virgin" relationship that researchers have toward killing. To those issues, I now turn.

CRUELTY IN A VIRGIN CULTURE

As suggested earlier, Grossman argues that the pseudospecification enacted by video games, such as *Doom* and *Quake,* separate youth from the reality of killing. For him, the instinctual posturing or feigning of power precedes the act of killing (the "masculine masquerade"), followed by the instinctual order to stand down. Aggression, apparently, is present in the posturing, but it is not a prelude to murder because species do not kill members of the same species. This is applied to soldiers in Grossman's analysis, but he later applies it to civilian boys.

However, the complex structure of the military is not given any discussion in Grossman's theory as it relates to power and aggression, except to say that somewhere around the Vietnam War the military changed. Aggression is assumed, but there is no cause of the aggression given, as in Milgram's study, except the assumption that we humans are born to be led. Beyond the midbrain, we are to assume, lies the aggression that slips through in the posturing (like a dog showing its teeth?), but it is really only a warning, not a sign of the violence to come. The order to kill must be forced by psychological training, as soldiers are introduced to killing by their superiors or, later, by the technology that comes to replace them in the form of video games and violent media.

The "leader," in some form, is necessary in the killing equation, both in keeping the soldiers restrained and in letting them loose when the time to kill comes. The leader acts as the "safety catch" on humans who do not instinctively want to kill each other. Thus, there is vagueness to the conceptualization in his theory. While we learn that soldiers in battle really do not want to kill each other, we are unable to discern the origin of their aggression that superiors (drill sergeants and technology) mobilize in the service of killing.

Is it caused by the military organization, as Milgram might have argued? The reader is left to discern that, by mystification, aggression is a natural, phenomenal term; that is, it explains itself. Paul de Man writes of this mystification, "What we call ideology is precisely the confusion of linguistic with natural reality, of reference with phenomenalism."[30] Aggression is something that we assume, in ideological form, to be a part of human life. True enough, but it does not spring from an abyss, it has causes and forces that bring it into the open.

In his brief elucidation of Milgram's text, Grossman cites his depiction of a businessman who became a torturer in the Obedience study.[31] He then compares this to the even greater influence that the military must have over men's minds in the service of killing: "If this kind of obedience could be obtained with a lab coat and a clipboard by an authority who has been known for only a few minutes, how much more would the trappings of military authority and months of bonding accomplish?"[32]

The implication that Milgram's lab coat and clipboard are relatively minor factors that induce killing (as compared with the bonding of the military) is problematic. Grossman, as noted earlier, has no *explicit* concept of socialization in his theory. Could not the lab coat and the clipboard signify the expert that Americans are socialized to respect and obey over a long period of their lives?[33] His assumption that "only a few minutes" establishes the degree of influence the figure in the lab coat has over the businessman is faulty and ignores the very same factors that stimulate students to act in certain ways under the influence of the hidden curriculum. Or that sports heroes undergo in the process of winning the big game.

The main point, however, is that Grossman also assumes that leadership and power lie in the individual human who assumes a direct relationship with the killer/torturer-in-training, not with ideas and things and what they signify. Is it the lab coat that "triggers" the rage or is it the man wearing it? Furthermore, where did these feelings of cruelty come from or are they really simply the effect of midbrain enabling? These are extremely important issues because if the enabling is not linked with a leader, but with the symptoms of society and how they influence publicity and behavior, then the logic of a paternal military does not apply.

The problem is not that a benevolent form of leadership (e.g., the father knows best when he operates within the boundaries of the law) should be encouraged to counter the violent ones, but that the locus of authority no longer lies in the leader. It lies in the form of the culture that is remarkably similar to reification because the identification does not take place with humans, but with things, such as spectral objects and fantasies. Though Grossman does argue that technology is the midbrain enabler that replaces the father, he harbors the false hope that it will be controlled if it "goes beyond print media and the flintlocks."[34] Finally, in a gross misappropriation of Milgram's study, he neglects the idea that "malevolent systems of authority" do not have to be centrally focused on an individual, but are "systems" and, as such, cover a wider range of culture than he imagines in *On Killing*.

Systems could cover capitalist logic, homophobia, bureaucratic efficiency schemes, and fad diets, all the regimes of intelligibility that make decision making more simplistic, but they also enact an unacknowledged violence on the subject who uses them. The problem is with the expert who operates outside the boundaries of practical experience to the detriment of people. The leader is a virtual dinosaur in contemporary life. If he commands, it is through myth and in the imaginary. In relatively prosperous times, Americans are more likely to be led by statistics in newspapers than charismatic leaders.

But let me return to the leader argument briefly. Grossman argues that Americans need positive role models and his primary example is the drill sergeant. In his chapter "Social Learning and Role Models," Grossman discusses "Drill Sergeant G," the most important role model in his life, who initiated him to military training on a "cold morning in 1974." Why the drill sergeant? Because while he trains men to kill, he also trains them to be disciplined and obedient and he never goes above the law. More importantly,

> [i]n the traditional nuclear family there is a stable father figure who serves as a role model for young boys. Boys who grow up without a stable male figure in their lives are desperately seeking a role model. Strong, powerful, high-status role models such as those offered in movies and on television fill the vacuum in their lives. We have taken away their fathers and replaced them with new role models whose successful response to every situation is violence. And then we wonder why our children have become ever more violent.[35]

Who took them away? What will get them back? Do we want them? Predatory culture has now driven the father away and taken hold of his children. And yet, the "off-switch" argument is not an option because, he argues, it is "profoundly racist. . . . [T]he black community in America is the 'culture' or 'nation' that has born the brunt of the electronic media's violence-enabling. In this case, poverty, drugs, gangs, discrimination, and the availability of firearms all predispose more blacks than whites toward violence. These factors defeat the first filter; then the absence of the second, midbrain filter becomes noticeable."[36]

He then likens this media dumping to the dumping of alcohol on the Native American population as a genocidal policy. So after all the other variables are controlled, media violence becomes the ultimate cause of the misery African Americans experience in the United States. Forget targeting racism, redistributing wealth, funding education and social services, or building a tax base for African Americans; just censor their cable.

Grossman's inability to confront a concept of society, except that given by a leader, is what allows for this disturbing (and seemingly politically correct) response to African American crime rates and incarceration. This is because, in grand conspiratorial form, he argues that the nation "pumps" violent television into the cities and this is what makes those spaces so violent. Kids in the African American community can "identify" with the negative role models on television and then seek to emulate them in their everyday lives. This keeps them from obeying the law or developing positive attachments to authority figures that do not promote unheroic violence.

As this debate takes place, the National Association for the Advancement of Colored People (NAACP) files a lawsuit against the media conglomerates because of a lack of African American programming (what then are these kids identifying with?). Or, as the press release from 1999 states, the "whitewash" of network television occurred during that same year, 1998–1999. Perhaps Grossman's argument is that nonwhite students are cross-identifying with hegemonic, negative television (i.e., that which represents the invisible white norm). If so, all the better to the theory that the breakdown of society is represented by the increase in school violence in "rural" areas. This simply means that the exploitation of youth, capital, and human decency has found expression in rural and suburban areas. This further delinks his argument about violence leaking from race; there is no reason to mention urban violence in his book since he cannot explain it without resorting to baseless arguments about cable television programming that sound more like conspiracies than the actuality of network hegemony, which implies racist neglect of adequate or proportional representation.[37]

Grossman dismisses the sociological insight that nonwhite communities develop a subculture and parallel informal economy in which to thrive while they are systematically discriminated against by the "legal" ones and doubly oppressed by the lack of a tax base when racist companies and their employees engage in "white flight" from those areas (e.g., Detroit). Grossman further writes, "Poverty and racism have always been a part of our society (often much more so than today), just as propaganda, class divisions and racism have always been manipulated in combat. And guns have always been present in American society, just as they have always been present in American wars."[38]

Let me go back to the "pumping" for a minute because perhaps Grossman is viewing this problem from a local perspective. A local Jonesboro resident writing into the Turn Left website notes that "[t]he local TCI cable system cuts off the air and blocks shows or movies that are not 'adequate' for Joneboro's audience, making me question if this practice is not a serious violation of Freedom of Speech."[39] This censorship was in place, in Jonesboro, before the shootings at Westside Middle School. It does not occur to Grossman that Jonesboro might be a unique place in its censorship of cable because he assumes that there is some sort of conspiratorial element involved in the cable of nonwhite communities when that is simply not the case. Furthermore, the censorship in Jonesboro does not seem to have protected Golden and Johnson from being enabled to kill.

ARTS AND ENTERTAINMENT SPECIAL "MEDIA CENSORSHIP"

From now on the cheap, and the tawdry, is out.

—Ralph Breen, Chairman, Motion Picture Association, 1934

As promised, Grossman's targeting of the need for "kilology" is an important part of our discussion of school violence. He argues that as we have repressed killing over the years, it has emerged in "bizarre form." Like the sex that was repressed by the Victorians, the killing that is repressed by American society takes place as we remove ourselves from the reality of death, moving funeral arranging outside the home and opposing the killing of animals.

Blending themes from Jean Baudrillard's *Symbolic Exchange and Death* and Michel Foucault's depiction and critique of the "repressive hypothesis" from the *History of Sexuality,* Grossman manages to obscure the argument once more.[40] But as we have seen, the question is not about the logic of the argument so much as it is about getting the agenda in place by showing the reader an explanation that, while not plausible, seems interesting.

As was noted earlier, guns are an object of fascination (and fetishes) in the United States as in no other nation-state. Prohibitions, disavowals, and hypocrisies surround national discourses concerning guns and their control. Though it may seem trite to compare Foucault's study of sexual liberation in the eighteenth century to the current fascination with firearms, this comparison is primarily prompted by Grossman's comparison of violence to sex and his claim that modern nations were "liberated" from sexual repression and that we need only to make a similar revolution concerning youth violence.

That is, Grossman, a military psychologist, maintains and promotes the "repressive hypothesis" while he talks incessantly about violence on national television, at book signings, school functions, and as a new expert in the quest to add a discourse to American violence. And, not coincidentally, this argument reinforces the position as an expert who listens to the repressed stories of killing. He writes, "Peace will not come until we have mastered both sex and war, and to master war we must study it with the diligence of Kinsey or Masters and Johnson. Every society has a blind spot, an area into which it has great difficulty looking. Today that blind spot is killing. A century ago it was sex."[41] Foucault would respond by saying that Western society has not "mastered" sex (or violence for that matter) but it has "economized" it and turned it into a project.

We do not get liberated from repression, but simply create a new list of categories and discourses about sex such that calling into question the taboo against publicly discussing sex is an "incitement to discourse." Baudrillard would say that in all this excessive attention to sex, we have managed to kill the pleasure of it, so that it no longer holds any fascination for us.

Similarly, in *The Perfect Crime* he argues that we have erased reality by simulating everything in social life.[42] How much more of a denial of practical experience is there? Practical experience is not to be understood as something utilitarian, as it is often supposed, but as something personal that takes place between individuals and their environment that shapes a profound respect for living a good life, not *the* good life, but a life free from constant surveillance and supervision.

In Grossman's plan for killing, we end up exactly where he does not want us to go: in the classifying and controlling study of killing that desensitizes the "population" to death even more than any movie could. Will we begin to "administer" killing and in this kill any vital impulse left in society? When society is disavowed totally, it is recuperated by the state and the enjoyment that comes with it is doled out in managed doses. Censorship replaces the freedom we *suppose* exists in liberal democracies. And this would be the point of the inquiry: If we are so free, why do we constantly need to censor our children and ourselves? There is a basic lack of trust in democracy and its citizenry, a trust that would come from a national respect for practical experience. For if we knew why, on an everyday level, we were performing routine acts (like watching television), we might not worry so much about the effects of its messages.

Lost in all of this is any mention of gun control or methods for understanding the national fascination with guns. Even though Jonesboro and its mediated aftermath was all about "the guns" in the end, the public is still unable to deal with the question directly. As victims' parents lobbied the Clinton administration for gun laws following the shootings at Jonesboro, they asked only that "gun locks" are required, not that guns be taken away or understood.[43] The "safety catch" became the metaphor for understanding school violence, but it would not stay in place much longer.

Given Grossman's avoidance of any theory of society, it is no wonder that in his last chapter he quotes Hobbes on the state of nature and on the lives of men being "poor, nasty, brutish and short." Unlike Hobbes, however, he does not argue that women have dominion over children because they, by and large, have the power in matters regarding childrearing.

Grossman would seem to agree with Scott Johnson that if he had been a stable presence in his son's life, the videos and movies would not have filled his head with negative thoughts and the shootings at Westside Middle School might never have taken place. The father is the "real" safety catch on the son and until we return to Oedipal politics, Americans run the risk of falling back into the state of nature. He does not count on the son fighting back and that is exactly what Kip Kinkel did the night before he shot up the commons area at Thurston High School two months later in the spring of 1998.

NOTES

1. Lt. Col. Dave Grossman, *On Killing: The Psychological Cost of Learning to Kill in War and Society* (Boston: Little, Brown, 1995), 304.

2. Stanley Milgram, *Obedience to Authority: An Experimental View* (New York: Harper and Row, 1974), 1.

3. Milgram, *Obedience to Authority;* Robert Jay Lifton, *Nazi Doctors: Medical Killing and the Psychology of Genocide* (New York: Basic, 1986); Hannah Arendt, *Eichmann in Jerusalem: A Report on the Banality of Evil* (New York: Penguin, 1963); Daniel Goldhagen, *Hitler's Willing Executioners: Ordinary Germans and the Holocaust* (New York: Knopf, 1996); Christopher R. Browning, *Ordinary Men: Reserve Police Battalion 101 and the Final Solution in Poland* (New York: HarperCollins, 1992).

4. Or as it seems now, the new media slogan following Columbine is "guns do not kill people, kids kill people."

5. Grossman, *On Killing,* 315.

6. Thomas Hobbes, *Leviathan* (1652; reprint, London: Everyman's Library, 1973).

7. Michel Foucault, *The History of Sexuality,* vol. 1, trans. Robert Hurley (New York: Vintage, 1978), 1–49. Foucault's argument is that sexuality was not "liberated" but rather freed up just enough to become categorized, controlled, and studied. It would remain subject to moral codes, civil law, reproductive aims, and identity politics despite the fact that during the nineteenth century the "age of multiplication" of sexuality produced a "dispersion of sexualities, a strengthening of their disparate forms, a multiple implantation of 'perversions'" (37). Recent attempts to study and regulate gun ownership, distribution, and control simply repeat a similar process, but by no means free up our relationship to violence in such as way as to understand its power over U.S. society. The same goes for sexuality. In short, any attempt to study or control violence and sexuality is a move that is saturated by the power-knowledge nexus that runs modern societies; there is no liberation.

8. Mikhail Bakunin, *Statism and Anarchy* (Cambridge: Cambridge University Press, 1991).

9. This is an extremely complicated connection that is explained by Deems D. Morrione, "Sublime Monsters and Virtual Children" (Ph.D. diss., Purdue University, 2002). My interest in this issue is only in the ways it allows kids to be mistreated in public schools and affects the relationship between generations in American society.

10. It is unclear if one of the two shooters pulled the fire alarm or another unidentified student. The reports are inconsistent and unclear, but none of the media seemed too terribly interested in sorting out this confusion. A later report claims that Golden went into school at 12:30 and asked to be excused. He then went to pull the fire alarm and ran out to meet Johnson on Cole Hill.

11. Immediately following the Jonesboro shootings, Arkansas governor Mike Huckabee called for the Arkansas state government to address legislation that was already under review to reform the juvenile justice system in Arkansas. The Extension of the Juvenile Justice (EJJ) Act 1999 (bill number 1192), the final product of this process, extends jurisdiction over adolescents accused of serious offenses like murder from eighteen to the age of twenty-one. This means that juveniles convicted of capital offenses can be sent to a number of different courts depending on the discretion of the judge in the case. They may be tried as adults or juveniles, but the amendment gives the judge the right to review and extend juvenile sentencing past the age of eighteen. In some cases, juveniles may be remanded to adult courts once they have finished their sentences in juvenile incarceration. This provision is contained in Arkansas Senate Bill 505 as an amendment to the EJJ. Previously, juveniles could not be reviewed as adults for crimes before the age of sixteen. Also, Arkansas was already setting the bill in motion when the Jonesboro shooting took place, but it was primarily to overhaul the juvenile justice system in the state that had been reporting widespread abuse for years. Arkansas was looking to states like Florida and Texas as models for its new system. See "Regular Legislative Sessions" for 1999 on the Arkansas Legislative website at www.arkleg.state.ar.us (accessed August 16, 2002).

12. "Reno Weighs Federal Charges in Shooting," *USA Today,* 31 March 1998, at www.usatoday.com/news/special/shoot/shoot015.htm (accessed February 3, 1999).

13. And, understandably so.

14. "School Shooting Numbers Actually Down," *Gottlieb-Tartaro Report* (Second Amendment Foundation), 4 April 1998, at www.saf.org/gottlieb-tartaro.html (accessed August 15, 2002).

15. "Mother Says Her Son Didn't Plan Attack," *USA Today,* 6 April 1998, at www.usatoday.com/news/special/shoot /shoot027.htm (accessed February 3, 1999).

16. Nadya Labi, "The Hunter and the Choir Boy," *Time,* 6 April 1998, 3.

17. American Association of University Women, *Hostile Hallways: The AAUW Survey of Sexual Harassment in America's Schools,* Research Report no. 923012 (Washington, D.C.: Harris/Scholastic Research, 1993). Ron Avi Astor, Heather Ann Meyer, and William J. Behre, "Unowned Places and Times: Maps and Interviews about Violence in High Schools," *American Educational Research Journal* 36, no. 1 (1999): 30–42.

18. American Association of University Women studies show that girls in public schools are extremely frightened on a daily basis by violence and sexual violence threats from boys. The subject of several fictionalized televised dramas (such as *Law and Order*), this problem is never addressed by the media coverage, except as an interesting detail. See American Association of University Women, *Hostile Hallways.*

19. Labi, "Hunter and the Choir Boy," 2.

20. William Pollack, *Real Boys: Rescuing Our Sons from the Myths of Boyhood* (New York: Henry Holt, 1998), xx.

21. Mary Bray Pipher, *Reviving Ophelia: Saving the Selves of Adolescent Girls* (New York: Putnam, 1994).

22. "Boys Charged in Jonesboro Shootings," *USA Today*, 11 August 1998, at www. usatoday.com/news/special/shoot/shoot013.htm (accessed February 3, 1999).

23. "Cold-Blooded, Evil Children," *The Record's Classified Online*, 26 March 1998.

24. Labi, "Hunter and the Choir Boy," 3.

25. The source claims Mitchell Johnson's aunt told the *Saint Paul Pioneer Press* following the shooting. Scott Johnson took Mitchell to the police station following the molestation incident and had him charged and sent to the juvenile court for evaluation. A decision was pending when the shooting took place. There was confusion about which state would process and rehabilitate Mitchell, Minnesota or Arkansas, since he lived with his mother in Arkansas. The alleged incident took place while he was visiting his father for the summer in Minnesota.

26. "Shooting Suspect Claims He Was Molested," *USA Today*, 6 April 1998, at www. usatoday.com/news/special/shoot/shoot029.htm (accessed 6 April 1998).

27. "Shooting Suspect Claims He Was Molested."

28. D. W. Winnicott, *Home Is Where We Start From: Essays by a Psycho-Analyst* (New York: Norton, 1986), 57.

29. "Teen Rage," *The Montel Williams Show* (October 8, 1998; replayed June 10, 1999).

30. Paul de Man, *The Resistance to Theory* (Minneapolis: University of Minnesota Press, 1993), 11.

31. Milgram conducted a voluntary study of obedience in New Haven, Connecticut, from 1960 to 1963 (see Milgram, *Obedience to Authority*). Milgram solicited voluntary participants in a newspaper ad to be paid in exchange for their involvement in a scientific experiment. Using actors to play victims and leaders, Milgram had the research participants take orders from a leader to shock the victim, who was ostensibly hooked up to an electrode. Each time the victim failed to learn the lesson given by the voluntary participant, he or she was directed to shock the victim, at increasing levels, until the victim complied or "learned." Milgram concluded that participants "obey" authority figures, particularly scientific ones, even if they believe the actions to be morally unjustifiable. What is more unjustifiable to them is to break allegiance to the authority figure.

32. Grossman, *On Killing*, 143.

33. As Milgram writes in his ninth recurring theme while searching the transcripts of My Lai and the Adolf Eichmann trial and the accounts of the trial of Lt. Henry Wirtz, "Obedience does not take the form of a dramatic confrontation of opposed wills or philosophies but is embedded in a larger atmosphere where social relationships, career aspirations, and technical routines set the dominant tone. Typically, we do not find a heroic figure struggling with conscience, nor with a pathologically aggressive man ruthlessly exploiting a position of power, but a functionary who has been given a job to do and who strives to create an impression of competence in his work." See Milgram, *Obedience to Authority*, 187.

34. Grossman, *On Killing*, 326.

35. Grossman, *On Killing*, 322.

36. Grossman, *On Killing*, xxi.

37. On July 12, 1999, the NAACP issued a press release announcing it would open a study to monitor network television for diversity, noting that further action may include "legal action against the networks and affiliates based on 1934 Communications Act that declared the airwaves belong to the public." On the same day, another press release announced a class action lawsuit led by the NAACP against gun manufacturers for their manner of distribution

and sales. It cites a 1998 Vital Statistics report that concludes that African American males aged fifteen to twenty-four are five times more likely to be injured by firearms than white males of the same age group. For African American females, the rate was four times as likely as white females in the same age group. By July 16, the NAACP announced a federal lawsuit against one hundred gun manufacturers in the U.S. Court for the Eastern District. All press releases may be found at www.naacp.org/news/releases.html (accessed August 17, 2002).

38. Grossman, *On Killing,* 303.

39. "Liberal Unfriendly Place: Jonesboro, Arkansas," at www.turnleft.com/places/jonesboro.html (accessed August 10, 2000).

40. Jean Baudrillard, *Symbolic Exchange and Death,* trans. Ian Hamilton Grant (London: Sage, 1993); Michel Foucault, *The History of Sexuality,* 3 vols, trans. Robert Hurley (New York: Vintage, 1980).

41. Grossman, *On Killing,* xxiv.

42. Jean Baudrillard, *The Perfect Crime,* trans. Chris Turner (New York: Verso, 1996).

43. "School Safety and Youth Violence, Panel I," White House Conference on School Safety, Departments of Education and Justice, Washington, D.C., October 15, 1998. The commentary came from Suzann Wilson's speech, a mother from Jonesboro, Arkansas. Courtesy of the C-SPAN Archives, Purdue Research Foundation, West Lafayette, Indiana.

3

Springfield, Oregon:
The Law of the Father and
Homicidal Rage

I had no other choice.

—Kip Kinkel on "Why?" in a taped interview with police[1]

Kip Kinkel had been expelled from school the day before his shooting spree
took place in the Thurston High School cafeteria on May 21, 1998. He was
expelled for having bought a gun from another student at school and for keeping
it in his locker that day. He had received a phone call the night before from a
classmate, Korey Ewart, who had stolen a .32 caliber pistol from another student's
father that evening. On the phone, he reportedly told Kinkel to bring money to
school the next day since he had a "surprise" for him. After the boys had made
the exchange in the early morning of the school day, the security guard on campus at the school heard rumors that a student had a gun in his locker. After further inquiries, he was led to Ewart's locker, then Kinkel's, where school officials
found the gun and called the Springfield police to have both boys arrested. Kinkel
was charged with five felonies and expelled from school for the rest of the year,
and Thurston counselors were busy looking for an alternative school for Kinkel
to attend in the coming fall.[2]

This case, however, opens with a father and ends with his death. Kinkel's rage combined a number of factors: his family's more than "good enough" mothering and his
father's alleged control. To get to the school that day, Kinkel had to kill his parents

and this aspect of the Springfield case added another element to the public's reaction and the experts' conclusions.

In this chapter, several themes are explored that changed the way student shooters would be viewed up to the Columbine event. As mentioned earlier, Kinkel killed his parents and he had been expelled from school the day before for having a gun in his locker that he had bought from another student. What is different about this case is that Kinkel was overprocessed. Psychiatrists, tutors, educational specialists, police authorities, and his parents had evaluated him. Up to the point when he entered the cafeteria for the shooting, everyone surrounding Kinkel had done everything "right" according to models of violence prevention lurking in the public's mind. "Why Kip?" posted on a theater marquis in downtown Springfield really signified the anxiety of a city and a nation whose solutions to that moment had all been used up.

His father went to the police station that afternoon to pick him up and later that day called the principal to talk about "what was to be done" about Kinkel. Kinkel's father reportedly also called the Oregon National Guard to inquire about summer youth programs for the problematic Kinkel. Kinkel would spend the summer grounded and repeat the current (now defunct) semester during the next school year, possibly in home schooling. He would spend the remainder of the month left in the term at home on restriction; no television, video games, music, guns, or contact with friends were in his immediate future. He would spend those days with his aging and retired parents, Bill and Faith Kinkel.

According to the *Rolling Stone* interview, the father took the son to lunch at a local hamburger joint, the proprietor of which was said to have reported them getting along "just fine" and even joking with the waitress behind the counter about the pace at which the food was prepared. They sat for an hour and left. No one saw them together again. The next event recorded in the sequence is by Nick Hiassen and Tony McCown, Kinkel's two best friends, who spoke with him on the phone later that evening. They said that Kinkel was waiting for his mother to return home and that he said his father was probably "out at a bar getting drunk."[3] Later, Kinkel's friends would learn that his father was already dead when they spoke to Kinkel and that he was waiting for his mother, probably to kill her as well.

All of Kinkel's friends and relatives who were interviewed recall him having virtually no violent reaction to the discipline and punishments he received from his parents over the years preceding the May 21 shootings. This includes the day at the police station with his father for the gun incident at school. The school authorities even said that when he was brought to the office to be questioned about the stolen gun, he simply admitted that it was in his locker and told them where to find it. They say he always appeared remorseful, even worried about the way his behavior would reflect on his parents, two highly valued and admired members of the Springfield educational community.

Randall Sullivan's portrait of Kinkel in *Rolling Stone* splices together reflections from those who claim to have remembered him as very calm each time he had been caught for some offense. Whether throwing a large rock off an overpass on a Bend, Oregon, snowboarding trip with a friend (his first felony) or the jokes he made to classmates about torturing animals, Kinkel's demeanor was rational and remorseful.[4] Sullivan's portrait of Kinkel leaves the reader with two basic (and conflicting) interpretations of him: either he was an average kid with a conscience (as everyone interviewed claimed) or he was a master of disguise, a calculating individual capable of hiding his true feelings and waiting for an opportune moment to vent his frustrations. Either way, the portrait is disturbing, right down to the clown-like caricature superimposed over Kinkel's real school picture that introduces the article. The insinuation of the image is psychopathology.

Kinkel was a "constant problem" for parents who needed to keep the truth under wraps. His mastery over his unacceptable emotions was so complete that he was able to produce masks to hide his real persona: an animal torturer and a boy scout, and a Goth who listened to Marilyn Manson and was also a football player on the Thurston High School junior varsity team. A disturbing fascination with gun collecting and explosive devices is juxtaposed to an enjoyment found while accompanying his family on trips to help others less fortunate.

Both Spanish teachers, Kinkel's parents had raised his sister to become a cheerleader, who eventually earned a scholarship to the University of Hawaii. Their troubles with Kinkel had started long before the shooting, according to friends, family, and colleagues. Kinkel had always been a disciplinary problem, refusing to get out of the pool on a family camping trip and making a scene when his father forced him to get out. Or insisting that his parents buy him a gun (and then several more) by pointing out the contradiction between their opposition to guns and his paternal grandfather's favor toward them as hunting tools.

Alone at home after school, with his father dead in the bathroom on the first floor, Kinkel planned his rampage in his bedroom, collecting bomb-making materials, guns, and ammunition he kept in a trunk and hidden in various places all over the house. Watching *South Park* and talking to his friends on a three-way phone connection, Kinkel enacted the life of a "normal" adolescent.

A few events leading up to the shooting alarmed his parents and alerted them to his possible antisocial behavior. On a trip to Bend, Oregon, with a friend and his family, Kinkel and his buddy dropped a large boulder off an overpass. A cop saw them and chased them down, and Kinkel's parents were awakened from their bed to drive all night to pick him up from the vacation. They began to check on him and searched his room, finding most of the guns and the ammunition, which were supposed to have been locked away until use at a firing range. He was grounded for that incident, as the Kinkels did not believe in corporal punishment. By the time Kinkel was facing a second felony for having a gun in his locker at school, Bill Kinkel was out of options. The day he brought Kinkel home he called the National Guard to inquire about enlisting him in the Youth Challenge Program, which takes kids "who are on the razor's edge, ready to fall on the dark side."[5] It was after this episode with his father at home that Kinkel decided to end it by shooting his father in the back of the head while he sat at the kitchen table.[6]

By all accounts, they were the perfect liberal, progressive family marred only by their troubled teenage son. Richard Bushnell, a family friend, says in the *Frontline* interview, "Bill and Faith had pride. They were highly, highly respected people. Highly intelligent people and it was one of those things where they had to bear whatever Kip did to 'em in the eyes of their friends and apparently there may have been some shame from them."[7] The omnipresence of the educational community in the Kinkel's lives may account for the pressure on Kinkel to be like his parents and his guilt and shame for failing to do so.

In fact, unlike the other cases, there is virtually no discussion of religion in the Kinkels' life, but rather, as Kristen Kinkel herself notes, her parents' overvaluation of "cultural experience." So intense was this attitude on her parents' part that they took a sabbatical year in Spain thinking that the trip would give the kids a head start by learning a language in its native atmosphere. Kinkel was in preschool at the time and his sister speculates that this experience actually held him back and was the beginning of his inferiority complex toward the rest of his family. They were able to pick up Spanish immediately and spoke that only while on the trip. Kinkel, she says, was just mastering English and then he had to be confronted with another language in order to keep up with the family. A friend recalls that they would speak Spanish at home and Kinkel would cover his ears and call out: "No more Spanish!"

The *Rolling Stone* exposé frequently references the family reading *Don Quixote* aloud as entertainment. Rather unlike the experiences of the other shooters in religious settings, Kinkel's upbringing was devoutly secular humanist. His parents opposed violence of any sort and Kinkel was never allowed to have toy soldiers or gun-like toys as a small child. As Kristin Kinkel has said, "violence, in our house, was a huge no-no."[8] But as we move on through Kinkel's life, we learn that he eventually "wore them down" on the gun issue as they began to think they had made a mistake in trying to shelter him from violence by making it into "forbidden fruit."[9]

This reading of Kinkel as a burden for his parents, whose need to keep his true personality under wraps out of fear of the judgment of others and whose mastery of his own emotions was extreme, leads the reader of these mediated stories to the conclusion that the school shooting phenomenon is closely linked to the figure of the serial killer in popular culture. The serial killer, like the image of Kinkel, has the ability to create and sustain several "masks" in order to hide his darker side from those close to him and his identity from the authorities, mystifying and eluding profiling, detection, and analysis.

The psychopathic juvenile adds intrigue to the public's ready attention to "true crime" as a form of entertainment. All of the indicators for serial killer behavior begin to match those of the possible school shooter. Jeffrey Dahmer was known to have tortured animals as a child as he worked his way up to humans. Similarly, the press amplifies the quips made by Kinkel at school concerning his fascination with blowing up squirrels and using them for target practice, but does not question the fact that Kinkel's friends willingly admit to participating in these rituals with him. Are they mad as well?

In chapter 1, it was noted that violent juvenile offenders are identified through the common symptom triad in the psychological literature: fire-setting, torturing animals, and bed-wetting. Bed-wetting is the simplest of the three to confirm because patients cannot readily admit to engaging in the other practices, knowing full well that it would spell further psychiatric inquiry and perhaps even removal from school. In this case, there is ample testimony that Kinkel told people that he tortured animals and enjoyed it, often describing the horror in vivid detail; but how would a boy whose parents kept such a close watch over him have allowed him to torture animals? And, as Sullivan notes in a flash of sympathy for the kid, why did not he torture his beloved dog? The sign-value attached to animal torture in the true crime genre is strong, much stronger than any proof revealed to back up such claims.

Furthermore, why would a kid brag about torturing animals if he were doing it as an unconscious manifestation of his pathology? Dahmer is reported as admitting to have tortured animals only after he was incarcerated and questioned about murdering several young boys; he is not reported to have gone to school and bragged about it. Part of the reason for this may be that, in Dahmer's case, he was trying less to torture animals for the sake of doing so than trying to funnel an impulse into a secret habit. Secret is the key word here, for if Dahmer "knew" he had murderous desires, then, true to the serial killer profile, he needed to keep them a secret at all costs. Kinkel was telling everyone about his angst. As D. W. Winnicott would say, he was crying out for a kind of help unavailable at the psychiatrist's office or in the prescription pill Prozac.

And what about the Goth linkage? Killers whose pasts include animal torture are linked with Gothic culture due to the ritualized aspects of the practice: sacrificing animals, bloodletting, and so on. The Gothic tradition, now so critically examined as a public health problem, used to be the butt of jokes, a form of novelistic entertainment or a refuge for castaways in the halls at high schools.

Saturday Night Live is perhaps the only popular culture venue that depicts Goth teens as harmless and makes them the butt of jokes in skits, a harmless portrayal of adolescent angst. Two teenagers and the regular guests hold a cable access show in the basement of their parents' home. The real humor of it is when the older brother of one of them routinely comes downstairs to beat him up or pick on them both while wearing a Michigan State t-shirt and drinking beer, an obvious reference to the tyranny of the Jocks or Sports. This relationship between the two cliques was only discussed after Eric Harris and Dylan Klebold made their displeasure at the Jocks obvious.

These insights aside, several interest groups took the claims about Kinkel's dabbling in Goth subculture so seriously that they issued public statements concerning animal torture. In perfect form, they argued the point that it is well-documented by the American Medical Association that people who torture animals will eventually move on to humans. But what about people who allegedly torture animals? And what about the fact that most boys find perfectly acceptable ways to torture animals, like hunting, trapping, and roadkill games? Where does one draw the line in all these categories between those who will and will not shoot up a school? What about the sacrificing of minorities by police officers who use profiling in cities like Los Angeles, New York, and Detroit, among others? Or of women and health care workers in abortion clinics?

The lines between the human and the animal are difficult to maintain in the face of all this murder and sacrifice of humans, *in their name,* as humanists! Friedrich Nietzsche's nihilistic democracy has seemingly come true. He points out in *On the Genealogy of Morals* that animal torture is a "conscience vivisection" of the human being, implying that torturing an animal is like torturing, not others, but one's self for being human ("We are weary of man"). "We modern men are the heirs of the conscience-vivisection and self-torture of the millennia: this is what we have practiced longest, it is our distinctive art perhaps, and in any case our subtlety in which we have acquired a refined taste. Man has all too long had an 'evil eye' for his natural inclinations, so that they have finally become inseparable from his bad 'conscience.'" Walter Kaufmann, the translator, notes that the German word "tierqualerei" Nietzsche uses to depict "self-torture" literally means "animal torture." Kaufmann further interprets Nietzsche's use of this term as signifying that his "coinage suggest that this kind of self-torture involves mortification of the animal nature of man."[10] This marks the need to view animal cruelty and torture as practices that are linked to the socialization patterns embedded in the type of political system enforcing them.

But there is yet another way to look at the connection between animal torture and human torture that appears in the American Gothic literary tradition. Edgar Allan Poe would describe the move from animal to human torture as one intimately linked with a torture of the self. In his story "The Black Cat," Poe depicts the emotions involved as a man graduates from murdering his pet cat to murdering his wife, two central figures in his life that he loved very much. The man is an average individual with seemingly normal qualities. The emotional subtext of the story shows how a person can become overburdened by the affections of loved ones, even when they do not intend it to be that way. He is in dread of the affection that his cat and wife show for him and this is connected to his possible guilt over a drinking problem. He says that this dread is linked to the denial of human perversity while discussing his feelings after torturing his beloved cat:

> He went about the house as usual, but, as might be expected, fled in extreme terror at my approach. I had so much of my old heart left, as to be at first grieved by this evident dislike on the part of a creature which had once so loved me. But this feeling soon gave place to irritation. And then came, as if to my final and irrevocable overthrow, the spirit of PERVERSENESS. Of this spirit philosophy takes no account. Yet I am not more sure that my soul lives, than I am that perverseness is one of the primitive impulses of the human heart—one of the indivisible primary faculties, or sentiments, which give direction to the character of Man. Who has not, a hundred times, found himself committing a vile or a silly action, for no other reason than because he knows he should not? Have we not a perpetual inclination, in the teeth of our best judgment, to violate that which is Law, merely because we understand it to be such? The spirit of perverseness, I say, came to my

final overthrow. It was this unfathomable longing of the soul to vex itself—to offer violence to its own nature—to do wrong for wrong's sake only—that urged me to continue and finally to consummate the injury I had inflicted upon the unoffending brute.[11]

THE EVENT

At school the morning after Kinkel was expelled, students recall seeing him walk into the building through a breezeway to the cafeteria where students normally gathered for breakfast and conversation. At that time, the school was hosting student government elections, so students were on the lookout for pranks by others who wanted to draw attention to themselves or away from others (think of Reese Witherspoon's character in *Election*).

Kinkel walked into the building wearing a tan trenchcoat, under which he had hidden a sawed-off semiautomatic .22-caliber rifle loaded with fifty rounds of ammunition. His first two bullets were aimed at point-blank range on the first students he encountered in the breezeway. He shot both of them without saying a word and they fell silently to the floor, one lived, one died. Next, he entered the cafeteria where the shooting took on an instantaneous and routine character, much like the others that go awry once the shooting begins.

Shooting from the hip, he fired off several rounds of his ammo from the large clip and rotated back and forth on his heels as he did so, spraying the room with bullets, knocking out windows, and indiscriminately hitting students both far and near in the room. He took a break from this "raging pattern" to walk over to a student lying on the floor, whom he shot in the back of the head as he placed his foot over the boy's neck to hold him down.

Next, he walked over to another student (also on the floor) and shot, but missed. He then corrected himself, but when he pulled back the trigger he found himself out of ammunition. When he reached into the waistband of his pants to pull out his prized 9-mm Ruger pistol, the student under him tackled him to the floor. Another student also lunged to tackle him and was shot by the gun going off in Kinkel's hands. Several more students then jumped on top of him, and the one nearest to him in the pile reported that he said, "Kill me, just kill me."

Later, in the *Frontline* interview, Kinkel's friend would recall him discussing the most recent school shootings (Pearl, West Paducah, and Jonesboro): "He reacted to the other school shootings with their shortcomings almost, like how they failed. He talked like, not that he would do it that exact way (like go to school and shoot people) but if he was going to go out he'd try and take as many people out with him. And also if he was gonna shoot people, like at school, that he'd kill himself. He couldn't believe the other kids didn't shoot themselves and just let themselves be arrested."[12]

WRITING THE HIDDEN CURRICULUM IN BULLETS

As soon as my hope is gone, people die.

—Kinkel's journal entry[13]

You can be whatever you wanna be
Cause a gun in your hand is a Ph.D.

—William Mastrosimone, *Bang, Bang, You're Dead*[14]

These lines from William Mastrosimone's play (written for kids following anonymous death threats at his daughter's school) express very clearly that one way of looking at school shootings, particularly the one in Springfield, off which this play is troping, is to reverse the typical focus of shootings to viewing the shooters as experts who are actively writing their school environments. The gun would seem to signal that highest form of knowledge, a Ph.D., which confers on the shooter the right to judge his surroundings and subjects with impunity. Though Mastrosimone's words are meant to perform Kinkel's ironic position, that of judge whose opinion was warranted by no one at Thurston High School, he nevertheless confirms a stereotype most adults hold about children (and academics): they do not and should not have the right to judge anything. Children have not yet earned the title to judge, therefore they should be prohibited from access to the tools of authoritative knowledge, like guns (or computers).

It is clear that this play was written from the perspective of adult anxiety. Mastrosimone says he wants kids to perform it for each other because "it is reasonable that there is a potential shooter in every school" and "[e]ven if we turn our schools into airtight security zones, stopping weapons at the door with X-ray machines, it's what's in a person's heart that can't be detected by those of us looking from the outside."[15] His paranoia is then projected back into the text as he comforts himself with this little ditty: "This is a drama to be performed by kids, for kids. I would never allow the play to be on video or film because it's important that kids see their peers on stage—kids they ride the bus with, kids they eat lunch with, kids they play sports and take class with."[16] He proves this by giving the victims a voice with which to confront their killer, imagining what it would be like for them to interrogate Kinkel in his jail cell. Mastrosimone's point, however, is that only this generation can save itself because adults are unable to grasp the situation; they will have to save themselves, within the boundaries set by another generation, but they must not test or attempt to go beyond those boundaries.[17]

Unlike José Ortega y Gasset's promotion of the generation as the chief concept for understanding history and more importantly pushing it forward, Mastrosimone's ambivalence concerning the "kids" is clear throughout the play. He seeks to understand their peer world by separating it from the adult world that corrals it. The only adult in the play is a psychiatrist and, of course, Kinkel's parents, whose primary purpose is to demonstrate his dysfunctional behavior toward firearms. Yet, the most important point made in the play is not in parading the victims' imaginaries around in order to mobilize guilt about what Kinkel did, but to establish a basis for pity for the victims and their lost futures. The scene between the parents and Josh (also known as Kinkel) demonstrates perfectly what Ortega calls the "essential anachronism of history," in this condition generations do not see one another correctly because they are in an ironic position. While they are contemporaries sharing the same space in history, they are doing so at different points in their lives, and so they are not "coevals." For Ortega, this is positive because the anachronism and possible antagonism that exists between generations keeps history moving forward by making present generations come of age strongly and giving them purpose and perspective. For Ortega, it is detrimental to history and progress if one tries to stop or block this "essential anachronism" taking place between generations. It must unfold uninterrupted; that way, the newer generation is able to come to know itself and come into maturity with a keen sense of "self" that is based on shared experience in time.

In Mastrosimone's play, the need to limit the students' expression to confronting the individual in his jail cell from the perspective of the victims is a symptom. This may explain why most models for violence prevention in the schools do not try to understand what the violence may indicate or transgress, but only to contain student expression, to isolate and extract problem students from the student population in order to preserve the older generation's dreams for the younger one. Unlike his other more famous work *Extremities,* a play in which a woman confronts her rapist, Mastrosimone promises that this work "won't make it to Broadway" because it is for the "kids."[18] By catering to this aggrieved minority, Mastrosimone brings liberal cruelty and the torture of remembrance into the world of kids—*Harper's* style. This is because remembering the event is a responsibility, as immediate history will become the new governess for the nation's kids.

Where can one locate history in a nation with no weight to hold it down for analysis? His point is Rousseauian: We must force them to be free, within the invisible boundaries set by the elder generation. The chorus in the play is composed of the five dead students who recite their pleas for Josh to kill himself, "Make your face a mask. A mask that hides your face. A face that hides the pain. A pain that eats your heart. A heart nobody knows."[19]

Here, it is worth mentioning Nietzsche's promotion of the "mask" in *On the Genealogy of Morals.* It is a mask that allows one to register a complaint with the ordering of values in a society, without anyone in that society becoming the wiser. Indeed, in most of the cases reviewed here, student shooters have been largely "unknown" or "withdrawn" from most of the other students at their schools. All the students' interviewed at school seem only to remember the masks they wore, such as Kinkel's childish smile, red hair, and freckles; some girls even thought he was kind of cute. It was only after the shooting that they claimed, "[H]e looked bigger that day, almost like a grown man." Later, when Kinkel was arraigned at the grand jury hearing, students in attendance said they were relieved to find he had "shrunk back down to size" and no longer projected the aura of terror and power they saw in the cafeteria that morning during the shooting.[20] It truly appears as a case of the "banality of evil."[21]

Mastrosimone, like other contemporary critics cited in this book, reifies one of America's greatest myths, that of the expert. It is fitting that this play attends to the peculiarities of the Springfield case because this was the shooting in which the nation should have learned that the expert was powerless to prevent or even to predict Kinkel's rampage. It is also fitting that Mastrosimone makes the principal adult character in the play a psychiatrist brought in to hold therapy sessions with Josh, an anonymous blackboard writer from his daughter's school. The kid at his daughter's school was expelled after writing on a classroom blackboard: "Tomorrow you are all dead meat." This incident was one of many copycat attempts or mimicries that followed the Springfield shooting. Mastrosimone's play blurs the copycat threat with the details and victims of the Springfield shooting, making the writing on the board and the shooting at Oregon a continuous crime, where each one feeds off the other, prompting the play's audience to view this as a serial crime restricted to the generation. Cause and effect are also blurred to ensure that the only lesson the audience learns is the reality and finality of death through murder. Another shaming interpellation will surely do the trick! Endless lines proclaiming activities the victims will never accomplish occupy the second half of the script as they berate Josh about what he has taken from them. A very normal boy who "went bad," Josh is depicted as suffering from a violent temper. Furthermore, his family's dysfunction is "dropped" into the text to insinuate that it accelerated Kinkel's lifelong social adjustment problem.

Why this case, Kip Kinkel and Springfield, Oregon, as the springboard for an educational play? The shooting events become good fodder for creating fiction even though they are also allegedly inspired by fiction (*Natural Born Killers, The Basketball Diaries, South Park,* and Stephen King's "Rage"). Reinjecting the reality principle through fiction is the aim of Mastrosimone's play, to make students experience the reality and finality of death, without considering the fact that they experience death on a routine basis.

What generation is he speaking to in this play and why is it assumed that the shootings will stop if its members are bombarded with stories that demonstrate the consequences of killing? This reality principle reinjects the simulacrum of cruelty already operating on every plane of American society (in the media, in government and court decisions, in the home, and in school) with power and adds to the drama of public life in the United States. For example, as the media feeds the need for serial killers to entertain the public, the public returns the favor by giving the media more killings to analyze and in the middle of this the only question asked is: Why do these killers pop up for no reason?

An event that can be neither reversed nor explained is a "senseless" tragedy and that makes it easy to leave it on a moral plane, a plane that has always served as a convenient foil for interest group politics in the United States.[22] Hypermoralism and the anti-intellectual disposition it effects (e.g., equating a Ph.D. with a gun) keeps citizenship tied to the specter of cruelty played out throughout corporate America. Even with the knowledge that many political decisions are calculated to benefit certain groups, most American citizens can only respond with sarcasm, indifference, or moral outrage, but never with a positive social demand. Mark Seltzer's commentary on the pathological public sphere connects the rise of serial killing to a postindustrial quality of life. In his essay "Wound Culture," he argues that the methods of serial killers correspond to the ordering principles of society, the pace at which public life is to take place, and the breakdown, not of the family or of values, but of publicity itself.[23] This is what accounts for the position of serial killer as one with whom many identify with even while they condemn the killer's crimes.

THE PSYCHIATRIC MODEL: THE EGO AND THE EGO-IDEAL

> Something's wrong with my brain.
>
> —Kip Kinkel, in his confession to police[24]

Kinkel was the stumbling block in devising "patterns in the rage," thereby making Mastrosimone's play so representative of the adult anxiety surrounding school violence at that time. Unable to figure this kid out, the media and concerned parents all over the nation began wondering if this event was only an inexplicable milestone in a continuous drama. Worried that the shootings would continue in the fall, schools and parents debated issues concerning security measures. Like the parents and authorities following the Paducah shooting, Springfield was on alert for signs of violence, but the questions remained: How would they know a school shooter when they saw him? How would they profile a normal kid? For his part, Kinkel had always appeared normal at school, getting average grades, playing on the junior varsity football team, and staying out of trouble that drew attention to him. The son of two "devoted and dearly loved teachers" in the same school district, Kinkel presented a serious anomaly to previous models used to predict violent children and, as such, he had to be refigured.

Even though he had severe discipline problems at home (he was constantly grounded) and had demonstrated evidence of emotional problems, he was never detected as having a problem at school, by either his peers or school authorities. He was very well liked, though perhaps not the most popular. As the girls interviewed following the shooting said in the *Rolling Stone* interview, "He was cute."

However, he was subject to and especially incensed by being called a "faggot" by other boys. He was suspended from school for kicking another male student in the head as they exited the school bus one day when the student called him an undisclosed name. As his two closest friends said later, he was not projecting his anger over a particular incident of name-calling two weeks earlier at the school for allowing this particularly repugnant aspect of the hidden curriculum to operate. Again, he was not angry with the principal or the police for arresting and expelling him for the gun in his locker. He was angry with the student who called him the name (perhaps the gun was for dealing with the student?). On the phone, his friends threatened to beat the kid up for him to try to get him to lighten up a bit, but he seemed, as the *Rolling Stone* reporter put it, "very intense and angry" about that particular incident and was unable to get over it, even though up to that point he had never responded to it.

Like Carneal, Kinkel was publicly humiliated by that particular name. Part of the hidden curriculum of schooling, this "trigger" word demonstrates very clearly the problems not yet dealt with concerning masculinity and homophobia, homoeroticism, and sexism faced by girls and boys at school. I will not separate these issues because they all work together to exploit identity categories in favor of an imaginary masculinity that is intimately connected to the contradictions students must perform and live with at school.

Where does the idea come from that communicates to students, in nonverbal ways, that they are bound to the bottom subject position by being labeled a "faggot"? This scapegoating uses an imaginary figure of the homosexual as a pariah. A "faggot" is not masculine, but feminine in this deployment and that is bad because femininity does not give one the power to achieve success in either school or society (whether real or imagined). Violent women are looked at as interesting characters in film plots or are immediately turned into freaks of nature (e.g., Lorena Bobbitt and Susan Smith) when they deviate from the feminine pursuit of "bottom." This will also be discussed in chapter 6, but it is important to note that this word "triggers" more school shootings than any movie scene, unlocked gun chest, or evil demon from birth.

However, it was this shooting that confused the categories experts had been using to detect violent kids because Kinkel had already been through all the appropriate institutional channels and had loving parents (both teachers), a successful older sister, several close friendships, and even girls who liked him. The problem the researchers faced was that Kinkel just could not fit into any of the negative developmental paradigms and they could not find the point at which he had deviated from the path of normalcy. His parents' spotless discipline and aid to him included tutoring, evaluation, and medication for depression and attention deficit disorder, avoiding corporal punishment, withholding cable television, monitoring his media influences, teaching him to shoot guns in the appropriate way, and keeping them locked away from him.

No matter what they tried, he subverted their attempts to make him into a "normal" kid. Kinkel's friends saw him as an okay guy who did not think he was getting fair treatment from the school or his parents for minor transgressions. Finally, Kinkel did not see his activities as a problem and did not want others around him calling attention to the fact that they did. More than anything else, he wanted to be able to do what he wanted and be seen as normal at the same time. But was it "normalcy" that Kinkel's parents were after or was it their standard of perfection? *Frontline* tells a very different story from the *Rolling Stone* interview; in the latter, his sister and family friends place much emphasis not only on Kinkel's troubled relationship with his father, but also his parents' uneven discipline. It was suggested earlier that Kinkel was forbade to play with violent toys and that violence in the Kinkel home was a "no-no," but as Kinkel's parents learned that he would transgress every boundary they set for him, they would give in to his demands.

It is interesting to note that after Kinkel had been sentenced, area newspapers released reports that Faith Kinkel's family had a history of paranoid schizophrenia. Specifically, the papers alleged that many people on her side of the family had been diagnosed with the disorder and that Kinkel's brain scan showed significant abnormalities.[25] At the trial, however, when Kinkel's lawyer attempted to get the confession thrown out on the grounds that Kinkel would plead to an insanity defense, the opposing attorneys and the judge balked, claiming that Kinkel was fit to stand trial and had waived his rights at the police confession. They further barred the testimony of the psychiatrist who evaluated Kinkel immediately after the shooting, claiming that she was unable to complete her evaluation (Kinkel's lawyer showed up and cut off the police interview).[26] But what is most interesting about this case is Kinkel's experience with psychiatry before the shooting. Kristin Kinkel points out in the interview, "My father didn't believe in psychiatrists. He thought they were like chiropractors or something." Kinkel's mother struggled to get him to a local psychiatrist and onto Prozac for a few months, but once he began to show signs of improvement everyone (included the psychiatrist) agreed he was better and could quit treatment.

As the media coverage began to unfold, Kinkel would begin to fit crime novelist Jonathan Kellerman's mold for the "savage spawn." The media also described Bill and Faith Kinkel as the beleaguered older parents who had children late in life and were "exhausted" by Kinkel's inability to follow simple directions and could not figure out "where they had gone wrong with him." So, following Springfield, the psychologists came out in full force, as did a new invention designed to aid mass shooting victims: the mobile trauma unit. Kellerman published his rendition of school shooters entitled *Savage Spawn: Reflections on Violent Children,* in which he argues that violent children are an effect of both nurture and nature, but that once they pass a certain point in their negative ways, they are incapable of being treated by psychiatrists or of ever functioning normally in society.[27] They become what those who favor moral interpretations of social problems call the "bad seed" or in Kellerman's terminology "savage spawn."

Kellerman offers a slightly different characterization of how kids go bad from the moralists by arguing that they are not born that way, but are encouraged by negative patterns of behavior fostered by the family unit throughout their lives. After a certain point, he argues, they should simply be incarcerated if they are causing problems in society, because neither they nor their parents are going to be willing to reverse the patterns.

In one interesting section of the book, he argues that part of the problem with violent kids is their parents and siblings, who having actively sought out help for their sons (he never mentions female children), actually give up on therapy when it starts to have positive results. He believes, based on years of clinical experience, that parents secretly need their sons to be bad (a form of Munchausen's?) and that they will make sure the child does not get better. He describes his reasoning for this claim like this:

> From what I could tell, this shift typically occurred when the child had been labeled the primary or sole problem in a *systematically dysfunctional family*. Focusing exclusively upon a problem child is easy to do even in cohesive families, because difficult kids do demand and receive a tremendous amount of attention. But there can also be a defensive value in scapegoating and concentrating solely on the identified patient, as it allows everyone else to ignore their own problems. Could that have been part of what was going on when Bill and Faith Kinkel rewarded their flagrantly dangerous son with an instant collection of lethal weapons? Was there a need to keep Kip *bad*?[28]

This insight is interesting when one considers that no single reporter or expert could uncover any parental responsibility or school liability for Kinkel's rage. They could only continuously report the good parenting and the school's correct decision to expel him. Kinkel's good-natured behavior in public was often commented on by family and friends of the Kinkels, who felt the parents were great role models for Kinkel and his sister. He was always isolated from the stellar record of his family as the problem for an otherwise perfect family.

However, it is unclear what makes a family "systematically dysfunctional" in contemporary society, when all kids are currently viewed as a problem for their otherwise perfect parents and teachers. Mastrosimone isolates the entire generation in his play in much the same way that Kellerman speaks of families isolating the problem child. Perhaps another look at the family as an organizing principle in contemporary society and as a powerful institution determining public policy would be helpful for understanding shootings, especially this one in Springfield.

The family has rhetorically reemerged in the United States as the preferred form of social organization, closely linked to issues concerning the subjectivity and moral development of children. To combat the more turbulent effects of global capitalism, mass communications, and all other structures that are believed to alienate families from one another (even Sigmund Freud admitted to having these feelings), the American Psychological Association has taken up the slack by holding this virtual humpty-dumpty together to maintain the fiction of an ideal America where families can stay together with the help of counseling.

One new concept and disorder that has been devised and widely used to keep focus on children is "conduct disorder," a psychological malfunction, usually found in children, who, while not displaying severe enough psychiatric symptoms to warrant hospitalization, present significant behavior problems that are strong enough to "dose" with medication. Personality dysfunction or conduct disorder is defined as "a repetitive and persistent pattern of behavior in which the basic rights of others or major age-appropriate societal norms or rules are violated."[29] This is not much different from the way that Hesiod defined adolescence at earlier periods in Western history. However, in this case adolescence emerges as a scientifically controlled and studied disorder that also implies a failure to meet societal expectations of discipline and conformity consonant with contemporary ideals of progress and efficiency. In contemporary times, this means a failure to perform according to the codes of neoliberal efficiency and standardized testing. However, this deontologizing move has obscured the contemporary psychologist's and educational researcher's ability to discern whether or not the adolescent's problems are the result of emphasis placed on outcome-based education or schemes that focus on methods of teaching and learning skills. In earlier formulations of adolescence, there was not an attempt to scientifically monitor and use behavior modification to change the adolescent's basic personality. Instead, there was more of an ironic acceptance of a difficult phase that the individual *must* pass through with firm discipline from an adult in his or her life, rather than with an examination, medication, or training. To behave as an adolescent is to have a disease that shakes the foundation of the family, causing it to break apart or become "systematically dysfunctional." The disorder is formed from within this mysteriously malformed individual whose rage is exacerbated by violent culture and a lack of a moral code.

In a similar argument, James Garbarino, the author of *Lost Boys,* cites an observation by psychologist Leonard Eron claiming that violent patterns of aggression are found in early childhood. Such clues to this behavior are when parents label their child "a terror" or "bad." He argues that the child will continue this behavior on into adulthood and that often one of the indicators of it is aggressive driving or "road rage."[30] Out of this, Garbarino draws another line of fallacious reasoning by suggesting that aggressive children engage in "tricycle rage." Interestingly, the tools used to vent the "rage" and the sign-value of their referents in popular culture is never questioned.

Perhaps, the elision of an objective and societal explanation for conduct disorder and child aggression is to be found in this rather American disavowal of psychoanalysis. Preferring to leave analysis of societal problems at the doorstep of the deviant individual, American behavioral psychology has made it virtually impossible for analysts who study aggression and rage to view it as anything other than a lack in individuals to be remedied by medications, and when financially possible (and time permits), therapy. Freud, as mentioned earlier, would point to the relationship between the child and the tricycle or the adult and the automobile, drawing no obvious distinctions between the child and the adult and noting that the objects are typically thought of as sources of enjoyment and efficiency, which nevertheless, frustrate the individual. Road rage, while certainly a behavior found in individuals, is not necessarily the result of their self-contained pathology and the inability to restrain themselves associated with pathology, but a result of their real lack of control over their environment. The tricycle and the car might be gifts from the progress of technology and cultural objects created to make life easier and pleasurable. Civilization, Freud writes, is discontenting because it offers so many beautiful and time-saving treasures that are inevitably bound to disappoint. This disappointment does not exist apart from the human condition, but is intimately linked to it, and society views it as a kink to be worked out through technological innovation. That the human lags behind his or her technology, coupled with the humiliation of the human by technology, is frustrating. The capacity to order and the challenge embedded in the notion of becoming civilized is a beneficial aspect of our nature to Freud:

[A] kind of compulsion to repeat which, when a regulation has been laid down once and for all, decides when, where and how a thing shall be done, so that in every similar circumstance one is spared hesitation and indecision. The benefits of order are incontestable. It enables men to use space and time to the best advantage, while conserving the psychical forces. We should have a right to expect that order would have taken its place in human activities from the start and without difficulty; and we may well wonder that this has not happened—that, on the contrary, human beings exhibit an inborn tendency to carelessness, irregularity, and unreliability in their work.[31]

The American societal quest for order has taken this insight to an extreme point, forgetting the second part of the dialectic that Freud lays out in the previous quotation. Zealously searching after the perfectly ordered ego ideal to saturate (because ideals always *ooze*) every aspect of social life, the public easily ignores the role that transitional objects, like technologies, play in everyday life, especially as means for venting frustration onto other humans. But what of the "compulsion to repeat" and its role in forging the disjunction between doing and knowing mentioned in the introduction? Also, what of the benefits provided by the order that Freud notes? Perhaps the emphasis has been placed on the negative aspect of this type of societal regulation, instead of on what it allows the collective psyche to disavow. Freud writes that it allows for a "conservation of psychical forces" to the benefit of a well-ordered society, so longed for by social contract theorists and even the "founding fathers" of American politics (who had to compartmentalize power). Where do these psychical forces collect and what are they used for?

The use-value of this contractarian idealism (and leap of faith to civilization) is that it enables (or demands) that the subject and the community forget this darker side of practice, the death drive, and even to a lesser extent parapraxes. Jean Baudrillard goes further than any other theorist of postmodern political culture to explain this underside of practice, especially in his mid-1980s text *America*. Cast as a revisiting of Alexis de Tocqueville's exploration of the American psyche over 150 years later, Baudrillard's text refigures Tocqueville's valorization of civil society in the United States as a blind moralism that works to the benefit of a hyperconsumerized culture. This culture has little respect for the psychology of its practices. The premise of the text is that in "America" there is no recognized (or grounded) reality principle that facilitates the death drive. America is defined by its aversion to the weight that might come from recognition of the "inborn tendency to carelessness, irregularity and unreliability" of humanism.[32] As for the mistake, the outlier, America stamps it out.

PARRICIDE

The equating of regicide with parricide is not intelligible unless it is linked with the family as a model of society.

—Blandine Barret-Kriegel, "Regicide and Parricide"[33]

I don't want anyone else to lose an arm or a leg or a child because of land mines.

—President Bill Clinton, speech to ethnic Albanian refugees in Macedonia, June
1999[34]

As described earlier, Kinkel shot both his parents the afternoon and evening before he opened fire on the cafeteria the morning of May 21. Luke Woodham's murder of his mother and Kinkel's case would be the only school shootings to be presaged by the murder of a parent. Both cases involved one or both parents being killed, not because they were actively involved in triggering the rage, but because they had, in some way, disappointed, blocked, or refused the son by their own representations. Woodham felt his mother was "weak" and unable to deal with the men in her life in an effective way, taking more abuse than she should have from them. He stabbed her with a knife, so there was none of the pseudospecification at work in the killing that Lt. Col. Dave Grossman is convinced is the primary instigator of juvenile homicide.

Similarly, Kinkel spent the night in the house with his dead parents, baiting the shroud that housed their bodies with bombs and leaving the compact disc player on repeat mode; the soundtrack from the Leonardo DiCaprio–Claire Danes version of *Romeo and Juliet* was playing. Talking to his two best friends on the aforementioned three-way call, he appeared calm, constantly murmuring to himself rhetorical questions about when his parents would arrive at home. Forensic tests later showed they were already dead when Kinkel participated in the call to his friends. The other concern he showed was that he did not miss the new episode of *South Park* (the cable had been removed from his house a month earlier according to reports). Kinkel said to his friends that his father was probably "out at a bar getting drunk," but did appear concerned for the arrival of his mother. Both Woodham and Kinkel killed their parents before school and, like Charlie Decker in "Rage," had expressed sensitive sides to their mothers in relation to the disappointment of their fathers.

If Mastrosimone's play is recalled, the fictional rendition of Kinkel has him reproaching his father for not taking after his grandfather and enjoying the culture of hunting and guns. He plays the anachronistic ideals of the two generations off one another by appealing to a paternal loyalty. Invoking the belief systems of the two men (father and grandfather), he implies that the age of the grandfather deserves more respect owing to the natural hierarchy implied in patrimony. Simply put, because Bill Kinkel's father thought guns were okay, he should, out of respect, feel the same way about Kinkel's fascination with guns. It is unclear if Mastrosimone paints this picture of Kinkel as a historical mediator because the media overemphasized Kinkel's abnormal intelligence, that is, the kind that does not match up with grade performance, but only with personal manipulation, or if it is because he views Kinkel as a 1990s version of Hamlet, arguing with ghosts to eradicate the antagonisms in the present between the "fake" father and the "real" primordial father. Mastrosimone's interpretation beckons to the search for the lost father, the real one who understands the need to get back to a father-son relationship based on shared pursuits, rather than shared ideals.

Kinkel's father relented, buying him the firearms he wanted with several conditions attached. He would be required to learn to shoot them responsibly at a firing range with the father present to supervise. He would also be required to keep his grades up, closing the gap between his actual performance and potential abilities. This is a particularly salient issue in the Springfield case, especially as it relates to the parricide involved. The parents had openly admitted to many in the community that they were disappointed with Kinkel's performance in school and were genuinely confused about why such high test scores did not translate into above average grades. Both teachers, they felt lost in their inability to make their own child come around to education's promise, a path they both shared with each other and their daughter.

Many American parents view their children as appendages to themselves. This thinking is not purposeful or malicious in every case, but it is written into the social body through political culture. As the Clinton quote makes clear, children, whether they are Kosovars or Americans, are an appendage to the nation and to the family, which are as Blandine Barret-Kriegel argues inextricably linked: the loss of one ensures loss of the other. To repeat the quotation heading this section, "The equating of regicide with parricide is not intelligible unless it is linked with the family as a model of society." Killing one's parents is a way of dealing with subjection.

There is a lot of discussion in the United States about the "lost" family and the attack on the family by secular and consumer culture, bureaucracy and violence, and sexism and racism, but there is no critical discussion about the negative effects of the "ideal" family underlying those arguments. The ideal element is an important ideological building block of political organization, but, at times, it seems to overstep its boundaries, forcing people to live up to imaginary expectations that frustrate and condemn them to self-hatred on a daily basis. Experts do no justice to people when they bemoan the lost family instead of figuring out how people can live with what they have. As the imaginary basis for political organization, the nuclear family run by the father is gone. Living as if they can bracket their will to careless, irregular, spontaneous, and unplanned life, Americans trigger the death drive into high gear and then wonder why all their cherished categories have fallen from grace.

DOING THE IDEAL, TRIGGERING THE DEATH DRIVE

The "trigger" is not a scene from a movie, an unlocked gun case, or a lack of psychiatric evaluation. It is a word, like "faggot," or an emotional reaction to being refused by the hidden curriculum of schooling through emotional discrimination or a lab coat. All of these triggers have codes attached to them because they mean a whole host of things to the people identifying with them, sometimes personal, sometimes public. But they always deal with them in public because on a noncognitive plane that is where the problem lies.[35] When theorists typically speak or write about discrimination, they focus on the rational advantages of being recognized in terms of political and material norms in society, not those left unsaid, such as the privilege of masculinity, popularity, or of emitting a trickle of the "true" self in public. The word "true" goes under erasure because it should not be understood as truth in the objective sense, but in the positive and vital sense that Michel Foucault and Nietzsche, in the tradition of Johann Goethe, might see as "becoming who you are."

NOTES

1. "Oregon Teen Shooting Suspect: 'I Had No Other Choice,'" *CNN Online,* 17 February 1999, at cnn.com/US/9902/17/school.shooting/index.html (accessed September 27, 1999).

2. Randall Sullivan, "A Boy's Life, Part I," *Rolling Stone,* 17 September 1998, 107.

3. Diane Dietz, Paul Neville, and Eric Mortenson, "Love against the Odds: A Kinkel Family Portrait," *The Register Guard,* 14 June 1998, at www.registerguard.com/news/19980614/la.kipkinkel.0614.html (accessed August 5, 1998).

4. In her letter to the judge at Kinkel's sentencing hearing, Kristen Kinkel explicitly refutes any rumors that her brother ever tortured animals by stating that she observed him to have been an extremely caring individual toward them.

5. Maureen Sielaff, "Prozac Implicated in Oregon School Shooting," *Vigo Examiner,* 30 May 1998, at www.cybersurf.co.uk/~johnny/dumblane/prozac.html (accessed April 28, 1999).

6. Same as note 5.

7. "The Killer at Thurston High," *Frontline,* 18 January 2000.

8. Barbara Walters interview on *20/20,* reprinted in "Interview with Sister of Kinkel Airs Tonight," *Oregonian,* 18 December 1998, at www.oregonlive.com:80/todaysnews/9812/st121816.html (accessed April 28, 1999).

9. Diane Dietz, Paul Neville, and Eric Mortenson, "Love against the Odds: A Kinkel Family Portrait," *Register Guard,* 14 June 1998, at www.registerguard.com/news/19980614/lakipkinkel.0614.html (accessed August 5, 1998).

10. Friedrich Nietzsche, *On the Genealogy of Morals,* trans. Walter Kaufmann and R. J. Hollingdale (1887; reprint, New York: Vintage, 1967), 95.

11. Edgar Allen Poe, "The Black Cat," in *Tales of Terror and Detection* (1843; reprint, New York: Dover, 1995), 110.

12. "Killer at Thurston High."

13. "Killer at Thurston High."

14. William Mastrosimone, *Bang, Bang, You're Dead,* 1999, 6, at www.bangbangyouredead.com (accessed April 8, 1999).

15. William Mastrosimone, "Notes from the Playwright," 1999, at www.bangbangyouredead.com/authornotes.html (accessed April 8, 1999).

16. Mastrosimone, "Notes from the Playwright."

17. This attitude is also indicated in the titles of books appearing in print during the 1998–1999 school year that were preoccupied by violent kids and gun violence. Titles like William Pollack's *Real Boys: Rescuing Our Sons from the Myths of Boyhood* (New York: Henry Holt, 1998) or James Garbarino's *Lost Boys: Why Our Sons Turn Violent and How We Can Save Them* (New York: Free Press, 1999) clearly signal that the experts are desperately trying to pin down the adolescent "spirit" in order to bring boys back to an imaginary space they have fallen

from (like grace?), such as the nuclear family, the monastery, the nonmediated world (natural), or the heteronormative relationship. In other words, these book titles and the arguments underneath them signify that the experts are profoundly alienated from their subjects and that they are trying to make the data "fit" their research design or theory, but without ever consulting the subjects themselves, especially those in the nonviolent range.

18. Mastrosimone, "Notes from the Playwright."

19. Mastrosimone, *Bang, Bang, You're Dead*, 50.

20. Jon Capell, "Kinkel Arraigned on 58 Counts," *MSNBC News*, 5 August 1998, at www.msnbc.com/local/KMTR/14815.asp (accessed August 5, 1998).

21. Hannah Arendt, *Eichmann in Jerusalem: A Report on the Banality of Evil* (New York: Penguin, 1963).

22. Recently, Congress rejected the Juvenile Crime Bill after having split the legislation to cater to the gun lobby. The part of the bill that did pass allowed the posting of the Ten Commandments on classroom walls. One representative even claims that had the Ten Commandments been posted at Columbine High School the shooting might never have taken place! The interesting aspect to this congressional refusal is not that national leaders rejected the bill because they felt that the problem of juvenile crime would best be handled as a state or local matter (which they could have easily done), that school violence is a multidimensional problem and that simply reacting to Columbine or Springfield would only confuse policy implementation, or even that student rights are violated by the swift decisions that the bill demands be met, but that they want to keep the issue in play because it is great entertainment for the coming presidential election. The Lott Amendment to the Senate version of the bill indicates that "Character Education" will supply part of the preventative efforts in the bill. In addition, the bill has caused controversy because it demands that public libraries with Internet access must use mandatory filters to keep underage kids away from questionable sites, such a pornography sites. The Lott Amendment can be accessed at www.eff.org/censorship1999/hr1501_sp1344_1999b_bill.html (accessed August 15, 2002).

23. Mark Seltzer, "Wound Culture: Trauma in the Pathological Public Sphere," *October* 80 (1997): 3–26.

24. Maxine Bernstein, "Kinkel Planned to Shoot Himself, Detective Testifies," *Oregonian*, 17 February 1999, at www.oregonlive.com:80/news/99/02/st021703.html (accessed April 28, 1999).

25. Elissa Swanson, "Killers Start Sad and Crazy: Mental Illness and the Betrayal of Kipland Kinkel," *Oregon Law Review* 79, no. 4 (Winter 2000): 1081–1120.

26. Maxine Bernstein, "Court Restricts Psychiatrist's Opinion of Kinkel," *Oregonian*, 6 March 1999, 2.

27. Jonathan Kellerman, *Savage Spawn: Reflections on Violent Children* (New York: Ballantine, 1999).

28. Kellerman, *Savage Spawn*, 104, emphasis in the original.

29. The general diagnostic criteria for personality disorders is "an enduring pattern of behavior that deviates markedly from expectations of culture," followed by cognitive and affective disturbances and low impulse control, and it must not be linked to other disorders (head trauma or disease) or medications. See *APA Diagnostic and Statistical Manual of Mental Disorders* (Washington, D.C.: American Psychological Association, 2000), 685–689.

30. Garbarino, *Lost Boys*, 66.

31. Sigmund Freud, *Civilization and Its Discontents*, trans. James Strachey (New York: Norton, 1961), 45–47.

32. Jean Baudrillard, *America*, trans. Chris Turner (1986; reprint, New York: Verso, 1988).

33. Blandine Barret-Kriegel, "Regicide and Parricide," in *I, Pierre Riviere, Having Slaughtered My Mother, My Sister and My Brother . . : A Case of Parricide in the Nineteenth Century,* ed. Michel Foucault (New York: Random House, 1975), 222.

34. "Refugees Cheer Clintons in Macedonian Camp," *CNN,* 22 June 1999, at www.cnn.com/WORLD/europe/9906/22/clinton.04/index.html (accessed February 6, 2002).

35. Kevin Jennings, "Be a Man," *The Advocate,* 29 September 1998, at www.findarticles.com/cf_dls/m1589/n769/21152495/print.jhtml (accessed January 18, 2002). Jennings describes how culturally the opposite of "man" and "grown up" is to be labeled "queer" or a "faggot," as if these are negative terms. The juxtaposition is silly, but true in popular—homophobic—use.

PART II

THEORIES OF VIOLENCE IN POLITICS AND SOCIETY

4

Witnessing and Salvation
at School

The disaster, unexperienced. It is what escapes the very possibility of experience—
it is the limit of writing. This must be repeated: the disaster de-scribes. Which does
not mean that the disaster, as a force of writing, is excluded from it, is beyond the
pale of writing or extra-textual.

—Maurice Blanchot, *The Writing of the Disaster*[1]

This chapter explores the ideological underpinnings of a countermovement that
has arisen in response to school shootings aimed at a totally different interpretation and cure for school violence: school prayer. The increasing number of Christian converts to school prayer is significant when one considers that part of the reason for the popularity of God and faith among today's youth is related to "the
disaster," a master signifier for the effect of school shootings.

Americans have a long love-hate affair with youth movements, from the roving
bands of boys eventually enclosed in public schools by the Women's Christian Tem-
perance Union in the last century, to the barricades and tear gas that squelched those
opposed to the Vietnam War. Regardless of the violence, the adult community has
long struggled with and eventually (though reluctantly) incorporated the ideals of
youth movements into the larger political structures and legal codes of the United
States. They have, as noted in chapter 3, learned to manipulate (or compromise
with) the Ortegan "essential anachronism of history" that exists between generations
living as "coevals."

However, the youth movement examined in this chapter labels itself as an exclusively "student-led" movement. It also seemingly dovetails with parental expectations, assuming a role as the alternative rebellion method for teens with no access to the secondary gains that will be discussed in chapter 6. Rebellion is no longer characterized by an organic and spontaneous gesture against a perceived hegemonic policy or force, but is instead channeled through bureaucratic procedures and parental desires, devitalizing the experience of it and making it predictable.

Instead of a "movement" that moves against a previous generation, this student-led prayer movement scripts its mission as one that reclaims the public schools for God. Therefore, it operates on a plane of reality unlike those in the past because its power lies at the nonsecular, spiritual level and is not concerned with formal political rights or equality (in fact, it fights governmental intrusion into private life even while it promotes its own lifestyle as truth), but with a more metaphysical and emotional program of healing.

Formerly, the school site was viewed by Christian activists as occupied by secular humanism that contributed to the devitalization of the public sphere through an assault on cherished ways of life such as family and spirituality. James Fraser points out that this assumption made by the Christian right wing is the result of Ronald Reagan's unending assault on public education as a secular humanist form of mind control. Indeed, Reagan's rhetoric misinformed the public by interpreting key U.S. Supreme Court decisions concerning religious practice in schools as antiprayer. Because of this misinformation, administrators banned students from praying even though it remained a legal activity.[2] Presently, it is a contested space where lobbying at the *meta*physical level is conducted by protocitizens, whose interests lie far beyond the realm of immediacy afforded by constitutional rights or rebellion/protest against an ongoing world event.

With the increasing array of alternative education such as distance education, vouchers, and private religious education, the public school has lost what little symbolic power it once had to negotiate in the interests of the free and experimental public space. It is now a far cry from what progressive educators like John Dewey or more appropriately William James had conceptualized as a creative and experimental laboratory merging fact and fiction, belief and verification. James himself sought a common ground between spirituality and science more ardently than any other pragmatist.

This leads to the question of what citizenship in the schoolyard looks like at present. In the next two sections, I will examine two cases involving the collision of scientific monitoring, secular humanism, tolerance, and spiritual belief in public schools. First, Michael Carneal's choice of the prayer circle at Heath High School is examined, followed by a reading of a popular prayer movement directly linked to a symbol of national identity: the American flag. Second, the story of Cassie Bernall is examined.

CITIZENSHIP IN THE SCHOOLYARD

In this section, I continue to interpret Carneal's intended target (from chapter 1) as having been the prayer circle rather than any specific person within that group. In other words, if any motive could be attributed to this case, it would have to be assumed that Carneal's intentional target was the practice of praying at school.

Many students at Heath High School have made claims indicating his ambivalence to the morning ritual in the lobby of the school. Ben Strong (the leader of the group) has said that Carneal hung out with other kids who openly expressed their atheism and at times would even tease members of the prayer group; and yet, he and Carneal were close friends. In fact, the charges of Carneal's alleged atheism as motivation for the shootings were so prevalent at the time of the incident that several national atheist organizations issued statements in the aftermath of the shooting arguing that they do not promote antireligious violence and, therefore, do not accept culpability for Carneal's behavior.[3] Yet, the strongest evidence that many believe the motivation was religious intolerance can be found in the community of West Paducah, Kentucky, itself.

In an alluring display of evangelical patriotism, many people have incited a movement called Prayer at the Pole, where a prayer circle is formed around the flagpole at the school. No longer content to have the prayer sessions in the lobby, this act binds school prayer to American citizenship (and perhaps normative masculinity), at the flagpole, in the aftermath of a great social wound. The question of intent is obliterated as groups take on their own victimhood and accept that they are targets. It may even be argued that to be targeted is the greatest victory for Christians in this case. Therefore, Carneal's state of mind no longer matters because his actions pave the way for a movement that bases its popularity on trauma and the wound.

These prayer sessions are reminiscent of Poland's Solidarity protests against Soviet control in the early 1980s. Members and supporters wore buttons bearing a picture of Pope John Paul II and the pope visited the country's religious landmarks twenty-seven times during the height of the movement's popularity. During this time in Poland, citizenship was not only negatively formed against Soviet control, but also through positive identification with the pope and Rome.

This citizen-forming practice functions along the lines of Kaja Silverman's rereading of Althusserian interpellation in *Male Subjectivity at the Margins*. Silverman argues that the fundamental misrecognition embedded in social practice is that people continually "take as an ontology what is only a point of address."[4] This process takes place in a noncognitive manner, simulated by visual signs and emotions such as the suturing of the figure of the pope to a political cause, the location of which is provided by the negative reaction to, in Slavoj Zizek's terminology, a Big Other such as the Soviet Union and makes a momentary identification *seem* like an ontological process. Indeed, most literature concerned with understanding citizenship as formulated through a process of noncognitive identifications (as opposed to liberal experiential interpretation) assumes that citizenship is never final, but is a continually stimulated process of identifications that produces the simulacrum "citizen." All of this ideological work functions at the level of nationalism.

It has been intimated in the media that Carneal was stimulated by the "trigger" scene in the film *The Basketball Diaries*. This passive argument indicates that he was doing nothing other than participating in a common form of citizenship that proceeds primarily through identification and misrecognition, not through participatory experience.

The crucial difference is that in the former, one acts according to Hobbesian laws of motion, either attracted to or averting from an object in the world with no principle guiding behavior or belief system derived from experience, while in the latter, one would participate because he or she experiences his or her citizenship as connected to the object in a fundamental way that is not tied to a momentary pulsion.

The students whom Carneal shot were finishing a ritual that bound them to their own form of citizenship, a form of irredentism (they claim to be taking back "ownership" of the schools) that signifies the reclamation of secular school grounds for the practice of prayer. Carneal's identification with Jim Carroll's character in the film makes perfect sense when viewed through this political lens. Carneal's choice of the prayer circle as the object of the shooting experiment demands a reading of the function and purpose of prayer at school. In the aftermath of the shooting, prayer circlers make legitimate claims on school grounds—even while they emphatically deny that Carneal targeted them—by using the wound opened in the lobby of Heath High School to lend credence to their mission.

THE MOVEMENT

We have a flagpole, and we have Jesus!

—See You at the Pole, September 16, 1998[5]

See You at the Pole (SYATP), a student-led prayer movement that began in 1990 in Texas, saw its membership and practice increase following the Kentucky shooting's exposure in the media. In fact, the prayer group at Heath High School saw its membership increase from a mere 30 students to 135 following the shooting (300 turned out the day after the shooting, 60 met daily, and the national turnout in 1998 was 3 million).[6] Traumatized by school violence around the country, this group's central focus and purpose shifted following the school shootings beginning in 1996 and, finally, by December 1997, was a permanent feature of school shooting coverage and public response, especially in relation to the "healing process" that begins literally minutes after news of a shooting.

Originally a movement to bring prayer back into public schools, the group was controversial and troublesome to those intent on maintaining a strict separation of church and state, but following the shootings, more and more students began praying at their school's flagpole with a resigned tolerance from school authorities.[7] Education secretary Richard Riley even announced the following message in advance of the national group's proposed meeting on September 16, 1998, to mark the students' return to school in the aftermath of Springfield, Oregon, a shooting that left the nation traumatized and afraid of what would happen when schools reopened in the fall: "Schools must give students the same right to engage in religious activity and discussion as they have to engage in other comparable activity. This means that students may pray in a non-disruptive [elsewhere cited as nondiscursive] manner during the school day when they are not engaged in school activities and instruction, subject to the same rules of order as apply to other student speech."[8]

Easily incorporated into the hidden curriculum of schools as a response to the shock experienced from the shootings, school prayer is (and has always been; this is what is erased by the movement as it accepts a societal status based on prejudice) acceptable if practiced in relative silence and in designated areas outside classrooms. As President Bill Clinton addressed the nation at a prayer breakfast following the memorial service for the three slain girls, he confirmed the nation's commitment to prayer as a healing practice by saying, "Our entire nation has been shaken by this tragedy. West Paducah, on the southern shore of the Ohio River, *is at the center of our circle of prayers.*"[9] These reactions to the shooting, especially since it appeared to target a prayer circle, gave increasing visibility to the SYATP movement.[10] As the school year and two more shootings passed, students around the country were ready to join in the prayer circles. With a nod from Washington and the memory of 1997–1998 being a bloody school year, they needed something to suture the wounds and calm the fears that followed them to school in the fall of 1998 and the SYATP supplied that for many.

The group's theme for the long-awaited day, September 16, was "For Such a Time As This" and drew on the Old Testament story of Esther, a young woman who saved fellow Jews from death at the hands of a king who also happened to be her unwitting husband. Students in the group believe that the persecution faced by Jews under this plot created by Haman, the king's disgruntled advisor, in 437 B.C., has strict parallels with the experiences of students in schools today. Specifically, believing that, as Christians and students, they are persecuted by violent media and the increasing secularization of the school's curriculum, activities, and official policies, the SYATP students link secular culture with violence and a retreat from what they see as the "traditional" values of American society. In a CNN interview marking the date of Kip Kinkel's arraignment, some students intimated that they also view prayer as a preventative measure, a method to block repeat occurrences of shootings.

The continuing violence reported at schools, coupled with three more extreme shootings, gave them proof of their righteousness. Increasingly, students are called to "witness" to others, challenging the "unsaved" to join the faith and bring Jesus into their lives at school. Witnessing takes place as students relate the specific problems they might face at their schools, such as fear of violence, guns, drugs, and the Goth culture. They further connect these problems to the culture of the communities in which the schools are housed. In this way, they make the causal link between secular culture and violence (and at times pornography). For them, the SYATP is a means to send a message to others that Jesus is watching over them in schools while they simultaneously argue that the fundamental problem causing school violence is the absence of God in school, which is caused by secular culture and law.

According to the National Council of Youth Ministries, the group that manages the chapters of the SYATP and organizes the fall event, God wants to "renew and revive the nation" and the SYATP event begins a year of prayer and devotion to God that will help bring him back into the schools. When asked in an interview what "systemic problems members see in public schools," Doug Clark, the director and promotion coordinator, responded:

> The roots of the problems in our schools—and in our culture as a whole—are spiritual in nature. When we stop following the principles God gave us in the Scripture, the results are the kinds of symptoms we see all around us: immorality, impurity, evil, hatred, murders and other moral decay. The Frenchman A. de Tocqueville, who came to the U.S. in the mid-1800s to find "the source of America's greatness," stated that he found it not in our industry but in our "pulpits aflame with righteousness." The Bible says that "righteousness exalts a nation, but sin is a reproach to any people." What goes for the culture as a whole will be true in the schools as well. The solution, then, is a return to God's values.[11]

Furthermore, the group distinguishes itself from other adult mass movements, such as the Promise Keepers, by arguing that its members are not redeeming themselves by making good on broken promises that might be the legacy of a traumatic family history, but are calling on God to come to them in times of need to instruct them at their schools. They have not forsaken God, as these adults have done, but are calling on God in expectation of further tragedy, asking for help and guidance as they confront what they perceive as the hostile culture in public schools. They also reclaim their schools in local settings, giving their mission a grassroots flavor that is more in tune with current political strategies to increase visibility and awareness through dispersion, thereby making the group's evangelical mission more effective.

These political considerations, while interesting, do not get at the belief structure that undergirds the formation of prayer circles, nor do they help sketch out the pattern of acceptance of prayer circles in public schools that can be traced from West Paducah to Littleton. What is more important is the circlers' identification with specific shootings and their use of them to exploit suffering and to authorize a political movement with an unrelated agenda.

Despite their claims that prayer circles are innocent gatherings where regular students pray for God to claim their schools, the circles can be read as a staging of what Mark Seltzer calls "the sociality of the wound," a general depiction of the crossing of private and public desire around trauma.[12]

To get an understanding of these processes, how they function, and what they accomplish for a political movement aimed at undermining the separation of church and state in the United States, I return to Silverman's reading of interpellation. As a citizen-forming process that works *as if* to reinstate or confirm a "dominant fiction" (much like the one outlined earlier by Clark concerning a return to Alexis de Tocqueville's claim about the "pulpits aflame with righteousness"), interpellation functions on the plane of ideology, not rationalism or even compromise, as in political pragmatism.

Linda Zerilli's argument concerning "knowing" is instructive to this discussion (detailed in chapter 7).[13] Zerilli argues that quotidian politics operates out of subjective certainty; an individual knows, but cannot formally validate his or her actions. In this case, the fiction is not an established one, but is conceived as willing the return of God, normative masculinity, and the heteronormative family to order the symbolic, or law. As willing fiction, the SYATP must compete with many other fictions but the wounds left by school shootings provide the perfect place to stage a comeback. As the membership brochure claims, "God wants to come back and renew his Covenant with students and parents."[14] More importantly, God must come back to fight evil.

In one article, Luke Woodham, the shooter at Pearl, Mississippi, is described as belonging to a satanic cult that worshipped the "God-killer Friedrich Nietzsche." This statement is of interest in that it signifies the Christian acceptance that God has been banished from the symbolic, even while he is always with his followers. Commentary on Nietzsche from a theological point of view is lacking in the SYATP literature, but this conceptualization of God appears to confirm Nietzsche's view of the Christian God as being the one who is dependent on human worship for survival.

Consider the omnipresence of billboards claiming to represent God's will and message across the country, a message that speaks directly to contemporary concerns as if it were the voice of a contemplative God: "I don't question *your* existence."— God; "Nice wedding. Now invite me to the marriage."—God; and so on. Unlike other Gods in Western society, the God of the proselytizing Christian can be banished (perhaps killed) if he is no longer allowed participation in the dominant fiction of the society. Finding ways to bring God back becomes the consuming task of students, and prayer at the flagpole is one such way to accomplish this task. Consider one description of the movement given by *Time* magazine:

> Blake Langhofer was the first to arrive. It was 6:40 A.M., and the sickle moon still hung in the dark sky over Maize High School near Wichita, Kansas. In sandals and shorts, Blake, 16, approached his school's blue flag pole. He leaned forward, placed his hands on it and bowed his head. Soon, he was joined by four friends, all jeans-clad and smelling sweetly of soap and shampoo. They formed a circle, and someone entreated the Lord aloud: "I pray you do wonders through the pole and let your wonders show through the pole." First a trickle, then dozens of students arrived; eventually more than 200 gathered in tight concentric circles around the pole.[15]

The coverage seems overtly erotic. The pole serves as a totemic marker that connects citizenship to the Christian God through an attempted re-Oedipalization of school grounds. Praying in "tight concentric circles" around the phallic object, students are revitalized by its magical tricklings. They are clean, "smelling sweetly of soap and shampoo," as they innocently jack off God at 6:40 A.M. (an early morning offering to help them ward off the vile and dirty images they will receive in school that day?). But is this primitive display of patriotism that so obviously longs for a representation of the male organ *important enough* to suture the wounds of students?

I read the shootings as a wound that is formative of trauma (after all, trauma is identified by Seltzer as a category that "leaks") in the next few paragraphs (strictly) as it relates to the pole. Finally, leaving the pole off to the side, except where it detaches itself and reattaches itself to the trauma and shock evinced by shootings, I read the "sociality of the wound" through Jane Gallop's rereading of Jacques Lacan's mirror phase. This reading is a bricolage of theories that pieces together some aspects of the SYATP ideology in order to sketch out some of the political implications of the group's growing membership.

One way to interpret the necessity of the pole is to accept it as an uncontested symbol of authority in contemporary life. Silverman argues that this "dominant fiction" needs the penis and phallus to line up: "Our dominant fiction calls upon the male subject to see himself, and the female subject to recognize and desire him, only through mediated images of an unimpaired masculinity. It urges both the male and female subject, that is, to deny all knowledge of male castration by believing in the commensurability of penis and phallus, actual and symbolic father."[16] The trauma of the shootings and the cognitive dissonance felt by Christians to be the direct result of secularization, as Silverman says later, smacks of the disposition that screams "your meaning or your life," or rather "the phallus or your life."

This threat of *subjective* destitution, experienced as one believes he or she is living in the proverbial cultural/spiritual void of late capitalist culture, fuels the need for an authority figure to bring the representations and spiraling identifications of post-Oedipal American culture back under the control of an ordering principle that is rigidly staged in dramatic prayer.[17] What better way to recover a lost father (masculine agency) than to center libidinal energies around a phallic object and assign magical properties to it that compel believers slowly to submit to the various cultural prohibitions that, once accepted as cultural convention, will reinstate a normative masculinity?

The covenant in the mission statement for the National Youth Ministries demands that assignees submit to "[a] life of discipleship which is *reproducing an on-going chain of maturing believers*," whose members will "in turn transfer ministry principles in such a way that they, too, will reproduce themselves."[18] According to the group, then, the students are not yet adult citizens, but are in the developmental phases that lead to the maturity of an ego structure that is responsible and reproductive, but only when mediated through the pole.

Prayer circling may then be conceived of as another developmental paradigm whose desired product is the formation of a subjectivity that will enact such responsibility and reproductivity in relation to masculine identification. The egos or "souls" of students who are "saved" in prayer circles are organized around the pole that speaks the word of God. This leads to a false socialization because, if we recall D. W. Winnicott's and Melanie Klein's theories concerning the developmental role of transitional objects in the emotional lives of children, they take great pains to show that the object must be freely chosen by the child in relation to their facilitating environment, which houses the individuals that give them care and love, and that this environment must be consistent and free of indoctrination. It is important that the object represent a real relationship with another person whom they know and share a bond with, not *mere* metaphysical speculation.

The next logical question is: Why is the ego made end-in-view? Why reconstitute, as Gallop says, the tragic story of Oedipal organization when one already knows (and is luxuriating in) a culture that prefers and thrives on *slack* representation? If the story is tragic, it is because it can only end in the failure of exacting reproduction, which produces not a stable ego molded along the lines of an idealization, but one that is tragic (for Gallop's Lacan) because it is propelled both by *retroactive* moves to contain a bodily image or "self" and by *anticipatory* moves to establish a foundational self from which to progress toward maturity. Working against each other, the two dispositions effect, as she puts it, the "violation of the very chronologies" that sustains the subject.[19]

This temporal disorientation is common in victims of school shootings, as evidenced by their inability to recover a complete memory of the event. Anachronisms abound in wound culture; according to Seltzer, "the basic uncertainty as to what counts as the 'real foundation' of trauma is, first, the wound, it is second, a wounding in the absence of a wound; trauma is in effect an effect in search of a cause."[20] Thus, the subject's affective history is the history of secondary identifications; the images that do "stick" with the subject must, on Gallop's reading of the mirror stage, be read as the primary ones. Thus, the mirror stage is, to borrow Thomas Keenan's term, the "conceptual hinge" on which the subject swings back and forth until a rigid conceptualization of the self is firmly rooted in an identity that allows it to believe in its totality and to disavow its psychic fragmentation.[21]

The conceptualization that provides this static conception of self is the resultant ego that uses its "armor" to shield against the vision of "the body in bits and pieces" (*corps morcelé*).[22] Although Lacan reads bodily fragmentation as a literal and singular stage (the space in late infancy where the ego's fate is sealed), Gallop allows for a reading that posits a plurality of stages that do not follow a rigid developmental model, but are contingent on "decisive" movements that "project" the subject into the future perfect (trauma?).

This opening of Lacan's text by Gallop is crucial to understanding contemporary identifications. The question of the subject can be read through what happens when the subject looks into the mirror (wound), but can no longer "anticipate" a totality smiling back at him or her in the mirror; he or she instead sees only recurring images of "the body in bits and pieces." The mirror stage is, then, a returning staging base for the subject's reactions to (and projections into) historical events (school shootings), where the body is literally rendered as "bits and pieces," while the mind that experiences also only recovers "bits and pieces" of those experiences as images. The wound circulates back and forth between shootings, prayer circling, and witnessing acts as the reverse Gestalt (the prototype that precedes the ego) of the one in Lacan's mirror phase; that is, the wound reflects back at the subject not as an ideal ego, but as an always already-fragmented subject. The identification is primarily with the wound while the pole attaches itself as a useful, but somewhat unnecessary accessory.

There is a collective wound that circulates between shootings that mirrors back at students an unmistakably fragmented subjectivity. As grief filled the first communities affected by the shootings, it soon turned into a school year that witnessed "a steady drumbeat of youthful murders [that] has been like a bandage ripped over and over again from a wound that just won't heal."[23]

Beginning with Pearl and ending with Springfield, the open wounds that mark the trauma of school shootings have a discrete beginning and ending signified by the summer hiatus. Throughout the summer, parents and students nationwide lived in fear of the first day back to school. There was an unmistakable collective fear that more shootings would surely follow and, unable to make clear sense out of the incidents, most traumatized victims repeatedly asked the empty and meaningless question "Why [shooter's name]?" in an unrestrained effort to understand the impossibility that always accompanies such a disastrous event.

As Seltzer argues, the usual answer to this question places responsibility on an event in the individual's past, such as abuse or neglect, which are forms of childhood trauma that are easy for the public to digest psychologically while also allowing for the disavowal of collective responsibility:

> The assumption that the cause of compulsive violence resides ultimately in childhood trauma has become canonical, in criminological and in popular accounts. This is scarcely surprising. On one level, the recourse to the trauma of child abuse or sexual abuse as explanation follows from "twentieth century beliefs" that childhood experience forms the adult (that is, the basic premise of psychoanalysis). Such an explanation has become virtually automatic in the literature (factual or fictional) on serial killing, assuming a peculiarly a priori status, even where evidence is conspicuously absent.[24]

In the case of West Paducah, however, the responsibility is temporarily reversed, since Carneal is "one of us." Explanations for the shooting all work to leave the wound open; interpretation is closure and this is refused by the community in order to reclaim the responsibility for a collective healing process operationalized in prayer circles. In order to have the wound, they have to assume responsibility for it, like a memorial or totem.

One may read the shooting series, up to Springfield, as provocative, leading more students on to adopt the strategy of prayer as an attempt to formulate a collective belief structure that serves to reinforce the individual ego or what Silverman calls the "*moi.*" Reading the interpellative act through trauma, Silverman views the process as one by which a subject misrecognizes his or her "self" in the address. Like Gallop's shattering of the mirror phase into several repetitive stagings that either push the subject toward or pull the subject away from an ego, Silverman's rereading of interpellation as a failed ontological quest provokes her to question the surfacing of the ego in popular films that follow traumas inflicted on masculinity after World War II.

Like Silverman's filmed analogies, the SYATP acts as a restorative (curative?) practice designed by participants to remain in traumatic suspension, consulting the wounding mirror over and over again as the shootings continue to erupt throughout the year. Until Littleton, there is no doubt that all the shootings are linked both in the media and through friendships formed via traumatic sharing sessions. Victims of the shootings become pen pals as prayer circle membership increases. Newspapers worry about the coverage of traumatic events like school shootings because they involve and affect "children," never questioning the nostalgic binary that separates childhood from adulthood in their response. After all, these shootings are traumatic because they are about kids killing kids, or is it that the kids no longer believe in the authority and power of adults to fight them in good faith and so they turn to God for that needed containment?

According to Juliet Flower-MacCannell's thesis in *The Regime of the Brother,* twentieth-century fascism, especially the Holocaust, eroded the confidence and trust that children had in their parents to protect and guide them. The governmental structure of a fascist regime, even fascist policies that may operate on a temporary basis under democratic control, undermines the parental role in order to garner power for the regime and make all citizens dependent on it for survival. She writes, "[Yet] fascism had stubbornly demonstrated the fragility of the parents, their vulnerability, their powerlessness. The Holocaust structurally reversed the parent-child relation. It did so to serve fascist, aggressive narcissistic ends: to be itself the survivor and the master, replacing the weak and feeble parents for good."[25] As social service and now media intrusions into the family abound and demonstrate to the public the weakness of the American family, no matter what form it takes, it continually represents this image of parental *lack.*

As the movement's popularity indicates, students can also no longer trust public school officials (or adults in general) to take charge of either the healing or the prevention of incidents like the shooting at Heath High School in West Paducah. Instead, they organize their fears and healing according to the designs of youth ministers who have in turn placed trust in a God to come; no more politics, no more community. Perhaps this reaction makes a good point about schooling and politics. Jamon Kent, the superintendent of schools in Springfield, admitted that school administrators, *because of the nature of their training,* could never imagine implementing the trauma care that other unofficial organizations contributed in the aftermath of the Thurston High School shooting.[26]

The wish for authority in this country looms large on the horizon and religion is one of the only actors capable of fulfilling it, perhaps with the exception of the police. Trauma victims at rallies have claimed to be reassured, even in a community church, only by spotting a police officer's uniform in the room. As they give their witnessing speeches, they still long for the authority of the state to be present in a public forum to stave off the agoraphobia that sets in after having been assaulted in school.

But there are also intolerant positions adopted in relation to the government's efforts to provide protection from further public assaults that are motivated by anger and hatred. In a direct move against the Clinton administration's zero-tolerance policy concerning guns, many SYATP members have claimed that the schools enact a similar zero-tolerance policy concerning prayer and some even support the National Rifle Association when they make this statement.

Several recent events, most notably the murder of Matthew Shepard, have brought many involved in the SYATP out against hate crime legislation, arguing (in the most twisted form of logic yet) that it is a direct attack on prayer in school. Their opposition to hate crimes legislation, they claim, brings on them unwarranted oppression against their status as Christians (are we seeing Nietzsche's democracy at work yet?). Each time a new trauma takes place, the group resutures itself to the wound in a way that allows for visibility and coherence to support its basic practical doctrines, such as prayer, *even if the tragedy is in no way linked* to previous ones.

Now in a position of semisymbolic power, prayer groups seek to protect the gains they have made from the tragedies at schools in the last two years. They need shooters and they need the "permissive" culture that nourishes them in order to maintain a stranglehold on school policy concerning the First Amendment. Each and every time the Left capitulates to this logic of violent culture, it gives the radical right wing another inch from the already open door that leads down the road to a reanimation of parochial masculinity. This movement is already reclaiming the political community by using the subjective destitution felt by students. The crowning event, however, that would open this wound completely and tear apart the idea of civil society among youth was Littleton. To its faithful conversion, I now turn.

TESTIMONY

Truth lives, in fact, for the most part on a credit system. Our thoughts and beliefs "pass," so long as nothing challenges them, just as bank-notes pass so long as nobody refuses them. But this all points to direct face-to-face verification somewhere, without which the fabric of truth collapses like a financial system with no cash-basis whatever. You accept my verification of one thing, I yours of another. We trade on each other's truth. But beliefs verified by *somebody* are the posts of the whole superstructure.

—William James, "Pragmatism's Conception of Truth"[27]

To be sure, some testimonies, like the ones discussed in the previous section, were exploitative. Cassie Bernall's alleged sacrifice to the cause of witnessing overshadowed much of the coverage of the post-Columbine discourse, but that testimony was later "proved" to be mistaken by "somebody." In an uncanny twist of events, one of *the survivors* of the Columbine massacre (a girl who was injured by shrapnel) was the authentic testifier to God's presence in her life, while the story told about Bernall was less than heroic: she was killed without being given a chance to speak.

Here is how the story goes: The parents of Bernall and the other student realized in the early days following the shooting that this misinformation was spread publicly. Not wanting to damage the effect of the message that they felt was so important, they decided to keep the misrecognition of Bernall as witness a secret. Martyrdom is the most effective vehicle of persuasion in the Christian faith. Witnessing presupposes a survivor to tell the story of the martyr's suffering. "Dying for one's faith" became the mantra of Christian witnesses after Columbine. Before Columbine, one witnessed to living the vital experience of God in one's life. Following Columbine, this shifted; one witnessed that he or she had survived in order to tell the story of how God's absence in school resulted in death. This is the point at which the war between good and evil begins in contemporary school politics: The secular culture that attempts to maintain a neutral stance on school prayer takes an assault from the prayers that want to see the political community reimagined in the image of the Bible.

And yet, as scholars of testimony argue pointedly, the goal of witnessing is never to access the truth of the event, but rather to interpret it for others. Shoshana Felman underscores that in "the underground of language" testimony is not conceptualized as a statement of truth but as a means to access it.[28] Taking her cue from Sigmund Freud's self-analysis of dreams, Felman understands testimony to be a function of truth making rather than truth telling. Thus, it makes little difference which account of the Columbine event one privileges as truth or declares inconsistent; as Maurice Blanchot declares, it is the writing of the event that matters. Like Freud's claim that he can write an interpretation of his dreams, so societies can read interpretations of events as they are told in the testimonies of witnesses. When huge collectives can no longer believe the events they are confronted with in the media, it becomes necessary to find "reliable" witnesses.

The 2000 theme for the SYATP was rather aptly titled "A Generation Seeking God." Again drawing on biblical premises, this theme focuses on the tenth anniversary of the movement (which is now, after Columbine, unabashedly referring to itself as a movement) and begins to link itself to shootings in more obvious ways. Whereas after West Paducah the group insisted that the shooting had nothing to do with the prayer circle, but could have taken place anywhere such as "at a basketball game or in a classroom," now it boldly proclaims that it fights Satan in the form of school shootings. As a recent brochure for the group exclaims: "Satan's effort to spread confusion and fear did not work in West Paducah, nor did it dampen the spirit of the Christian students in Littleton. It appears that he will lose the battle in Ft. Worth as well. To paraphrase the words of Joseph in Genesis 50:20, 'What man meant for evil, God intended for Good.'"[29]

Perhaps part of the reason why this sudden revelation of intent, previously veiled by the wound, is coming out is because immediately following Columbine several students who survived the carnage in the library and the cafeteria went on speaking tours to churches throughout the country. At one such event at a First Assembly of God Church in Lafayette, Indiana, two students came with their mothers to witness to the event and discuss the important role of God in it and their lives. Other parents whose children were killed in the shooting found different ways to attract public attention. Some, like Rachel Scott's parents, lobbied Congress for tolerance for Christian values in public schools. Rachel's father, Darrell, wrote a poem to express the feelings of those arguing for a return to the "principle" on which, he claims, the United States was founded: "simple trust in God."

> Your laws ignore our deepest needs
> Your words are empty air

You've stripped away our heritage
You've outlawed simple prayer

Now gunshots fill our classrooms
And precious children die
You seek for answers everywhere
And ask the question, "Why?"

You regulate restrictive laws
Through legislative creed
And yet you fail to understand
That God is what we need![30]

Scott's father now tours the country and supports his family by giving lectures about his daughter's tragic death and the renewal they (and she) found in salvation. Isaiah Shoels's parents also tour the country giving lectures and speeches to parents and kids about the racism experienced by their son that led to his death in the library. In addition, they discuss the role of God and good parenting as necessary for preventing further shooting tragedies.

What is more interesting, though, is the way in which the families and the media describe the effect of school shootings as similar to a natural disaster, making responsibility for the events one that is not reducible to the objects the media would condemn, nor to human individuals, such as the parents of the shooters or the administrators at the school site. Consider the way Michael Shoels, Isaiah's father, describes the aftermath of the shootings, "We are like the victims of an earthquake or a hurricane."[31]

Shoels argues that the discrimination and hatred experienced by his family prior to and after the killings at Columbine make their case for aid even more urgent. Living in hotels while traveling on the speaking tour "Let's Stomp Out the Hate before It's Too Late," Shoels and his family had, at the time of this statement, used up their portion of the aid contributed to Columbine victims. For them, the effects of the shooting and the death of their son *is* experienced as a natural disaster; something that comes out of nowhere and destroys lives.

Kai Erickson states that the effect of trauma can both bind and dismantle a community, especially in the case of a natural disaster such as an earthquake or flood. But the lines between a natural disaster and a technological one are blurred in contemporary society and as technology begins to "protect" us from natural disasters, Erickson argues, we learn of a "whole new category that specialists have come to call technological disasters—meaning everything that can go wrong when systems fail, humans err, engines misfire, designs prove faulty, and so on. Earthquakes, floods, hurricanes, and volcanic eruptions are 'natural'; collisions, explosions, breakdowns, collapses, leaks and of course, crises like the one at Three Mile Island, are 'technological.'"[32] Erickson notes that it is difficult to distinguish between a "human error" and a "systemic error," meaning that it could either be that human irregularity (its link to the death drive) that Freud makes the central thesis of his psychoanalytic writings or it could be an error in the programming and organization of the system itself, designed however, by humans.

This is reminiscent of Stanley Milgram's reflections on human organization as a complex and potentially dangerous thing *in itself* and the effect of these systems going bad, as in the case of school shootings, seriously undermines the collective belief in human control. That is why Michael Shoels's reflection is so poignant; he *is* the victim of what society now conceptualizes as a "natural disaster." In school shooting coverage and therapeutic solutions, one finds that virtually all critically modern responses to tragedies like the death of Isaiah Shoels have vanished. In the media, one finds little representative space for criticism of the systemic racism, sexism, and homophobia found in both the shooting events or the critical responses.

The spaces destroyed by school shootings and the responses to them in the media might attempt an analysis that can respond to the crises of human interaction and the failure of publicity they represent. In the postmodern period, one finds critical responses of this sort lacking. It remains to be seen, then, what type of criticism can help remedy a situation where those who are suffering from systematic exclusion, punishment, and abuse can only blame an abstract notion of the environment for their problems.

The ancients, Erickson is careful to note, when faced with a natural disaster, prayed to an otherworldly figure to help save them, recuperate them, and rebuild their destroyed communities. After the birth of reason and technology in the modern period, one finds the answer to natural disasters in careful planning and management of them by referencing science and reason. The hidden curriculum is one example of this technological control over natural phenomenon, specifically, human interaction in public spaces. The hidden curriculum used to "hold" students whose potential for violence and targeted anger was strong, because, like an efficient technological device, it absorbed dissent, produced compromise formations, and basically gave these students an outlet in fantasy or in an alternative community.

Now that it has failed a few times and come back at students with alarming disciplinary measures in the form of monitoring, surveillance, and profiling, the community no longer believes in the schools' potential to reproduce students who are adjusted to the needs of a plural society. It is no wonder then that many students and parents have returned to the idea of God with widespread popularity, despite the negative consequences this movement poses to the idea of public schooling. School shootings (alongside other technological disasters now conceptualized as natural ones) have disabused Americans of the belief in human control or design over technology, understood very broadly as human control and responsibility for the environment of both civil society and the polity. Now, it is only God or a higher form of technological monitoring that seems plausible as the savior of community.

The reason for this abandonment is that while one can analyze the violence at work in contemporary society with a view to understanding its precipitants and processes, one cannot predict the *effect* that it will have on its victims, both real and imagined. By imagined, it is meant that "anyone" can be a potential shooter, therefore, anyone is a potential victim. The more this thinking is publicized and made into the moral lesson for living in contemporary society, the more likely it is that everyone will begin thinking like a victim. While quoting Robert Jay Lifton's "broken connection" thesis, Erickson states:

The most important point to be made, however, is that when the dread is lasting and pronounced—as often happens in trauma—the spectacle of failed technology can become the spectacle of a failed environment as well. This is a view of life borne of the sense that the universe is not regulated by order and continuity, as clerics and schoolteachers have been telling us for so many centuries, but by change and a kind of natural malice that lurks everywhere. That is the "broken connection" of which Robert Jay Lifton speaks.[33]

And so, as many become traumatized by school violence, others search for answers that lie backward in history such as the "return" to God or the demonization of secular culture with its limited spiritual and moral potential to reinstate the trust between citizens so necessary to democratic life. But there are things to be feared in this response to school violence. For one thing, students of other religious or spiritual persuasion do not want to see the flagpole at school occupied by Christians. Of the few symbols of national unity in the United States, the flag binds the polity through the misrecognition process that Silverman outlines. This means that each individual has a different relationship to the flag and conceives of his or her citizenship through very different ideological beliefs, with Christianity being but one among many religions that also exist among cultural and political beliefs drawn from a wide array of experiences.

For one group to suggest that God should be allowed (by the federal government) to reclaim the school is very exclusionary and insensitive to those with dissimilar beliefs. As school districts around the country ban student-led assembly simply because of one sector of the community's homophobia, students are learning that their options for participation are severely limited. Furthermore, the symbols and imagery of groups like the SYATP for all their patriotic and therapeutic zeal are parochial in their representation of gender and symbolic power. Traditional masculinity and its supplement, femininity, modeled along the lines of the Oedipal family unit, is one among many *ideals* that cannot respond to the needs of real students in contemporary American life, especially to those whose families are organized along many different lines and whose trajectories are by no means limited to married heterosexual couples, but extend to adoptive parents and extended family members.

Even more important than the representational aspects of the group is its proselytizing function at the school site. The problem hinges on the definition or practical implications of "witnessing" because as some say, witnessing is simply about Christian students pledging the existence of God in their lives to "other" students. However, when those other students do not want to be witnessed to, prayed for, or condemned for believing in something other than the highly contentious "principle" on which the United States was founded, it becomes a problem of public law and policy.

Already, SYATP affiliates have filed a lawsuit against the Corpus Christi Independent School District and with support from the Rutherford Institute have won a settlement. They have also managed to use their alleged persecution ("They [the government] took prayer out of the schools!") in connection with school trauma to forge a community based not on reinstalling a common faith in human potential or trust, but negatively by exploiting its failures. Furthermore, as Brian Landsberg, the chair of the Sacramento Jewish Community Relations Council, states, "Our kids don't feel they need to be prayed for. Praying for them is denigrating."[34] Indeed, many groups in the private sector of the United States do not want public policy or school policy to alienate them by reflecting the views of one particular interest group. For that is what the SYATP has become, an interest group, as it has expanded its message from fulfilling a voluntary need in civil society, to insisting that its very Christian and patriarchal message applies to all Americans.

There is one more important question with regard to the SYATP and youth groups with similar school orientations. As noted earlier, the movement insists that it is "student led." Youth groups must label themselves that way in order to bypass the law stating that the only constitutionally protected groups that can meet on school grounds outside classes are those that are freely formed and chosen by students. The groups cannot be engineered or managed by adults unless students request adult assistance. This criterion has been the basis for approval of student groups nationwide. One question arises here: What does it mean when other forms of student assembly are banned and the only options left are youth ministries? Following Columbine, policy was headed in that narrow direction having discredited Goth students or alternative forms of music and play by crediting those same groups with at least partial responsibility for school shootings. The SYATP, as it has gained members, has changed the look of its national forum by absorbing aspects of those discredited groups into its presentation.

For example, the movement's t-shirts and paraphernalia borrow the *form* of popular culture and implant in it the message of Christianity. Christian rock, except for the lyrics, is virtually indistinguishable from popular musical genres like R&B and techno. T-shirts are designed to mimic those of popular bands and rock band names such as the Nine Inch Nails are reclaimed for Jesus' martyrdom as the Ten Inch Spikes. Youth assemblies feature dramatic presentations and reenactments of school violence to students using the real guns, musical lyrics, dress, and attitudes now banned by the hidden curriculum of schooling.

In one such presentation in Texas, youth ministers constructed a haunted house for the purpose of teaching violence prevention in which they fired real guns holding blanks while simulating the events at Columbine High School. When a judge shut down the house, the head youth minister claimed that "the church is using the Columbine skit, complete with earsplitting gunshots, to scare teens and others into accepting Jesus."[35] Once assured they were only blanks, the judge reopened the house. It is interesting that while the Supreme Court passes legislation making it legal for police to chase suspicious individuals without probable cause, this group can use real guns to scare students into believing in Jesus. Furthermore, as more and more "suspects" are murdered for pulling wallets, flashlights, and other non-weapon-like artifacts from their person, the police who shoot and brutalize them are set free. While the problem is also about which group gets protection from the government to operate freely in civil society, it is also increasingly about the way in which the options for living creatively in public are diminishing so that only one option remains: God. Students in school can no longer dress freely or enjoy popular culture in an experimental way, but they can have the same form of popular culture at the SYATP and related functions and this is one of the primary places where they find it. With these observations concerning youth ministries and their strategies for attracting students to their witnessing causes in mind, I now examine the story of Cassie Bernall, as represented by her mother, Misty, in the controversial book *She Said Yes.*

THE MARTYRDOM THAT WAS NOT

Misty Bernall's book, written as a tribute to her daughter only a few weeks following her death in the Columbine High School library, is an interesting and thought-provoking text for reasons wholly other than those debated by it critics and supporters. While the media criticism has focused on the issue of whether or not Cassie Bernall's martyrdom is deserved, they have ignored the interesting story of her life before the shootings.

Here, I expand the reflections that I will make at the end of chapter 6, where I intimate that Cassie's story is, in many ways, representative of the treatment most teenagers are faced with at school, by their parents, and by the popular cultural artifacts that triangulate this relationship.

For starters, Cassie had only recently been "saved" and traveled over to the Christian fellowship she belonged to at the time of her death. Prior to this conversion, Cassie had been a fairly representative Goth teen and her friends were less than suitable to her parents' tastes. Her music far surpassed the lyrics of Marilyn Manson in their intense hatred of parents and authority figures and she and her best friend "Mona" wrote letters to each other describing the deaths of several people (Cassie's parents included) in light of what they perceived to be the parents' harsh forms of discipline. Like a normal teenager, Cassie lied to her parents about these activities and they never bothered to ask about the song lyrics or to inquire about her actual whereabouts with friends until after they found the notes describing their imagined deaths at the hands of Cassie and Mona.

Here again, one meets the virtual space of adolescence described by Winnicott. Cassie's parents, seemingly uninterested in her life until they found letters describing her hatred of them, had now to decide whether or not she really would try to kill them, or if she was simply doing it on the level of fantasy, which, according to Winnicott, would be a normal process in adolescent behavior. Winnicott's point is that it is normal for adolescents to fantasize about destroying their parents because it signifies that they are attempting to make the necessary break from dependence on them.

The tension between fantasizing their "destruction" and the reality of their omnipresence as total caregivers parallels with the adolescents' need to vent about the contradiction in fantasy. Unfortunately, it has become a common sentiment in American society to believe that the demographic category "youth" is correlated with criminality and even murder. Therefore, people believe too much in the reality of fantasy as a precursor to an act, rather than as a subterfuge that helps the subjects mediate their conflicting emotions, desires, and contradictory moods. This society not only alienates youth from each other, but also from their fantasy lives. The Bernalls' reaction to reading Cassie's letters to Mona was not normal, while her fantasied destruction of them, according to Winnicott's premise, was normal.

Misty's close friend often listened to her tell stories about how she felt alienated from her daughter's out-of-control behavior and finally became exasperated, telling her that she had to remember that she was the mother, not the friend of her daughter. It was only later, after Cassie's conversion to fellowship and the containment measures that preceded it, that Misty conceded to herself: "[But] through Susan I began to see my role as a parent in a new way—as a mentor and a confidante, rather than as a buddy. I stopped trying to please Cassie and make her like me, and started trying to guide her more consistently. Unbelievably, instead of rebelling, she accepted the boundaries I set for her and even seemed grateful for them."[36]

But the Bernalls did not take control in this way at the beginning of the story. Instead, they let their hurt feelings (understandable) combined with the environmental frenzy concerning murderous Goth teens (i.e., stereotyping) dictate their response to the letter. And so, when they found Mona's handwritten and illustrated letters to Cassie describing their shared hatred for "Ma and Pa Bernall," replete with headstones marked "R.I.P.," they *depersonalized* their relationship to their daughter by calling the police and turning her and Mona in to them, saying it was in the girls' best interest (recall the parental relationship to police discussed earlier).

Cassie became an alienated person to them, as one of those Goth teens taken over by evil cultures. They did not view the graphic letters as the product of an emotional teenager as Mona's parents did; when confronted by the Bernalls about Mona's behavior, they looked on them as if the Bernalls were the villains and offered to let Cassie come live with them if she could get away.

After notifying the police, the Bernalls banned her music, her after-school activities (she could not even get an after-school job), moved to a different house, and changed their phone number. The first step was to contain Cassie from her peer group—something that is brutally important to a fifteen-year-old.

Cassie's response to this treatment was twofold: first, she argued that "in using her letters against her (as she put it), we had trampled on her rights," and second, she felt that "we were holding her prisoner in her own home."[37] After they moved, Cassie's friends began harassing them and committing small acts of violence against their property. Again, they called the police and promptly switched Cassie to a Christian school. They cut off every means that Cassie had to sublimate the anger and rage that accompany adolescent development. Misty admits that after Cassie began sneaking out of the house when they left to run an errand,

> [w]hat we ended up doing—and I know it sounds highly intrusive—was to remove every opportunity for deceit from Cassie's personal life. We went through her backpack

on a daily basis; we searched her room repeatedly to make sure there was nothing amiss (we found new notes); we even installed a voice-activated recording device on our own telephone. Drastic as they were, we felt in order to save Cassie from the path she insisted going down, we had to take these measures.[38]

By not trusting her with her "personal life" and failing to understand the subtle power of "holding firm," they let her down at the "critical moment," the moment when she tested them to not be destroyed by her anger, to survive the assault intact and emerge as total persons. In this exhausted form of containment, they showed Cassie that she was indeed the threatening person she feigned in her letters; they showed fear and she fought them even harder for control over the parent-child relationship.

It is important to point out that holding firm does not mean withdrawing from responsibility by letting a strategy of containment take over the disciplinary act. The Bernalls' containment of Cassie from her friends, school, phone, and popular culture only made her more determined to fight back and further alienated them from her as a real person. The specter of the murderous adolescent is rampant in this culture and it forces youth to take on the persona reserved for them by the generation of their parents. Without the necessary adaptation tools and the space to work through the emotions of adolescence that are fraught with a tension between reality and fantasy itself, youth will "not rest" as Winnicott says and they should not anyway.

These tensions have been rehearsed earlier in this writing, but they are worth reiterating: "adolescence" is a socially constructed term, but it is experienced by real human beings. Adolescents are dependent on their parents for support and permission for every activity while at the same time expected to behave like mature, independent adults. If our culture viewed adolescence as the testing period it has been set up as, instead of as a dreaded and hateful stage in human development, we might not hate the kids who experience it as much as the public, the juvenile justice system, the police, and the media demonstrate.

The true radicality of an act is determined by measuring it against the environment in which it takes place. The environment that youth are currently forced to fight anticipates progressivism along the lines of a humanist and enlightenment ideal; kids are *required* to care about the environment, social justice, and equality because these are the ideals of their parents' generation. A radical act in the era of Clintonian liberalism was to be socially conservative and generally opposed to secular culture. Now, in the era of George W. Bush, we can also see the importance of religion to young people with virtually no future prospects economically or politically. The fallout over social security, corporate greed, and the increasing security culture inaugurated by the September 11, 2001, attacks on the World Trade Center and the Pentagon have only compounded the hostility of the environment in which adolescents are reared. Since most of their parents represent the generation of those in power, and every example of corruption (from corporate greed to serial killers) is of the generation that thrived under secular humanism and neoliberalism, we can only anticipate more conversion to religion—possibly fundamentalist—as a way of rebelling and trying to make sense out of their role in this country. The truly radical act for youth today is to become a fundamentalist Christian. To be sure, it is a retroactive move when one considers the history of the battle between secular and religious values in the school and the society. But adolescents today do not experience it as a backward step; rather, they consider it the only freedom left for them to choose.

"Bringing God back" is a convenient myth for youth today because it contains all the elements necessary to satisfy the voids in culture. Oedipus can come back through God and can address all the uncertainty that accompanies living in a secular world that failed to address the question of values. Baby Boomers wanted equality between the sexes, but conveniently forgot to address the competitiveness that equality breeds when not accompanied by a standard of conduct. Christian life implies a heteronormative ethic for gender arrangements with the male figure at the center ensuring that each gender knows its place. Capitalism provided all the social goods necessary to living in an equal society, but many groups were left out of this plan when the invisible hand forgot them. The Christian life promotes charity through service to others, even though it is inevitably followed by a debt to God. Sexuality was freed only to become an object of intense scrutiny—a lifestyle choice—devoid of any of the aura and imagination that makes it pleasurable. The Christian ideal makes reproductive sexuality into a gift bestowed by God and shuns the scientific study of this process in schools. Yes, it is a trade-off and a suspect one at that, but what I am pointing out here is that people need to be able to believe in things and feel secure in their environment. The liberal humanist ideal went too far and pulled the rug out from under an entire generation, but failed to realize that the very essence of the experience of adolescence is not to conform to parental desires. Therefore, any deviation from them, no matter how conservative it might seem in terms of a history of progressivism, is necessary and desirable. Cassie Bernall is the first martyr in a backlash generation.

As Misty takes great pains to point out, she and her husband were not Christian enthusiasts by any means. They simply wanted to get their daughter away from the negative influences at the public school she was attending when all her behavior problems began. When Cassie began attending the new school, she stood out from the other students and they recall her as having been an aloof and cynical presence at the school. It was not until her parents cut off every form of contact with her old friends that Cassie decided to attend a retreat hosted by the new school where she instantly converted, had a change of heart, and came home to her parents proclaiming her saved status. Misty is careful to note that neither she nor her husband was terribly excited about Cassie's conversion to religion, but that if it kept her peaceful, they were accepting of it. After a while at the Christian school, Cassie decided she needed to return to public school so that she could help others and spread the message to them; she simply could not make a difference at a school where the kids had already accepted religious salvation. She needed a challenging mission.

NOTES

1. Maurice Blanchot, *The Writing of the Disaster,* trans. Ann Smock (Lincoln: University of Nebraska Press, 1995), 7.

2. James W. Fraser, *Between Church and State: Religion and Public Education in a Multicultural America* (New York: St. Martin's, 1999), 179.

3. *Marantha Christian Journal* (1998), 1.

4. Kaja Silverman, *Male Subjectivity at the Margins* (London: Routledge, 1992), 21.

5. Doug Clark, Director and Promotion Coordinator of the National Network of Youth Ministries, at www.syatp.com/stories.htm (accessed February 2, 1999).

6. Stacey MacGlashan, "Prayer Circles: Students Gather to Pray for Schools," *Times-Picayune,* 17 September 1998, B1.

7. Schools have the option of banning limited forums, but only if the ban is applied to all groups. It is interesting that most have chosen not to ban them in response to prayer, but when one considers the controversy surrounding gay and lesbian forums in states such as Colorado, Michigan, and Utah, it seems odd that the prayer circles gained credibility (or are at least viewed as relatively benign) after the shootings began, especially West Paducah.

8. This widely circulated statement was given to the press by Richard Riley for this purpose.

9. Radio Address by the President to the Nation, 6 December 1997, emphasis mine.

10. Reactions by those involved in the shooting are mixed. Ben Strong has decided that "there's just no way to explain it," while officials who run the SYATP from the National Youth Ministry argue that from their talks with prayer circlers, they have formed the conclusion that Carneal's target "could just as easily have been a basketball game." Another student and close friend of Carneal's said, "Well, you'd just have to know Michael. It was just a Michael thing, I guess."

11. Doug Clark, Director and Promotion Coordinator of the National Network of Youth Ministries, e-mail to the author, 12 April 1999.

12. Mark Seltzer, "Wound Culture: Trauma in the Pathological Public Sphere," *October* 80 (1997): 3–26.

13. Linda Zerilli, "Doing without Knowing," *Political Theory* 26, no. 4 (1998): 435–58.

14. The web site address is www.syatp.com (accessed February 2, 1999).

15. David Van Beima, reported by Emily Mitchell, "O, Say, Can You Pray? A Grass-Roots Ritual by Young Christians Test Church and State Borders," *Time,* 28 September 1998, 68.

16. Silverman, *Male Subjectivity at the Margins,* 42.

17. The idea to read this event as a challenge to the post-Oedipal was inspired by Diane S. Rubenstein's "Chicks with Dicks: Transgendering the Presidency," which "questions the extent to which the phenomenon commonly referred to as 'Hillary hating/Hillary bashing' is a resentment not so much of Hillary [Rodham Clinton] (or Hillary bashers) but a referendum concerning the possibility of a post-Oedipal feminine identification." See Diane S. Rubenstein, "Chicks with Dicks: Transgendering the Presidency" (paper presented at the annual meeting of the Western Political Science Association, Los Angeles, California, March 1998), 5. I want to test the notion of post-Oedipal masculine identification. This means putting the pole up against the most salient features of the wound.

18. National Network of Youth Ministries, "Network Covenant," at www.nnym.org (accessed February 2, 1999), emphasis mine.

19. Jane Gallop, *Reading Lacan* (Ithaca, N.Y.: Cornell University Press, 1985).

20. Seltzer, "Wound Culture."

21. Thomas Keenan, *Fables of Responsibility* (Palo Alto, Calif.: Stanford University Press, 1997), 177.

22. Gallop, *Reading Lacan*, 80.

23. Rick Bragg, "Past Victims Relive Pain As Tragedy Is Repeated," *New York Times*, 25 May 1998, A8.

24. Seltzer, "Wound Culture," 10. As was demonstrated in the three previous chapters, the student shooters have been labeled animal torturers and some had been previously accused of sexually abusing other children. The animal torture connection is as tenuous as the childhood experience argument when it is applied to the figure of the serial killer.

25. Juliet Flower-MacCannell, *The Regime of the Brother* (New York: Routledge, 1993), 14.

26. Jamon Kent, Springfield Superintendent of Schools, *School Violence Prevention*, Part 2, White House, 15 October 1998.

27. William James, "Pragmatism's Conception of Truth," in *Pragmatism and the Meaning of Truth*, ed. A. J. Ayer (Cambridge, Mass.: Harvard University Press, 1975), 100.

28. Shoshana Felman, "Education and Crisis, or the Vicissitudes of Teaching," in *Trauma: Explorations in Memory*, ed. Cathy Caruth (Baltimore, Md.: Johns Hopkins University Press, 1995), 13–61.

29. See www.syatp.com.

30. Testimony of Darrell Scott, Father of Two Victims of Columbine High School Shootings, Littleton, Colorado, before the Subcommittee on Crime, House Judiciary Committee, United States House of Representatives, 27 May 1999, 2:00 P.M.

31. Lisa Belkin, "Parents Blaming Parents," *New York Times Magazine*, 31 October 1999, 63.

32. Kai Erickson, "Notes on Trauma and Community," in *Trauma: Explorations in Memory*, ed. Cathy Caruth (Baltimore, Md.: Johns Hopkins University Press, 1995), 191.

33. Erickson, "Notes on Trauma and Community," 196. He ends this section by writing: "When one begins to doubt the findings of scientists and the calculations of engineers, one can begin to lose confidence in the use of logic and reason as ways to discern what is going on. And that is a truly frightening thought, for it has been understood for a long time that deeply felt upheavals, at their worst, can act to upset the established order of things, and, in doing so, create a cultural mood in which dark but familiar old exuberances flourish— millennial movements, witchcraft, the occult, and a thousand other systems of explanation that seem to make sense of bewildering events and offer a means for coping with them."

34. Quoted in Jan Ferris, "Christian Clubs on Campus Crusade," *Sacramento Bee*, 17 September 1998, A1.

35. "Columbine-Themed Haunted House Shut Briefly," *Denver Post*, 30 October 1999, at wysiwyg://20/http://www.denverpost.com/news/shot1030c.htm (accessed November 3, 1999).

36. Misty Bernall, *She Said Yes: The Unlikely Martyrdom of Cassie Bernall* (Farmington, Penn: Plough, 1999), 71.

37. Bernall, *She Said Yes*, 64–65.

38. Bernall, *She Said Yes*, 67.

5

Why Can't We Be
Deweyan Citizens?

We don't know now and we may never fully understand what could have driven
two youths to deliberately shoot into a crowd of their classmates.

—Statement by the president, Office of the Press Secretary, Kampala, Uganda,
March 24, 1998[1]

Why are individuals compelled to act out violently in the least regulated spaces
of democratic institutions like schools?[2] Is it because they are not regulated,
as the authorities would have the public believe, or is it because they are already regulated by codes of conduct undetected by the witnessing public? This chapter suggests that student violence is an effect of the hidden curriculum of schooling that
extends beyond the boundaries of the classroom, past the comprehension of ordinary (and to date, formulaic) interpretations and into the motivational sentiments
behind American culture and citizenship. Such effective discursive regimes are analyzed by curriculum theorists with the intention of marking out the territory covered by the hidden curriculum of schooling. Acting as a counterdiscourse, hidden
curriculum theorizing seeks to find concepts with which to apprehend the nonvo-
calized aspects of the schooling process that promote conflicting ideals, goals, and
ways of life for students. The objective is to discover the ways that conflict is managed in schools and to work out the effects of this unacknowledged processing of
student bodies and minds.

Sometimes, however, the hidden curriculum research is too formal, focusing only on the ways in which the material adopted as official subject matter produces conflicts of *interest* in *classrooms*. Little of the material focuses on the ways in which the hidden curriculum produces conflicts of *conduct* and *identity* in *extracurricular spaces*. With the intent of amending the literature on hidden curriculum theorizing by looking at different effects of the hidden curriculum produced by the disciplinary apparatuses at work in the extracurricular spaces of school, this chapter looks *beyond the school* to American culture in order to understand the rules underwriting practice in these spaces. These are the spaces where students are ostensibly "free" to conduct themselves as they wish, but in which they are actually forced to conform to a hidden norm of conduct that validates and inscribes a specific cultural ethos onto student bodies.[3]

When researchers speak of curriculum theorizing, they typically focus on the cognitive aspects of the curriculum (i.e., what ideas students are supposed to learn from subject matter) and leave little room for discussion of the noncognitive aspects of the school's official curriculum practices. The noncognitive aspects of the hidden curriculum are those practices and rules of conduct that validate the customary dispositions of American citizenship. For example, conflicting emotions and violent impulses are displaced onto areas deemed appropriate for such expression (such as extracurricular activities like sports or extrasocial juridical procedures like lawsuits), whether as participant or spectator, in an effort to deny the reality or validity of dissenting opinion or practice.

Another way of denying the reality of conflict—especially conflicts with no easy resolution, like those pertaining to cultural difference—is to insist on a "normal" mode of behavior.[4] In the United States, one either conforms to the herd mentality cultivated and reproduced at school and in the society, or one (as the most ardent defenders of this mentality claim) *has* to allow oneself to be targeted as a scapegoat for the voyeuristic enjoyment and vented frustration of the rest. The hidden curriculum of school not only communicates to students that it is appropriate to displace conflict in this way, it also actively promotes it at a noncognitive level.

By noncognitive, I mean to say that there is no verbally expressed policy concerning this displaced conflict, but that the same message is communicated via denial and avoidance throughout the entire culture surrounding the school site. In a precise psychoanalytic sense, it is "a mode of defence which consists in the subject's refusing to recognise the reality of a traumatic perception."[5]

Now, this avoidance phenomenon has always existed at schools, even in workplaces and the institutions of civil society like churches, sporting events, television, and rock concerts. The difference is that, at present, the school and the culture, because of the increasing interest in school violence, can no longer simply ignore the conflict, but must find new ways to contain it and to protect the hidden curriculum's effects from harm.

The school, with the approval and demand of the larger society, insists that these outlying elements get erased (through expulsion, home schooling, jail, pharmaceutical and psychiatric containment, and so on) and since they can never be eradicated, they are seemingly repressed. This chapter contends that student violence (erupting in a variety of forms) mimics a return of repressed elements to do battle with a debased form of community that not only cannot assimilate these individuals into its customary functions, but cannot even *bear witness* to the validity of re-pressed claims.

To date, this is the most damaging form of conformity conjured up by the Amer-ican political imagination and yet it goes undetected because it is, quite simply, an intensification and extension of previous conduct to those practices that have previ-ously been ignored or scapegoated without dissent. To use a phrase from Louis Al-thusser, the "relative autonomy" that individuals once enjoyed in schools has been curtailed in favor of a policy of strict interpellation that reinscribes a norm of be-havior in schools that will make it function efficiently.[6]

I want to question this efficiency, what it allows for, what type of denial it enables, and the psychological motivations behind it. As Michael W. Apple puts it, the hid-den curriculum is a powerful mechanism that "denies the reality of conflict" in favor of conformity with certain norms of procedure and behavior.[7] In surveying the pub-lic response to school violence, one can see that this phenomenon is operating not only at the level of the school, but also at a community-building process that ignores or attempts to silence those members who impede its progress. When the ignored and ridiculed resist the tendencies of the hidden curriculum, the community elimi-nates every detectable signpost of their existence.

The practices that are said to reflect the norm are written into the scene of the American political culture. The norms are those aspects of citizenship practice deemed appropriate by default. The public, unable to see an alternative method of dealing with student violence due to shock and political indolence, allows the processing of students by the now panicked hidden curriculum to continue without acknowledg-ing the negative effects of such socialization. Shiftless in front of the television screen, the public blinks at the policy of containment operating in schools and only seeks comfort in the visible signs of security (police uniforms, clear backpacks, camera lenses, and children paraded in front of courthouses donning bulletproof vests).

What I mean to imply is that the public consumes these crimes with great fervor and the media is only too happy to supply the images, but the point is that through this televisual consumption, the public is allowed to disavow the implications of shootings. Concerned with the uncanny and grotesque details of the shootings and preferring to draw conclusions that only further its fear of public gatherings, the public is able to remain firmly planted in front of the television set (where it is safe). Instead of demanding to know and understand the extent to which episodes of vio-lence, like shootings, affect the quality of the democratic community, it encourages and welcomes every intrusion into its right to privacy and that of students; censor-ship is then exchanged for the chimera of security.

The public that accepts this discounted version of community protection is the same one that is only motivated to engage community when it dovetails with efficiency. As one of the results of the bureaucratic mindset, efficiency, when adopted as the supreme value of a society, indicates that what citizens value most in their everyday life is to have their Being managed by others (it is even more important for their children). This dis-placing of political ontology onto "experts" who interpret the motivations behind school violence is what accounts for the apathetic character of American citizenship.

DEWEY AND NIETZSCHE

With these insights in mind, I will sketch out the type of culture that breeds the reactionary behavior that gets decontextualized by the referent "school violence." Using two philosophers who have been chosen for the diagnostic and prescriptive strengths they can bring to bear on the subject of school violence—not because they have directly confronted this topic, but because they have analyzed political culture in detail—I describe the hidden curriculum's messages as the standard for citizenship in American society.

In the spirit of confrontation, the hidden curriculum sparks the provocative question: Why can't we be Deweyan citizens? To answer this question, it describes democratic practices through the eyes of Friedrich Nietzsche, one of the greatest critics of democratic practices, and responds via John Dewey, a philosopher who gave enormous credibility to the democratic model.[8] A third, perhaps suspect character, Sigmund Freud, is brought in to aid Dewey in putting his prescriptions into effect. As Freud states, in a Deweyan spirit, "one remembers that it is only by dire experience that mankind ever learns sense," and so we shall see if American democracy promotes this Deweyan experimental ideal or fosters the reactionary indolence that Nietzsche describes. The problem ultimately lies in the American resistance to practical experience, the sort of experience that might lead to the adoption of a pedagogy approaching "sense."

My reading of citizen practice veers toward Kenneth Burke's reading of the function of the scene in *A Grammar of Motives*. In the opening pages to his book, he argues that the scene of a dramatic production "contains the act" and will condition and determine the actor's motives.[9] I read culture as just such a scene determining the character of acting in public institutions and in life in general and especially in schools where children are molded according to the scripts of administrators and policymakers. Dewey's scene is nature, a variable force that he describes as "a source of philosophic enlightenment" if only "the mind is weaned from partisan and egocentric interest" so that nature is viewed "as a scene of incessant beginnings and endings."[10] Nietzsche scripts the scene from the perspective of this partisan and egocentric interest, describing the dispositions that both produce in the public: bad conscience and ressentiment. Thus, both philosophers are intent on theorizing the possible motives that an individual might give for engaging in public life in democratic societies.

Both writers concern themselves with theorizing the noncognitive aspects of practice, especially as they relate to morality and custom. Both question the operation of a phrenetic gap that exists between knowing and doing, act and intention. Though they share an emphasis on the doing part of the binary, they each believe that the justifications for action are supplied by different societal mechanisms or attitudes. For Dewey, nature and the experiences that nature provokes (though he later added culture to the mix) supplies the variation in habitual practices, which are the most common forms of doing that concern him. Because nature is perpetually changing, the objects that confront us in our practice will always appear different by some small variation. When we do not notice that they have changed, we are supposed to be acting habitually. Thus, only judgments (intellectual or cognitive) make us notice the differences, even though the differences are always already present in the action.

When we are not making judgments, we are taking up an aesthetic attitude toward the world and its objects. Dewey makes this point more clearly by pointing out that "proper" conventional philosophy never makes use of examples from our everyday practices to demonstrate the use of reason. Instead, it chooses examples of actions that are always already calling up an intellectual attitude precisely because they have been signified as pertaining to the intellect. The proper philosopher always reifies activity by questioning only acts that already have cognitive markers attached to them, taking for granted that this type of philosophical questioning ensures that ways of doing things in the world are reproduced. Thus, the proper philosopher, more precisely the "epistemological realist," never asks whether, when we eat food, we really analyze it and decide that it is food; instead, he asks whether or not we doubt the existence of God or the appearance of a bent stick.[11] As such, Dewey's notion of noncognitive practice is simplistic (this by no means disparages it) and optimistic. It is optimistic simply because it does not allow for a normative evaluation of practice based on intentions, but evaluates practice on the basis of options presented in the variations of the natural world. In this sense, Dewey's theory is completely social and the objectivity that he assumes early on prefigures his staunch scientific stance in his later works.

Recently, some scholars have compared Dewey's and Nietzsche's work in an effort to underscore their philosophical symmetry, especially the ways in which comparison between the two thinkers might inform educational philosophy in democratic societies. What is represented in these analyses is often a comparison of the two thinkers' *idealisms*, which are scattered throughout their large number of works. These *idealisms* might be compared to the foam at the top of the barrel of cream, representing the best part of their thought and, not coincidentally, the reason we read, think, and ruminate about them: they taste best to us. It is easy to think that the positive parts of a philosopher are also the most real and true, because educators are often seen as the most progressive and forward-thinking scholars in the social sciences. One never thinks about how trauma might be confronted by Dewey, because Dewey is always read as the promoter of the ideal of the inevitability of progress; therefore, he is always read as an idealist. There is, I want to suggest, something about Dewey's early works that can be read as a mark on idealism, a wounding that ends up recovered in the notion of practicality.

Nietzsche, perhaps because of the way in which he upsets and offends so many idealists (much as Jean Baudrillard, the "nihilist," does in contemporary theoretical circles), confronts cruelty as it enacts itself through idealism with ruses and aphorisms. Nietzsche's style inheres not so much in his ability to offend as in his use of irony to protect his text from idealistic banditry. Neither thinker, it is fairly clear, wishes to deal directly with the subject of cruelty. This is obvious in both their styles and the social topics they choose to confront in their writing. In the following pages, I dig out their positions and put them into play with one another in order to view more closely their shared belief that there is a critical lapse in judgment through practice.

NIETZSCHE ON THE NEGATIVE TELEOLOGY OF MOTIVATION

> A living thing seeks above all else to *discharge* its strength—life itself is *will to power;* self-preservation is only one of the indirect and most frequent results.
>
> —Friedrich Nietzsche, *Beyond Good and Evil*[12]

Nietzsche, in contrast to most philosophers in the nineteenth century, decided that neither sheer will nor the inherent positivity attached to teleological principles explained why people act. For Nietzsche, to live—as expressed in the previous epigraph—is to will. To act in order to "discharge" its vital possibilities, whether or not they secured the human subject's self, was the modus vivendi of the species. From this perspective, human beings have a surplus of energy so powerful that it is not capable of being directed through stages of development toward enlightened self-knowledge or even toward the maintenance of the memory of the origins of its trajectory.

Instead, our actings and thinkings constitute our will to power in more or less successful ways, depending on our capacity to tell stories about these acts that are not to be judged for their truth. The vital lies supplied by our moral systems allow us to maintain a semblance of truth with regard to ourselves. As necessary fictions, vital lies allow individuals to pretend that their doings and thinkings were not in the interest of self-preservation, but were done out of selflessness, perhaps even charity—all conditioned by good habits. Thus, self-knowledge is impossible, precisely because behind whatever knowledge we think we possess, there is no self, properly speaking, to secure it in the world of power. To describe this will or force, Nietzsche writes:

> A quantum of force is equivalent to a quantum of drive, will, effect—more, it is nothing other than precisely this very driving, willing, effecting, and only owing to the seduction of language (and the fundamental errors of reason that are petrified in it) which conceives and misconceives all effects as conditioned by something that causes effects, by a "subject," can it appear otherwise. For just as the popular mind separates the lightning from a flash and takes the latter for an action, for the operation of a subject called lightning, so popular morality also separates strength from expressions of strength, as if there were a neutral substratum behind the strong man, which was free to express strength or not to do so. But there is no such substratum; there is no "being" behind doing, effecting, becoming; "the doer" is merely a fiction added to the deed—the deed is everything.[13]

As a modernist responding to the progressive and constructivist philosophies of the modern period, Nietzsche may be viewed as whittling away at the subject, the "substratum" on which the political order of modernity rests; specifically, the subject of law, of reason, of judgment, and of responsibility—the sovereign and autonomous being.[14] The political order that laws corral into moral schema needs a rational subject, the individual, to ground it and to reinforce its prerogatives through judgment. Judgment is an act that is reinforced by conscience, the development of which has been the sole aim of educational and penal institutions reaching back to at least the medieval period.

According to Nietzsche, with the decline of the nobility, in both Greek and Roman society, there began the ascendancy of the morality of the servile, who seek to redress the wounds inflicted on them by the nobility through propagating guilt. The repetitive aspect of this guilt-inducing process throughout the protracted history of Western society has formed within and between individuals two symptoms: bad conscience and ressentiment.

Ressentiment presents itself as an acting out against the guilty party in order to redress a previous wrong. It is the belief in justice, specifically the belief that punishments can be devised that are equal to the crimes that they seek to redress and that allow ressentiment to flourish. Paradoxically, a culture committed to the idealistic ethos of progress, one that aims at undoing the history of harm and freeing the individuals from servitude to produce in their place autonomous, calculating, and rational subjects, is the site where ressentiment becomes the sovereign act that justifies and sanctions a new type of cruelty. Nietzsche calls it a "psychical cruelty" that hurts much more than the direct, physical cruelty that characterized the masses when they were closer to their animal impulses in earlier times. Instead, this new form of cruelty convinces the animal to place itself in a cage called civilization. This caged animal creates for itself a new type of conscience, the "bad conscience," which represents the torture and psychic anguish of the confused subject. Nietzsche writes:

> The man who, from lack of external enemies and resistances and forcibly confined to the oppressive narrowness and punctiliousness of custom, impatiently lacerated, persecuted, gnawed at, assaulted and mistreated himself; this animal that rubbed itself raw against the bars of its cage as one tried to "tame" it; this deprived creature, racked with homesickness for the wild, who had to turn himself into an adventure, a torture chamber, an uncertain and dangerous wilderness—this fool, this yearning and desperate prisoner became the inventor of bad "conscience."[15]

A *bad* conscience is formed by actions performed out of weakness and is associated with the morality of the servile, whose code and form of action is characteristically reactive. This happens because the servile have been positing new values to underpin the social and political order that arose only in reference to an original evil or injustice that had been done to them. According to Nietzsche, this posturing of the sovereign individual is a sign of weakness and a symptom of the degeneration of the human species. A stronger morality than that of the servile is that of the nobility who, at least, according to Nietzsche's reading of history, had the confidence to posit values narcissistically, that is, only in reference to themselves.

The inability of the morality of the noble to combat that of the servile has produced the dominant moral fallacies that attribute goodness and happiness to some otherworldly figure, such as God, justice, or some equally metaphysical ideal, ultimately produced for this world in some other one. For Nietzsche, the decline of the notion that the measure of "good" is produced elsewhere is a sign of increasing vitality, if and only if this diminished belief does not manifest itself in some form of bad faith encouraged by another ideal that springs up to take its place.

Although Nietzsche is not explicit about what agent might best produce the will he seeks to cultivate in the world, many answers have been supplied by his interpreters. In a relatively traditional interpretation of Nietzsche's views, Maudemarie Clark and Brian Leiter introduce *Daybreak* with the following argument, "Nietzsche assumed that explaining human behavior naturally (i.e. non-metaphysically) meant explaining it egoistically."[16] Therefore, to say that a critique of moral values simultaneously questions the foundations of those values (i.e., their metaphysical source) is to say in this case that values are rooted in nature and do not have a metaphysical source. Clark and Leiter become positivists by omission, reflecting a scientific interpretation of Nietzsche's critique of morality.

This is further evident when they align him with Freud and interpret Nietzsche's view of motivation through Freud's notion of drives. Though Nietzsche does admit in *On the Genealogy of Morals* that "our organism is an oligarchy"—implying that when one drive abates another takes over—and that our inability to know which drive is in control of the organism is a function of our constant interplay for control over our outward appearances and actions, he does not seem to imply a scientific basis for understanding the drives.[17] He implies, rather, that we suspect that the drives exist in multiple forms because of our erratic outward behavior; that is, our neurosis implies a multiplicity of competing drives. It also implies, when read in the context of Nietzsche's discussion of "forgetting," that large portions of our activities and their justifications are inaccessible to us in an intellectual fashion. This noncognitive aspect of knowledge is what makes possible any form of acting at all. A symptomatic reading of this passage would have Nietzsche situated not within a traditional scientific approach, but in a postpositivist and perhaps psychoanalytic position. Furthermore, though the correlation is indeed remarkable, it does not mean that Nietzsche is retroactively responsible for a Freudian science. In fact, it simply means that Nietzsche has now been scientifically determined and judged by the very causal fallacies that he diagnoses in *On the Genealogy of Morals*.

Recent social thought has consistently identified Nietzsche with poststructuralism, because his works on morality (*Daybreak* through *On the Genealogy of Morals*) confront the problem of language. These works are said to build on one another in a combined effort, through which Nietzsche attempts to make thinking progressively clearer to his students and detractors. Because "nature" can be scripted through linguistic means, it is unclear which Nietzsche, the positivist or the poststructuralist, is key to understanding motivation in his thought.

Since poststructuralism is readily identifiable with a critique of the metaphysical foundations of all systems of thought as they are constituted and rewritten through language, a poststructural interpretation might be more plausible than a positivist one, given Nietzsche's grammatical predilections. Positivism generally has either a scientific or a naturalistic justification that supports its claims to truth and objectivity. As for Dewey, Nietzsche argues that positivists (contemporary examples include behaviorist psychologists, social scientists using quantitative methods, and everyday individuals who only believe what they see) support their claims by demonstrating, through the use of reason, that deeds always match the intention of the doer. The belief and the practice can coincide to produce a convincing form of objectivity. However, their incorporation into an act or interpretation is often misleading. Many convince themselves that an interpretation of an event makes it real, whereas others are convinced that only reality itself (read through physical signs) can effect something so miraculous. Predictions at the end of the century made this disparity alarmingly clear. Though Dewey and Nietzsche find themselves writing against both forms of philosophical deception, they differ in the ways in which they read the "event." This is important for understanding the politics of school violence. In the last four chapters, I have strung together media coverage of several school shooting events; however, I have not implied that my story, told through the narrative placement of events in the media, is the truth. Indeed, there can be no such thing in media coverage, only convincing interpretations of a "bare" fact that we can never again access.

The event is the material or linguistic construction of an active reality at a certain place and time. It is *usually* and popularly interpreted by reference to the motives of individuals, as material placeholders who participate in it. Being the human subjects that we are, we always interpret specific acts or, in Nietzsche's words, deeds through the motivations of the subject (an individual in a subordinate position to a politicophilosophical system) or of the individual freed from unnecessary constraints acting according to his or her desires, which, ironically, if they are actual, nevertheless conform to a predictive logic or morality that may be read as an absent causality. In other words, both Dewey and Nietzsche take great pains to understand how we eventually make sense out of certain events in our history and how codes (of conduct, morality, custom, habit, and even will) have enabled us to *fit* them to our practices. Nietzsche's "great separation," if taken figuratively, would seem to indicate that he views our valuing as a semiotic process that takes place in relation to our need to script an event in a certain way.[18]

Dewey, taking an objective view of the subject rather than Nietzsche's perspectivism, views the event as a "bare, existential fact" to be interpreted by the observers and participants in ways that, practically speaking, promote vitality.[19] The trouble that arises between the two is that Nietzsche assumes that we generally interpret the event through bad conscience and thereby engage in a reactive response as if we are possessed by a dysfunctional or degenerate social illness. Our bad conscience is always present to make sure that we react to events in devitalizing ways. Dewey has a sort of naivete concerning this point in the judgmental process; assuming that we are open to deciding in many ways, he argues that sense qualities are more important for determining the outcome of an event than are any psychological predispositions. If

Dewey needs a place in contemporary thought, it may be more appropriate to put him in the context of theories of the body and its role in interpreting social practice.

Perhaps it is because of Nietzsche's perspectivism that he has so often been interpreted as the postmodern philosopher before his time, as the thinker from the modern canon of political philosophy who is most closely aligned with the erasure of the self and the erection of the ambiguous subject in poststructuralist theories of politics. For Nietzsche, while there is a fictional subject before the law, the juridical subject, there is no confirmed self behind it that critically interrogates that law. There is, then, no "real" citizen, only subjects who continually mistake their role in democratic societies as a participatory one. Indeed, Nietzsche's aim might be said to be the deconstruction of the citizen as that subject position produced and informed by democratic sentimentalism. This is clear in his discussion of the state. As the modern political construction that would serve as the "cage" in Nietzsche's theory of bad conscience, the state, an "oppressive and remorseless machine," processes a "raw material of people" while wearing the veil of democratic sentimentalism. For Nietzsche, as for other poststructuralist thinkers, the subject of politics is only a result or inevitable remainder of ideology and act. Accidental self-knowledge is the only way in which we "know" whom, in fact, we are. Nietzsche's will to power stresses the nonconformity of human agency to stagnant political processes or valuing systems and the noncomplicity of human nature with nature itself and especially with nature's distorted mirror reflection: culture. This culture is the expression of the will to power in its operative condition; in its postmodern condition, it is predatory because all are assumed to be exercising this will to power with no objective, no goal, even if only small, and, finally, no pleasure.[20]

DEWEY AND THE POSITIVE TELEOLOGY FOR MOTIVATION

Dewey, by contrast to Nietzsche, posits that humans have the capacity for more integrity and offers a critique of Nietzsche's "impossible" notion of "self-overcoming." Integrity is the subject's capacity for communicating its will to the world around it in a meaningful and practical manner. For Dewey, we overcome ourselves every time we experience the world in ways that reinforce our addiction to the pleasurable *feeling* of power that we get when we act in a manner that is consistent with our thoughts and activities and that is not presumed to coincide with those of others or with our guilty conscience. For Dewey, these are *our* thoughts and though they may be borrowed from others and amended to our purposes, we own them in the sense that they serve a *practical* purpose for us in our everyday lives. Experiences, repetitive and yet different, renew confidence and attach positivity to our actions and, through their borrowed aspect, are not entirely individually formed.

According to Dewey, we know that we carry others within ourselves and pay homage to them when we use them to enrich our life. This notion of the other would seem to fly in the face of many political theories currently in circulation that are concerned with the stability and ownership of identity. Multiculturalism has been the signifier for the debate that epitomizes this identity crisis. While the goal of naive multiculturalism (simply the idea of learning about others' cultural artifacts and relations to common political artifacts) has been to force a puritanical political minority to absorb the others within the social body, critical multiculturalism has reacted to ensure that those others, as cultural artifacts, retain their specificity and do not get co-opted or used.

The tension between incorporation and resistance to incorporation centers on the notion of cultural and political identity. Identity is presumed stable on both accounts, though the critical arguments in play would seem to indicate that self-preservation of identity is in crisis and that people need to police the borders of culture in the public sphere (in fact, for some to ride this border as teachers) in order to ensure that the category of identity itself does not come into question. Nietzsche and Dewey share disdain for such attitudes for different reasons. Nietzsche underscores the point that culture and values constantly shift, thereby undermining any stable basis for self-knowledge and the memory that would sustain its story from origins to end. Dewey also understands that culture and values shift, but does not bemoan the fact that self-knowledge is impossible; it is, quite simply, not that important so long as desire and energy continually reinvent themselves in the organism and its environment.

Dewey's point in *Essays in Experimental Logic* reaffirms this desiring perspective by pointing out an error in logical theory that is often made by epistemologists who argue for a rational and, therefore, stable basis for action. Many argue that when we judge an object or an act we assume that we have done it from an intellectual or cognitive perspective. Against this, Dewey argues that if philosophy were to "condescend to a concrete experience," it would find that, more often than not, our judgments are not yet intellectual (nor should they necessarily be forced to an intellectual level), but are the expression of what he calls an "aesthetic" attitude.

For Dewey, we choose objects to enjoy without giving an intellectual justification for desiring them; that is, without discriminating between them and other possible objects of enjoyment through a deliberate intellectual decision. Instead, we choose an object of attention or enjoyment because a "surplusage" forces a choice on us. "The tendency is for actual perception to limit itself to the minimum which will serve as sign. But, in the second place, since it is never wholly so limited, since there is always a surplusage of perceived object, the fact stated in the objection is admitted. But it is precisely this surplusage which has no cognitive status. It does not serve as sign, but neither is it known, or a term in knowledge."[21]

Therefore, noncognitive aspects of practice make possible the difference between acts. To see how and why this works, consider that Dewey's explanation of perception is both physical and semiotic. Thus, if we were to address Dewey's theory in relation to motives for acting, it would seem to him that motives are always retroactively placed over an act discursively and, though they may be bound up with characteristics of the actions and objects involved, that by no means makes them constitutive of that act in its initial phases. It is, rather, a surplus of perception that makes them possible.

The example that Dewey uses to demonstrate the aesthetic attitude is pedestrian, specifically that of a person recalling aspects of a lamppost that he or she might have passed on a daily walk. Similar to the poststructuralists' preoccupation with popular culture, Dewey's philosophy makes more out of average experiences (how to digest a lobster or buy a suit of clothing) than exemplary instances with which philosophical discourse is so often preoccupied. Dewey's goal is to elide traditional forms of knowing by switching the context of the analysis from an institutional or deferential "work" environment to one that he believes is significantly less coded: the street. In this operation, Dewey attempts to shift the argument concerning motivation for action in a positive direction by addressing Nietzsche's pessimism.

Dewey turns to Nietzsche's pessimism on the subject of value at the end of *Essays in Experimental Logic* in order to adumbrate the forms of epistemology that are possible to describe motivation in action. In a subtle move against Nietzsche's position, he writes, "Nietzsche would probably not have made so much of a sensation, but he would have been within the limits of wisdom, if he had confined himself to the assertion that all judgment, in the degree in which it is critically intelligent, is a transvaluation of prior values."[22] Therefore, Dewey's belief that custom and habit are subject to change because of the variation provided by the flux of the social world (and its excess of signs) is what explains Nietzsche's antipathy toward the assertion of the impossibility of incremental change and perhaps even progress in politics. The ability to make more of sensation is the ability to "condescend to a concrete experience" and to analyze the factors involved in making judgments according to our simple aesthetic enjoyment of objects.

Though Nietzsche is made out to be a numb philosopher in the previous passage, the implication is clear that, for Dewey, just because change does not reach out of an ordinary activity (such as eating or viewing a lamppost that one passes each day on the street) and announce itself, does not mean it is not occurring. Change is subject to many variations in force, which will not always be apparent to people undergoing it. Dewey states that "we have to remember that habit operates to make us overlook differences and presume identity where it does not exist—to the misleading of judgment."[23]

How, then, might this difference be noticed if it is not obvious? Dewey's frequent use of the phrase "critically intelligent" in reference to judgments in this section of his book makes clear that he views critical intelligence as the ability to see and realize differences in actions where none are presumed to be perceptually apparent. Noticing these differences does not amount to noticing supposedly proper differences (as Immanuel Kant might have ordered them in relation to imperatives), but to noticing any differences. The amended realist prescription for social change might then read, "Try to realize the difference in this situation," rather than "Try to see the good in this situation."

Based on their versions of the self, Nietzsche and Dewey share an aversion to the Enlightenment project, specifically to Kant's thesis of, and hope for, an autonomous self, whose practice is consistent with a stable social morality that permits social progress. Kant holds that judgments are made with reference to some transcendental eternal value, the categorical imperative. Thus, the morality of action ultimately rests with the judgment of a value given outside of any social medium (action, history, or language) or even, especially for Dewey, sense data. For both Dewey and Nietzsche, the judgment does not come into play by reference to an ahistoric value, but from either the judgment in action (Dewey) or from conscience/language (Nietzsche).

Dewey's perspective on this is clear in *Essays in Experimental Logic* when he notes that the "epistemological realist" always mistakes emphasis on the change brought about through judgment as the "survival of an idealist epistemology" that misrecognizes unabashed repetition as progress. According to Dewey, neither idealists nor realists judge progress in terms of "approximating a given value." Instead, Dewey inverts the assumption and yet still agrees with Nietzsche's critique of idealism:

> [P]rogress is never judged (as I have had repeated occasion to point out) by reference to a transcendental eternal value, but in reference to the success of the end-in-view in meeting the needs and conditions of the specific situation—a surrender of the doctrine in favor of one set forth in the text. Logically, the notion of progress as approximation has no place. The thesis should read that we always try to repeat a given value, but always fail as a matter of fact. And constant failure is a queer name for progress."[24]

Thus, Dewey casually accepts Nietzsche's pessimistic claim that we are creatures of habit but, for Dewey, habitual activity itself constantly disappoints us (again, if we notice the differences) by not recurring in exactly the same way; though we may desire habit, we never succeed in operationalizing it fully. Furthermore, Dewey points out that "success" is not the outcome of following "doctrine," but of what is "set forth in the text," indicating that, contrary to Kant's thesis, "given values" are supplied by the situation in which one finds him- or herself operating, not by what is "taught," in the strictest sense of that word, via doctrine. Therefore, the Word (of Reason or God) is not instructive, because it cannot immerse itself in every conceivable situation (even though it tries desperately to do so); there is no such thing as an effective prescriptive morality (we might question the effectiveness of the Ten Commandments to prevent violence in light of this claim).

Nietzsche, by contrast, seems to mimic Kant's structure; bad conscience is the cumulative effect of years of habit and punishment that the subject has experienced (not in the Deweyan sense, but more like the simple receiving of what Nietzsche calls "disinterested malice") through linguistic customs and language: It is the memory of the will, the remembrance of those instinctual acts prevented from satisfaction in the artificial domains of ethics and politics.

Nietzsche's bad conscience mirrors or builds on Kant's categorical imperative, reflecting back at the Enlightenment a critical disenchantment with transsocial valuing systems, that is, value systems said to transcend the problems associated with social contradictions. Nietzsche argues that we need a critique of the "morality of moral values" and consequently a transvaluation of values, but, as shown earlier, Nietzsche plays Karl Marx to Kant's transcendental ego, merely reifying it, leaving it there untouched.

Thus, Nietzsche's beyond can be nothing other than a form of transsociality itself. It, like Marx's inevitable revolution, can only come into existence after the metaphysics of the dominant Enlightenment concepts is put down and cast out of the social altogether; yet amazingly, according to a poststructuralist interpretation of Nietzsche, this would be an utterly futile undertaking. The inability of Nietzsche as a modernist to accept that change might be taking place through practice is what accounts for the stability of the bad conscience and the necessary remedy for getting rid of it.

DEWEY AND NIETZSCHE COMPARED

Through examining each thinker's critique, it becomes clear that the metaphysics necessary for securing the respective positions is different. The anchoring points, or, as Dewey says in *Experience and Nature,* the "generic traits of existence" that are claimed to account for judgment's repetition or variation, are different for each. For Dewey, the teleological direction comes from a conjunction of the individual and the incomplete social situation; the guiding thought or emotional aspect to action is brought forward by tendencies operating within the individual that excite and inhibit the tendency toward a given end that is never, given the flux that Dewey grants the social world, a discrete end, but is more like a fruition or consummation. The variation of characteristics and attitudes attributed to individuals is provided by nature, a constantly shifting component of the world, that, while in flux, only appears to produce stability through the *effect* of habit.

While a judgment exists in crude form within the individual, in its emotional aspects it becomes an object of consciousness through its realization in intellectual form. Thus, when we have ideas that we defend, they are not immediate things that come to us in one fell swoop; they have already been formed through a deliberative process that is emotional, intellectual, and most importantly physical. We might not have consciously known that our ideas were formed that way, but they always already were. Thoughts have a crude beginning that predates their expression in intellectual form; there was always a period of working through what Dewey calls, in *Art As Experience,* an undergoing, when thoughts were acted out in some form.[25] It does not really matter how they were acted out as long as they were realized and added to the intellectual processes of the individual through some form of practical activity. Thus, we never know until we do. The only way in which this doing is able to take place freely is within a social arrangement that provides for the widest possible variation of opportunity to do, that is, the most incomplete form of arrangement.

Social arrangements, such as the democratic state, are, therefore, extremely practical forums for conducting experimental activity, according to Dewey. Dewey's perspective on the democratic state makes his preference clear, contra Nietzsche, that rather than imposing a cage on subjects, the state brackets an impersonal space, the public sphere, that allows individuals to communicate with one another through objective means. When the social contract is entered, science begins:

Science or theory means a system of objects detached from any particular personal standpoint, and therefore available for any and every possible personal standpoint. Even the exigencies of ordinary social life require a slight amount of such detachment or abstraction. I must neglect my own personal ends enough to take some account of my neighbor if I am going to be intelligible to him. I must at least find some common ground. Science systematizes and indefinitely extends this principle.[26]

Science, like the state and the social contract it enforces, is a practical invention agreed to by participants so that they may *expand* their personal activity. Dewey does not argue that the state and the science that makes it possible simply protect personal expression; they actually promote it. The practical character of activity is the key to Dewey's understanding of practice and its relation to cognition or theory: "The paradox of theory and practice is that theory is with respect to all other modes of practice the most practical of all things, and the more impartial and impersonal it is, the more truly practical it is. And this is the sole paradox."[27]

Indeed, it is a paradox, but charging it as such does not alleviate the ambiguity of the public-private binary as it is enacted in contemporary politics. Moreover, the charge that there is a direct flow of information and activity between the two supposedly separate spheres draws out critics intent on redefining the boundaries for specific moral interests. For example, these boundaries are never drawn "impartially" or "impersonally," but always suture themselves around certain objects. An example is youth as a social category and the relation between youth and popular culture. If popular culture is the pedestrian arena representing "concrete experience," where prudence and "critical intelligence" are necessary for action, then the demonstrated ability to follow moral codes and ethical procedures is what reveals degrees of intelligence.

That moral codes and ethical procedures only appear to be objectively formulated would be Nietzsche's critical rejoinder to Dewey. That we think that the rules that govern the public sphere and its assemblies are in our best interest because they supposedly apply to everyone, on an objective basis, does not mean that they are formulated out of objective, or even practical intentions. Nietzsche's point is that public morality and law are formulated in response to social wounds and traumatic figures that gain popularity and attention as reactionary critical causes and movements in the public sphere. These figures terrorize populations into believing that they need protection from harmful acts and influences that come from that very same public sphere. The ironic implication is that while most democratic societies believe that their laws are formulated on a contractual basis that seeks to protect their rights, the public sphere that is created and protected by the contract is tainted by the very pathologies that it seeks to cast out.

This brings us back to Nietzsche's formulation of the bad conscience as a reactionary form of desire whose negative motivations (i.e., to keep offending objects at bay or to castrate them socially) build on one another and create a collective sphere of law and morality that cannot be presumed to be objective or innocent. Dewey's inability to view motivation as reactive and drawn out from negative motivations (even though perhaps "baited" by a sick world portraying itself as healthy) renders his theory impotent (as a progressive thesis) when faced with traumatic events and their spectres.

Nietzsche's "conscience," however, is much different from Dewey's incremental change thesis. For Nietzsche, we come to moral decisions, not by an individual deliberative process, but through a communal heritage. Morality, on this view, would seem to be a canon of fixed sentiments, pressed into our consciousness from outside and reinforced by the language that we use in our everyday encounters. We do not consciously know why we follow moral dictates; we simply follow them because they are impressed on our memory through the form of customs, institutions, and traditions that, above all else in our modern society, must be preserved.

This process of preservation exists in a historical movement that begins with Socrates and, through several mutations, ends with the democratic "sentiment." The process of preserving morality is of a certain type that exists in opposition to another: it is a dialectic of conscience. Its telos must be some form of weak thinking that subordinates its actors to an ideal that they are incapable of sustaining in either language or law. Slave morality is reactive (hence, our inability to be conscious of its origins) and it reacts to Master morality. Critical intelligence is a compromise formation with powerful interests, simultaneously allowing people to believe that they are making good judgments and reproducing the power structure. Thus, even with the positive motive of learning from experience, Dewey's theory of motivation cannot respond to the charge that nature might be an arena of traumatic events or, as Nietzsche puts it, "a festival of cruelty." Already saturated by wounded subjects and their various forms of ressentiment, the public sphere represents a serious stumbling block to Dewey's theory of motivation.

Consider Dewey's and Nietzsche's respective positions on desire, or what has been referred to as motivation throughout the previous section of this chapter. For Dewey, desire is a continuous yet repetitive action, not the continuation of a fixed decision to desire some thing or object. The object is not what constitutes the excitation; rather, the action accounts for the object itself: The object is realized only after the desiring process has abated temporarily.

Like Nietzsche, for Dewey, to will is to live, without regard to the character of the will, and yet, the character of the will is precisely their point of contention. Dewey writes, "When desires discharges itself it finds out what its object is." This discharging of desire does not necessarily constitute a single act either. "My experience is that we keep recurring, either in fact or imagination, to the conditions which excite desire; we think of those or we look at those, and that keeps up this perpetual partial discharge; just as the child will keep his eye going back to the sugar and thus maintain the discharge."[28]

According to Dewey, desiring is much like what contemporary psychology calls addiction. Assuming that we can change objects altogether, popular psychology, by contrast, focuses on changing habits by emphasizing the importance of obtaining external objects and incorporating them within our habitual desiring processes. The therapeutic implication is that we can simply change desires because we are sovereign individuals capable of making decisions outside our desiring mechanisms. Have a salad instead of those french fries or a cigarette instead of a drink. For behavioral therapy, there is no gap between knowing and doing. Not so in Dewey; indeed, we never know *cognitively.*

According to the reigning psychology of the day, however, we must somehow know in advance. Every act is interpreted as the result of what Dewey would call an intellectual decision. But this is not so according to Dewey, because our desires are inseparable from actions that corealize them and the aesthetic, noncognitive attitudes that make them possible. Therefore, the intellectual decision is only a part of the desiring process that by itself is an incomplete desiring act.

We can make intellectual decisions by themselves, but they are always made out of habit, because we remember that we made them successfully at some time in the past and that they were the result of full experimental activity. In other words, we remember or realize that decision relates to an object of desire that we have previously chosen through our experience of it. Every desiring act is made possible by an incomplete situation. Therefore, every desiring act (which is to say every act) is the result of an open situation and, if it is to be "critically intelligent," calls for prudence, a good judgment based on consideration of the factors involved in the situation. This incomplete situation and the phrenetic gap it presupposes must consult a prudent ethical position.

The ethics involved in embracing the Deweyan "doing" of desire require that people vigilantly pursue their desires with the public interest in view. While the public sphere is theoretically incomplete, it is practically determined by the personal pursuits of those who strongly advocate their interests, writing them into policy that will stand for the public interest. This means that whatever stands for "critical intelligence" is representing the interests of the dominant voices in policymaking and, furthermore, that "critical intelligence" is nothing less than an expression of dogmatic thinking.

This thinking is dogmatic because it demands that "my interests, *determined by my experience,* ought to apply to everyone for their own good, *irrespective of their experiences.*" Add to this the argument that "I have put this interest on the public table to save everyone the time and pain of having to experience it for themselves; that is my contribution to the public welfare." This is the difference between a public policy constructed out of the *sentiment* bad conscience (Nietzsche's theoretical description) and a public policy that might reverse this motivation by actively engaging the problem at hand.

Such policy is effected by the individual demand that "the public interest is that which secures the greatest good; my experience and my interests confirm this interest to be valid, therefore, I am in favor of it"; this latter statement is consistent with Dewey's democratic theory. What separates the two perspectives is motivation at the individual level. The first implies that public policy is a service provided so that the great majority do not have to formulate their interests through experience, the second that individuals must do the work of experience in order to justify validating public policy.

Now, this is an obvious description of the arguments that are made in favor of democracy. As Kant said, enlightenment requires that the public detach itself from "the go-cart to which it is harnessed" to make use of the faculty of practical reason.[29] This would be simple if experience were simply a neutral facet of modern life, devoid of positive or negative emotions and sensations, but humans are not yet the machines that science has provided to alleviate the work of experience. We still use them for that purpose but are *not yet them* for that purpose. In order to take Dewey's political prescription, individuals must detach themselves from the servile morality that both Nietzsche and Kant diagnosed. The political violence that we witness in contemporary society that appears to erupt without explanation ("senseless," "random," or "motiveless") is really the result of repressed experiences that are ignored in contemporary society.

Dewey thought that we could detach ourselves from the emotions that accompany experience by moving forward and refusing to look back at the pain or joy it caused, but in that avoidance, we have only internalized the affective aspects of experience. "Going through the motions" is an apt phrase for most of the practical activity that constitutes contemporary human life, where individuals simply follow the instructions to get what they need by taking dictation from bureaucracies.

In this sense, the Word has become the only means of instruction. Without an instruction manual, there is no motivation to act and desire becomes embedded, calculated, and inscribed into the hidden curriculum of schooling. We should desire only what we decided in advance by the instructions, not what we find in the world while we are discharging our desire. Objectives are not formulated inside practice, but are determined beforehand. The will that Nietzsche assumed was part of our being is slowly streamlined into procedures and policy proclamations.

Dewey gives a sign that he understood this possible lack of will or desire when he writes, "The problem [of desires] is to get up steam enough to move on toward their realization. It is a question, in other words, of keeping up the stimulus rather than of discovering the proper mode of control, for *the proper mode of control will be to a considerable extent organized into our system.*"[30] It is here that Dewey concedes to Nietzsche and gives an anticipatory nod to Michel Foucault, who argues that such a regulatory ideal, like a "proper mode of control," does indeed come into play to shape our practice by infiltrating our political system through discourse. A modernist Nietzsche might call it a cage, implying that it has a stable and foreseeable existence, whereas Foucault, more in line with Deweyan thinking, arrests critique at the edge of the cage and sees a fluid and moving spiral of power/knowledge that shapes Dewey's "mode of control" that gets "organized into our system." To follow Foucault's reasoning, however, it is necessary to admit, as Dewey does not, that this is a form of power.

The key point in Dewey's quotation alerts us to the problem of momentum, since he implies that motivation is only sustained if it is continually stimulated. Read against Nietzsche's will to power, Dewey's motivation is dependent on an uncertain fear that the will needs to be maintained and is manufactured by certain social factors, probably those at higher social echelons. (Is not this why Dewey takes his philosophical stand in the study of pedagogy?)

It is here, it seems, at the intersection of will and desire, that the two thinkers reverse positions, since Dewey does not believe in the energy of the animal that Nietzsche claims is "rubbing against the bars of the cage"; he instead falls into the trap of thinking that the animal accepts incarceration when it should not be doing so. Dewey's critical project for motivation fails on two accounts: it does not account for negativity in the pubic sphere and it gives insufficient cause for momentum that is located in the individual whom he so valiantly defends as the locus of social change.

That desires are a "problem" for Dewey signifies his presupposition that he is addressing a depressed (or, in Freudian terms, repressed) population, not willing to communicate or use "critical intelligence" to confront practical problems in civil society. For Dewey, the problem of desires is simply one of lack of motivation, not motivation stifled or repressed by tortured memories from history. Dewey's lack of reverence for history places him in opposition to Nietzsche's overt reliance on a cruel past to decipher present problems. Dewey's perspective is precisely that of objectivity in the sense that his term "practical" is a substitute for either good or evil in Nietzschean terms. That Dewey refuses to confront history attests to his belief that all judgment is not a rehashing of old valuing systems and moralities, an eternal return of the same, but that it is always, in Baudrillard's terms, a "cool" judgment. Neither good nor evil, Dewey's judgment is simply indifferent, as is science and the methods that it supports. Dewey's memory of history is a "cool" one.

As Dewey's later works testify, the coolness of science is the precise antidote to the very negativity that Dewey, in the same vein, refuses to acknowledge. Whereas others may view the benefit of science in utilitarian terms—it provides the goods and progress necessary to enhance the quality and duration of life through controlled experimentation with the natural world that is bounded by the availability of status and profit—Dewey, by contrast, views the positive benefits of science as instrumentally therapeutic.

Since science "extends the principle of abstractness" to virtually every avenue of the social, it will necessarily force the individual living in a scientifically directed society to forgo selfishness in the interest of communicating its experiential conclusions. The individual cultivated by this abstractness is not barred from experimentation by financial or moral sanctions; indeed, this individual neither needs nor wants validation from the Nietzschean herd. The profit-motive that prioritizes the valuing system in contemporary society leads to the debased community that Nietzsche describes as a "herd."

Dewey believes he is confronting an apathetic public whose desiring mechanisms have deflated; thus, he does not acknowledge the negative teleology that Nietzsche rightly reveals. For Nietzsche, the will to do harm outweighs the will to solve practical problems, especially when bad conscience and ressentiment become the primary vehicles for profit gain and policy formation. As Dewey admits, the public does have problems, but they are not so severe as to reduce prescription to imaginary remedies or, worse, Hobbesian models that will once again cast out perceived pathologies through strategies of containment.

THE LIMITS TO FORGETTING

Getting to a place (*beyond* good and evil) in which one can solve practical problems requires something that both Dewey and Nietzsche value in different ways: an *active* sense of forgetting. To take Dewey's path at this juncture would be futile; one cannot deny what has already been put on the table: A tortured history that is brought out into the open cannot be repressed, but it is managed, unfortunately, by others, not ourselves. Forgetting entails that one can and should put aside one's egotism and get on with the difficult task of willing a different priority for public decision making, instead of waiting for it to appear in the scene at the orders of, say, the play's director. This is the passive spectator approach to progress that waits for others to decide what experiences are valid and how they should be interpreted.

Obviously, this means that the individual, rather than the society or culture, takes up the task of ignoring the bad conscience and ressentiment swirling in the lunchroom, the library, and the parking lot in order to engage these public spaces in vital ways. But, as this chapter suggests, the cultural backdrops that motivate individuals to act in public in defunct ways demand a societal answer for which the individual alone cannot account.

While Nietzsche, nagged by this debased community in all his writings, leaves us with little but imaginary and utopian answers to material problems, his description is nevertheless apt and instructive, in ways that Dewey's naive analysis cannot perceive due to its intense denial of history. And yet, Dewey takes no solace in imaginary answers to real problems. Perhaps Dewey reinvents the Nietzschean dare to live without throwing down the anchor at some convenient social milieu (i.e., cliques, hate groups, or lawsuits) and his philosophy of positive motivation urges the individual to do so while remaining in the public sphere. Dewey's positive materialism is the scene that sparks this motivation so lacking in current public life, but it needs to be maintained and this means hard work for the public, not just for those who claim to speak on its behalf.

Imagine what students would do in schools if the curriculum taught them to value the differences of each educational experience, rather than viewing educational experiences as means to ends that have no guarantee of satisfaction? Imagine abolishing final causes in the form of the grade transcript, the Standard Achievement Test score, and the opinions of college admission boards? Realize that these are not imaginaries, but rather decisions made by societies about how to view the nature and quality of democratic life: The public school is the critical site for ensuring the reproduction of this view and for resisting the lure of the negative telos that is haunted by bad memories and bad conscience. And yet the question remains: How are we to deal with the twin sicknesses of bad conscience and ressentiment in order to put students onto the path of Deweyan experimentalism?

Keep in mind that Americans already possess a certain capability for forgetting that is expressed in their cultural enjoyments and their "aesthetic attitudes," and as Dewey states, "The history of man shows . . . that man takes his enjoyment neat, and at as short range as possible."[31] This should alert us to the weaknesses of American culture, that, if exploited in meaningful ways, might lead to an experimental future, but, as it is, the public is content with the manufactured models of containment and the feeling of safety provided by video cameras, locker searches, uniforms, and memorials. It will not be long until, like animals, we finally begin to rub up against the bars of our cages, knowing that we put ourselves there, but blaming others.

Why can't we be Deweyan citizens? While we can deny certain elements of the community, we can't forget them for long because they return to haunt the public sphere with a physical vengeance—a surreal haunting that we interpret as an affront to an efficient and normal way of life. The codes of conduct for this normality are embedded in the hidden curriculum of schooling. The more we contain and deny experience—whether good or bad—the greater the chances are for multiplying the number of repressed returns. When words no longer work, the best way to get attention is to act out.

As school shooters have done throughout their tenure in the spotlight, one of the best ways to get the attention in this shiftless norm is to interrupt its functional path. Instead of voicing their concerns through socially acceptable modes of expression, students express their feelings concerning the hidden curriculum in their actions in the very places where they find the hidden curriculum to be the most incarcerating: the "free" spaces. Peter McLaren makes this point while discussing the dialectical tension between reproduction and resistance that takes place under the hidden curriculum of schooling: "We need to change reality rather than simply changing our conception of reality, although the latter is certainly prerequisite to the former. . . . In psychoanalytic terms, we might fear that our own ignorance of the contradictions which inform us as human subjects may lead to a 'return of the repressed'."[32]

McLaren's admission that "changing our conception of reality" is a prerequisite to changing practice signals the Deweyan and Freudian claim that we need to view our "contradictions" as experiences that can inform us about the nature of our practices. Yet, Americans do not easily slide into the suit of experience that Dewey wishes them to wear, nor do they understand, as Freud emphasizes, that the knowledge of sense comes from "dire experience." Instead, they prefer to interrupt it, cut it off, and deny it in favor of the dominant conception of progress. This progress is only measured by the *pace* at which social life is carried out, and in the quest for efficiency, experience is left behind, repressed, and never "sensed." What happens to this repressed material? It returns.

No doubt, but it also returns by means of what denied it. The means of the return are what is repressed in the original disavowal of the hidden curriculum. *It returns as a failed attempt at finding sensation.* Resistance takes the form of a physical violence that cannot be understood by the debased community whose interpretative paradigm is unable to apprehend that a material expression of violence is directed at those practices taking place in the free spaces. Because they are "free" does not mean they are without signification, as containment policymakers would like us to believe; they are imbued with their own highly significant and complex forms of meaning. This misapprehension is embedded in arguments that claim that "bad objects" like guns, video games, movies, and Internet resources, the mere symptoms of the violence, cause student violence. We should not look to the objects themselves to communicate the answer to the nagging "Why?" of school violence, but to what ends they service and what practices they make possible that cannot be communicated or heard by the public and the curriculum.

Freud explains in his essay "Repetition, Recollection and Working Through" that some patients undergoing analysis would, in the process of repression, forget the causes and associations of their resistances entirely, and the only available signs alerting the analyst to their existence were physical ones. Reading the patient's practices would, in Freud's view, give the analyst a clue about the nature of the repression, its associations, its drives, and its characteristics. He writes, "The patient reproduces instead of remembering, *and he reproduces according to the conditions of the resistance;* we may now ask what it is exactly that he reproduces or expresses in action . . . the patient remembers nothing of what is forgotten and repressed [*sic*] he expresses it in action. He reproduces it not in his memory but in his behaviour; he repeats it, without of course knowing that he is repeating it."[33]

When Americans analyze school violence, they look at the accessories of violence and seek to keep them from students. They do not analyze what the practice of violence "reproduces" and how it does so "according to the conditions of the resistance," as mimicry of their treatment in the throes of the hidden curriculum. Freud further explains that the patient will protest to the analyst that the attempt to heal through a talking cure leaves the patient open to engage in all sorts of potentially destructive forms of behavior and that we (parents, society, politicians, and school administrators) must "wrest these weapons from him one by one" in order for the "success" of analysis to proceed.

Americans "wrest" the weapons all right, but they see the weapons not as symptoms of a larger form of repression, but as the object cause of the desire to use them. This is the great denial, not of the patient, but of the analyst, who, wanting to go no further in attempting to understand the repression *he* (read: the public) brings to bear on the analytic process, is content to dissolve the transference prematurely. Hence the patient's practices continue as more and more students mimic the resistances of others who have gone before them and even threaten to "finish the job." In a sense, they are right; the job is unfinished and the work of transference continues one-sidedly as the students, in conformity with the fundamental psychoanalytic rule, continue to "go on in their symptoms."

American culture encourages a forgetting that is at odds with any form of remembering (or even recall or recognition) because it is artificial. Living in a society in which one finds numerous ways to avoid remembering, ressentiment and bad conscience become the primary forms of denying experiences, whether good or bad, in order to avoid the pain of working through to avoid the sensations that accompany experience. Bad conscience and ressentiment become, as Nietzsche says, "sovereign"—that is, fully developed ideologies with projects of their own; keeping involved in the projects enables one to continue the denial of experience. As school violence comes to foreground discussions of American society (indeed it is almost always the pretext for such discussions), it is scripted in ways that allow these ideologies to flourish.

And yet, the repressed subject does not *know* ideological boundaries. As much as the public wants to believe that school shootings are *motivated* by fully developed ideologies, it fails to notice that the vile acts are performed in a temporal continuum (recall Dewey's statement that "when desire discharges itself it finds out what its object is"). The only cognates marking the practices are to target students en masse, in extracurricular spaces. What accounts for the public's misrecognition of shootings is a disavowal in which its privations are retroactively imposed onto the acts as interpretive schematics that allow it to turn the tragedy into a "project" of another sort. The impulse to engage in student violence is to get to the real of experience, to bring back "sensation" in a retroactive move against a society moving away from it into the virtual. Finally, its ultimate (embedded) aim is to make others feel one's own pain, ressentiment as deliverance from a tortured history ("I'm making you pay for what happened to me last year!"). As the Colorado students are purported to have exclaimed while committing their school atrocity, "It's only a flesh wound!"—an allusion to the film they had seen in the weeks preceding the carnage, *Monty Python and the Holy Grail*, whose message problematizes the singular or tangible reality and mourns the experience of sensation.

Regardless of political identification, the fundamental psychoanalytic rule of American society is not that practice moves in a certain direction, but that it runs away from the experience of sensation and all the messy (inefficient) feelings that accompany it. The containment policy operating in schools only intensifies the violent humanism that students practice when they resist and, at the same time, reproduce the unsaid, unfelt experiences of the hidden curriculum. The alibi for this society-wide denial is the paradigm of efficiency communicated by the hidden curriculum of schooling that is present in both the school and the society.

NOTES

A slightly different version of this chapter was published as "Why Can't We Be Deweyan Citizens?" *Educational Theory* 51, no. 2 (Spring 2001).

1. Published in the *Jonesboro Sun,* 25 March 1998, A1.

2. Ron Avi Astor, Heather Ann Meyer, and William J. Behre, "Unowned Spaces and Time: Maps and Interviews about Violence in High Schools," *American Educational Research Journal* 36, no. 1 (1990): sections 9–11.

3. One way to think of this ethos that inscribes certain behaviors and practices is by way of Pierre Bourdieu's "habitus." See Pierre Bourdieu, *The Logic of Practice,* trans. Richard

Nice (Stanford, Calif.: Stanford University Press, 1976). But a closer approximation is found in Charles Taylor's summary of Bourdieu's thoughts on practice in his essay "To Follow a Rule . . ." In this essay he writes, "We do frame representations: we explicitly formulate what our world is like, what we aim at, what we are doing. But much of our intelligent action in the world, sensitive as it usually is to our situation and goals, is carried on unformulated. It flows from an understanding which is largely inarticulate. This understanding is more fundamental in two ways: first, it is always there, whereas sometimes we frame representations and sometimes we do not, and, second, the representations we do make are only comprehensible against the background provided by this inarticulate understanding." See Charles Taylor, "To Follow a Rule . . . ," in *Pierre Bourdieu: Critical Investigations,* ed. Craig J. Calhoun, Edward Lipuma, and Moishe Postone (Chicago: University of Chicago Press, 1993), 50.

4. One can reference the increase in "character disorders" reported to the American Psychological Association as a sign, not that appropriate and tolerant behavior (liberal democratic) is in decline, but that it is discouraged by both the school's overemphasis on scholastic performance and the society's competitive and antagonistic drive toward efficient educational standards. When do parents and teachers have the time to encourage tolerance when they are encouraged to ignore it themselves? Furthermore, given the recent controversy over teachers helping students cheat on standardized exams, it is relevant to ask: Where is the agency or integrity of teachers supposed to be derived from when the teacher-training curriculum, standardization of the field, and administration of teachers' tasks are increasingly oriented toward these tests? How does a curriculum that is designed to ease teaching to these tests, eliminate teacher error, and objectify information encourage the practical ethics implied in teacher honesty?

5. Jean Laplanche and J.-B. Pontalis, *The Language of Psycho-Analysis,* trans. D. Nicholson-Smith (New York: Norton, 1973), 118–20. At stake is the notion of "traumatic perception" for surely the public reaction is mediated through the trauma of school shootings. All the sacred notions of youth held by American society are violated by school violence (e.g., that they are "innocent" and "nonviolent") and this perception must be denied for then the collective belief system would have to be reconsidered, including the way we think about children and the purpose of education.

6. Louis Althusser, *Lenin and Philosophy,* trans. Ben Brewster (New York: New Left, 1971), 127–86.

7. Michael W. Apple, "The Hidden Curriculum and the Nature of Conflict," in *Curriculum Theorizing: The Reconceptualists,* ed. William Pinar (Berkeley, Calif.: McCutchan, 1975), 99.

8. No, the democracy that Dewey promotes is not the same one that Nietzsche rejects (see Shannon Sullivan, "Democracy and the Individual: To What Extent Is Dewey's Reconstruction Nietzsche's Self-Overcoming?" *Philosophy Today* [Summer 1997]: 299–312), but the democracy that Dewey promotes is also not the one operating in the United States at present. Theoretically, the philosophers are at odds with one another, but the problem is not which democracy sounds better, but rather which one actually motivates citizenship. Dewey's democracy is a fantasy space—unrealized in contemporary society—while Nietzsche's describes the democratic sentiment of those exercising power in what passes for democracy in contemporary society.

9. Kenneth Burke, *A Grammar of Motives* (Los Angeles: University of California Press, 1969).

10. John Dewey, *Experience and Nature* (1938; reprint, New York: Dover, 1952), 98.

11. John Dewey, *Essays in Experimental Logic* (New York: Dover, 1916), vi.

12. Friedrich Nietzsche, *Beyond Good and Evil: Prelude to a Philosophy of the Future,* trans. Walter Kaufmann (1886; reprint, New York: Vintage, 1966), 21.

13. Friedrich Nietzsche, *On the Genealogy of Morals,* trans. Walter Kaufmann and R. J. Hollingdale (1887; reprint, New York: Vintage, 1967), 45.

14. Michel Foucault, "Nietzsche, Genealogy, History," in *The Foucault Reader,* ed. Paul Rabinow (1971; reprint, New York: Pantheon, 1984), 85.

15. Nietzsche, *On the Genealogy of Morals,* 45.

16. Friedrich Nietzsche, *Daybreak: Thoughts on the Prejudices of Morality,* ed. Maudemarie Clark and Brian Leiter, and trans. R. J. Hollingdale (1881; reprint, New York: Cambridge University Press, 1997), xxiii.

17. Nietzsche, *On the Genealogy of Morals,* 58.

18. Nietzsche, *Beyond Good and Evil,* 6.

19. Barry E. Durry, "Event in Dewey's Philosophy," *Educational Theory* 40, no. 4 (Winter 1990): 463–70; Dewey, *Experience and Nature,* 71.

20. Peter McLaren is the first educational theorist to call culture "predatory" in a way that separates it from the individuals who make and experience it. For an example of his performative style, see the first chapter of Peter McLaren, *Critical Pedagogy and Predatory Culture* (New York: Routledge), 1995.

21. Dewey, *Essays in Experimental Logic,* 393.

22. Dewey, *Essays in Experimental Logic,* 386.

23. Dewey, *Essays in Experimental Logic,* 386.

24. Dewey, *Essays in Experimental Logic,* 387n1.

25. John Dewey, *Art As Experience* (1934; reprint, New York: Capricorn, 1959).

26. Dewey, *Essays in Experimental Logic,* 440.

27. Dewey, *Essays in Experimental Logic,* 441.

28. John Dewey, *Lectures on the Psychological and Political Ethics: 1898* (1898; reprint, New York: Hafner, 1976), 160.

29. Immanuel Kant, *Perpetual Peace and Other Essays,* trans. Ted Humphrey (1784; reprint, Indianapolis, Ind.: Hackett, 1983), 41.

30. Dewey, *Lectures on the Psychological and Political Ethics,* 160, emphasis mine.

31. Dewey, *Experience and Nature,* 78.

32. Peter McLaren, "Decentering Culture: Postmodernism, Resistance, and Critical Pedagogy," in *Current Perspectives on the Culture of Schools,* ed. Nancy B. Wyner (Cambridge, Mass.: Brookline, 1991), 252.

33. Sigmund Freud, "Recollection, Repetition and Working Through," in *Collected Papers: Clinical Papers, Papers on Technique,* trans. Joan Riviere (1924; reprint, London: Hogarth, 1957), 369, emphasis mine.

6

The "Facilitating Environment" and Generational Change

Let the young alter society and teach grown-ups how to see the world afresh; but, where there is the challenge of the growing boy or girl, there let an adult meet the challenge. And it will not necessarily be nice.
In the unconscious fantasy these are matters of life and death.

—D. W. Winnicott, "Adolescent Immaturity"[1]

One of the key understandings backing the investigation of school violence thus far has been from Sigmund Freud's *Clinical Papers* and "Notes on Technique."[2] These notes demonstrate that the patient operating under the sway of repression has physical symptoms that can cue observers into the nature and cause of the repression. But Freud's clinical notes can only help if we understand the pedagogical and developmental processes of adolescents through a mentor relation that relies heavily on the analyst's role in helping the patient "work through" the repression.

Freud believes that this repression stems from internal disturbances (that are the result of familial factors experienced in early childhood) and that it is not motivated or released by objects in the patient's environment per se, but is heavily dependent on the role of the analyst in transference. According to Angelika Rauch, this bias, based on an "early Freudian assumption that the child's primary narcissism is a 'normal' state of being," has been carried over into American ego psychology.[3] This "ideology of the ego's independence" presumes that the patient (even the child patient) has achieved a stable ego without the benefit of a consistent environment or reliable objects; thus, this theory ignores both environmental factors and transitional objects.[4] The "return of the repressed" is provoked by complex environmental factors that, as was suggested in the previous chapter, are the result of the primary environment of the child, the hidden curriculum of schooling.

Furthermore, we cannot claim that the school violence analyzed by the media is practiced by all students irrespective of their particular identifications with the hidden curriculum. The student shooters are marked by their overidentification with the national fantasy of progress and the promise of education that is transmitted by the hidden curriculum. Indeed, how can young white males from middle-class backgrounds constitute the repressed?[5] Peter McLaren's passage in the last chapter is seductive because it enables us to view conflict in schools as the product of a hegemony that is monolithic and affects students in equal measure. We would be remiss, however, if we did not point out that the repression is not based on societal representation, but overidentification with a hegemonic norm that is in decline.

While Freud is helpful in showing new ways of looking at the problem of school violence, especially its physical manifestations (as a doing detached from cognition), it cannot aid us in understanding the larger societal response to youth violence or to prescribe remedies for it. It also cannot explain how these social dynamics in the school environment ignored by the school and the society reveal this ego bias in contemporary education and developmental modeling that effaces the environment's role in fostering hate and aggression in developing adolescents.

This chapter is chiefly concerned with detailing the processes of school violence and diagnosing them through their appropriate categories—that is, categories that speak to the concerns of adolescents, not adults. This means viewing school violence with a concern for the development of the individual in a certain cultural environment. To do this, I will examine the work of child psychologists and developmental theorists who, while remaining loyal to many important Freudian theses, depart from his traditional analytic style (reflective monologue). Placing emphasis on the temporal continuum so necessary for understanding child development (i.e., the child's active experiences in time and history) accounts for the role of objects in a child's environment—as well as the continuity of that environment—as shapers of personality and character on the road to selfhood. This will mean looking seriously at a Deweyan antidote to the problematic public sphere that Friedrich Nietzsche helped outline in the previous chapter. As was seen, John Dewey's theories, while extremely relevant for contemporary discussions of democracy and education, lack an adequate theoretical acknowledgment of cruelty, suffering, and resentment as common features of public life.

These are features of life that, given the media's overwhelming focus on their negativity, continually haunt subjects in public life and make living in a democracy less about enjoying the freedom to do things, than living under constant threat of being judged, named, evaluated, and reminded of past mistakes. This feature must be dealt with if we are to understand education as a "practice of freedom,"[6] rather than as a

Foucauldian "carceral experience."[7] This means looking at ways around the current education policies that focus on containing students from harmful cultural artifacts or that stem from a lack of understanding or care on the part of school officials.

If we seriously believe that youth violence is unconsciously motivated by the desire to get to the "real" of experience, then we need to outline how the real has been foreclosed from youth in contemporary society, by whom, and for what purposes. In the last chapter, it was hinted that part of the problem is the extension of containment policy, a reaction to school violence that restricts youth to "school arrest." This negative containment policy has been applied across the board to all students and treats them as if they were potential school shooters from the moment they enter the school facility. Furthermore, by taking away from youth any means of expression that the public has deemed inappropriate and the objective cause of the violence, adult society has also taken away this generation's facilitating environment.

Acknowledging that parents in the United States are reasonably worried about their children's safety at school, there is a better, more positive form of containment that can be applied in schools in order to allow adolescents to work through their difficulties as they abandon childhood and become adults. Hard truths are revealed in this space to parents, teachers, and administrators; alienation is necessary to this maturational process, but society needs to acknowledge this as a part of the development of children and to learn how to distinguish hate that is real from hate that is phantasied. The facilitating environment is one in which youth are able to destroy, in fantasy, the ideals of the generations that have gone before them.

The crucial point is to know what happens in the gap between knowing and doing that marks the difference between imagining blowing up the school and really doing such a thing. Here is the difference between the virtual space and the real space of adolescent life, one that researchers have shown to be of extreme importance for adolescents caught in the space between childhood dependence and adult autonomy in a "free" society.

Today, there is considerable debate taking place in curriculum studies over whether or not this space is marked by a generational problematic or a multicultural one.[8] School shootings opened up the school to the outside world. The media was able to turn out the inner processes of schools for the public as each event erupted, showing and telling the difficult lives of adolescents in contemporary society. Things were revealed that adult society is normally not privy to, unless they happen to know other adults who work in the schools who are willing to discuss the trials of youth, their demeanor and frustration.

The shootings at Columbine High School revealed the deep divisions between students as they formed "cliques" operating in a hierarchical relation that is justified and celebrated by the school officials (to wit: the recent celebration of the "jocks" with the victory of the state championship as an appropriate healing therapy for the wound opened in April 1998). Racism, sexism, and exploitation based on class differences mark the lives of adolescents, more so sometimes than adults. Their frustration is vented through the more prominent categories of discrimination; they are more open about the hate they feel, an experience that adults are prone to repress in order to live in "civilization."

The main problem that characterizes school violence is that it is a response to the school environment because it takes place at school, not in the home or in other public spaces. School shooters do not direct their rage at the hated teacher or even necessarily target their enemies; they target their peers, other students. So, I want to suggest that school violence of this sort is motivated at an unconscious level that cannot be detected by either the students committing it or those witnessing the event and that it is also directly related to anger and frustration experienced at the school (or perhaps an intersection of the school and the society, or home).

The hidden curriculum of school foments this antagonistic relationship between students because they are required to rebel against one another instead of against the values of the society in which they live. If one looks at previous generations, for example, they all have a peculiar experience of rebellion or cohesion that motivates them to band together and create a *vital* movement related to their existential experience (e.g., the World War II generation united against fascism and Baby Boomers united against the Vietnam War). But there is no common bond forged between today's students, a shared problem or cause that is external to them that they are able to perceive or know cognitively, at least on a level that might encourage a cohesive movement.

José Ortega y Gasset would mourn the fact that they have lost the ability to project a disagreeable personality trait onto a previous generation in order to exact an imaginary revenge and possible historical change. He writes in *Man and Crisis:*

> We are all contemporaries, we live at the same time, in the same atmosphere—in the same world—but we contribute to their forming in very different ways. This way is identical only for coevals. In history it is important to distinguish between that which is contemporary and that which is coeval. Dwelling in the same external and chronological time, they live together in three very different periods of life. This is what I usually call the essential anachronism of history. Thanks to that internal disequilibrium, it moves, changes, wheels, and flows. If all of us who are contemporaries were also coevals, history would be stopped in a state of paralysis, petrified, having only one face, with no possibility of radical innovation.[9]

As D. W. Winnicott would say, youth have lost the capacity to "play" and use imagination to rebel against their situation in a "firm, holding environment." In fact, my argument is that rebellion is co-opted or absorbed by adult society to such an extent that youth today cannot find any means to rebel that are their "own." Furthermore, they do not have the environment necessary for realizing that type of generational angst. To do that, they would need to be able to perceive the differences between themselves and the other generations controlling their futures, but with continual control and the retreat of their parents from adulthood, they can only see their parents as "friends" or "mentors," not as worthy historical adversaries.

In order to understand the morbid movement of students we witness today—who would rather kill each other for attention (with no positive political program or contribution to society) than to go against the ideals of their society in order to contribute to historical change and possible progress—an adequate mapping of the ideological environment is necessary. As they are continually "interpellated" into politics and public thinking through consumerism and into adulthood through their parents' emotional investments in them and their futures, they have no "relative autonomy," as Louis Althusser would say. That is, they do not have emotional or political room to figure out that they might be able to choose their own future or at least change it to conform to their desires in some small way that might add to or improve the polity. In fact, they believe (I think) that they have no other option than the fascist gestures of school shooters; that is why so many write into the school on web postings and scrawl threats on the walls of classrooms and schoolyard walls following a shooting, threatening to "finish the job" and proclaiming their adoration for the shooters. Each time a new threat is posed through leaking information from peer reporting or anonymous phone calls to the school, the district is forced to shut down school and take each threat seriously. This gives students enormous power over schools and authority figures but the administrators capitulate out of fear of litigation in the event that a shooting might occur. Girls fall in love with them as heroes and others bring weapons to school, thereby increasing the terror of the school officials. The truly radical gesture depends on the environment in which it takes place, who is there to realize its significance, and what it is registering a complaint against.

Adults may well wonder why the youth of today are not protesting against American bombing campaigns in Afghanistan or worried about growing corporate control over every aspect of political and social life, but it is clear that that type of resistance has been co-opted, as the adults and advertisers choreograph resistance to ensure reproduction of a very limited political and social view of life. Is it any wonder that youth would rather live in imaginary worlds of video games and the Web where they can feel some autonomy in a space free from total supervision?

I now turn to some insights from psychoanalysis, specifically the British school of object relations, in order to sketch out the contours of the environment that youth experience currently and an environment that would be "good enough" for them.[10]

WINNICOTT AND THE HOLDING ENVIRONMENT

Winnicott, one of Freud's interlocutors, gave public lectures to teachers, social workers, and child specialists, and in doing so shed considerable light on the difficult processes of adolescence and the fantasy spaces of children as they relate to the larger environment in which children develop and become adults.

Winnicott's greatest discovery was the "facilitating environment," a space that may be viewed as formally similar to Kenneth Burke's "stage" discussed earlier as the motivational factor for American citizenship. Winnicott, however, viewed the facilitating environment not as a destructive or negative space, like Nietzsche's democratic public, but more like Dewey's laboratory school, a space where children and adolescents could learn experientially without fearing punishment for failure or transgression.

Winnicott, unlike Dewey, goes further in describing the importance of the facilitating environment to the development of "healthy" individuals in democratic societies. His concern is that adolescence is largely misunderstood at certain periods in history and that this leads to the deprivation of individuals who experience the "reactive" policies of their caregivers (e.g., such as a war or economic depression, when many children lose their parents and their holding environment).[11] Looking at youth delinquency or deviance from the vantage point provided by the environment can explain why some generations lack vitality in their social practices. What is most important about Winnicott's environmental consideration, however, is that it does not focus on the influence of material aspects, but on the continuity of the environment and perhaps its "good enough" marker. When youth are "deprived" of this environment, they become outwardly transgressive or act in ways that observers find difficult to fathom.

The signs of decline we witness in *lesser* forms of school violence Winnicott would view as a "sign of hope," in that they signal the child's necessary destruction of outward objects and societal values. Indeed, what Winnicott calls the "antisocial tendency" that is found in nearly all adolescents, is necessary and implies hope: "At the moment of hope the child reaches out and steals an object. This is a compulsive act and the child does not know why he or she does it. Often the child feels mad because of having the compulsion to do something without knowing why. Naturally, the fountain pen stolen from Woolworth's is not satisfactory: it is not the object that was being sought, and in any case the child is looking for the capacity to find, not for an object."[12]

For example, all of the students found guilty of shooting up schools had previous incidents of destruction or transgression that were only later uncovered as proof of these individuals' pathological natures. They were viewed as signs, retroactively, that the students should have been incarcerated, not that they should have received help or understanding from the society.

Part of the problem is that we, as a society, treat students like children, but want them to behave like adults. And, conversely, we treat them like adults, but want them to behave like children. There is no consistency to public policy concerning child welfare (e.g., child labor laws are good at times and unnecessary at others); a juvenile justice system that emphasizes therapeutic punishment for delinquents is continually dismantled then rebuilt when detention centers are overcrowded or kids "run free." We want them to behave like adults because this will make things "go smoothly" for the adult portion of society, or at least keep them out of the way (daycare management). This *environmental* inconsistency is what Winnicott deems deprivation. According to him,

> [t]here is one kind of classification that is of vital importance for all those who think in terms of educational systems, and yet this form of classification is not always given due place. It cuts right across the classification according to type of neurotic or psychotic defence organization, and it even includes (at one extreme) some boys and girls who are potentially normal. This classification is in terms of deprivation. The deprived or relatively deprived child has had environmental provision that was good enough so that there was a

continuity of personal being, and then became deprived of this: deprived at an age (in emotional development) at which the process could be felt and perceived. The reaction to a deprivation (i.e. not to a privation) is one that holds the child in its grip—henceforth the world must be made to acknowledge and repair the injury. But as this process is largely working in the unconscious, the world does not succeed or does so by paying heavily.[13]

Thus, the notion of deprivation has nothing to do with material satisfaction—as is so often a theme in public policy and critical pedagogy—but with environmental and emotional consistency. Deprivation has to do with a lack of stability in the environment of the child's emotional life. If a child had always been treated with a lack of concern, a sudden avalanche of attention would cause the child to feel deprived, deprived of neglect. It is the same for the reverse proposition. Empty consumerism that is given to a child in lieu of love and attention to *subjective* needs breeds the unhappy adolescent.

The title of one of Winnicott's books, *Home Is Where We Start From,* is an allusion to the foundational environment children come to know and rely on as they develop, which, when altered radically, sets in motion a period of antisocial behavior that appears inexplicable to those witnessing their children's actions. This statement is important because most of the discourse surrounding therapeutic solutions focuses on the individual as conceptualized in ego psychology, a theoretical disposition that assumes the personality of the child is complete (this is what accounts for the popularity of the "bad seed" child-figure that runs throughout American cultural mythology and current discourse).[14]

Winnicott's formulation brings to our attention the fact that when we are discussing the development of children, we should not only be concerned with material factors or moral factors, but also with the fact that they are in the process of forming *personalities*. Personalities are a reflection of the environment in which they are formed. This means that ego function is, at best, a mimicking of the adults surrounding the child. What is most interesting in the school shooting accounts is the way in which the media and observers avoid discussing the personality of the youth in question. It is as if they never had a personality or they were truly evil; school shooters become a blank screen onto which the public can project its anxieties about youth in general. This is what accounts for the widespread acceptance of the notion that there is a "potential shooter in every school" and that society must "get inside their heads" to profile them and prevent the inevitable shooting.[15] But this misrecognition by the public of adolescents is symptomatic of the way most Americans view them, as acting in a vacuum under the influence of predatory culture.

The reaction on the Left is to argue for material changes and for more money for education, without thinking about how the money could be allocated to help students achieve their own goals and develop into autonomous citizens. On the Right, the emphasis is placed on the lack of values that are taught to students, combined with the break up or assault on the family, without an understanding of how values are incorporated into personality (experience!) or of how the family that is non-nuclear and non-Oedipal can encourage this personality formation in children without indoctrination. Even though there is much lip-service paid to instructional technologies that free the student to experiment and new school organizational structures that provide more classroom time devoted to "hands on" learning and objective-oriented projects, much of the "free" time traditionally accorded to students is limited in favor of strict objective learning (e.g., cutting recess, lunch periods, and classroom exchanges).

The safety regulations put in place as a widespread reaction to school shootings have far exceeded the emotional and punitive consequences of the crimes themselves. As educators like to remind the public, school violence has declined by 50 percent since its record high in 1992–1993.[16] Why then has the reaction been so extreme? What is it about the public sphere and the conduct of citizenship in the United States that has encouraged such reactionary and uncaring thinking toward adolescents?

It is clear that the response has not been focused on alleviating or understanding the emotional life of youth, but is comforting only to parents (who necessarily worry, but also want to control their children), to politicians (who use the issue as an opportunity to look good), to administrators (who are tired of being liable for regulating student conduct), and to police and psychiatric institutions (who want the parents' attention). These responses ignore youth and their desires; focusing on the "safety" of youth also shields them from experiencing and also keeps them from learning and developing a sense of self and integrity. Rather than ditch the impulse to revenge or funnel it onto the appropriate public figures, the media, along with politicians, schools, and experts, indirectly punish the students by containing them for their safety. These policies are perhaps more harmful to the behavior and character development of youth than any other development thus far. Yet, the question remains: Why such a strong response to a few shootings?

Winnicott, early on, understood that the public's response to youth delinquency would arrive in the form of feelings of public revenge. In an address to magistrates in England, he argued that the public needed to understand and have more sympathy for the "antisocial tendency" that is displayed in youth violence, because these tendencies that are most often found in adolescent behavior are a sign of hope. Furthermore, public revenge needs to be managed by the lawmakers of the society, not by abstract law (lawsuits) that channels the anger out indirectly. The anger is never projected onto a personality, which would make people more responsible for their anger. Instead, in a world where objectives and objects (in the literal sense of non-human objects or representations) bear the brunt of responsibility for human actions, leaders no longer have a function other than finding new objects to circulate and use in their perfidy.

Magistrates, he argued, need to give expression to that feeling of revenge before "the foundation can be laid for the humane treatment of the offender."[17] This is because even though many societies and educational systems find it desirable to cultivate a sentimental attitude toward crime in their citizenry, this sentimentality is, after a traumatic event, simply a means to repress the unconscious hatred they feel for the offender. Like Nietzsche's democratic sentiment, this care in advance for the offender does not presuppose that the public "works through" and experiences its anger toward the individual who disregards its laws and risks hurting its members. Instead, the sentimentality is a waste of time, foreplay to the revenge to come, because as Winnicott says, "sooner or later the hate turns up." This is because "no offence can be committed without an addition being made to the general pool of unconscious public revenge feelings."[18]

In contemporary democratic society, public revenge is commonplace. Furthermore, it goes hand in hand with other citizenship developments theorized by Mark Seltzer and Lauren Berlant. For Seltzer, as was noted in the last chapter, the wound is that which binds citizens in a community of suffering, and for Berlant the highest achievement of the citizen is that of "victim" via the infantile longings of adults.[19]

All of the school policies developed to anticipate school violence ensure that student behavior is in conformity with the rules and procedures that ensure that education takes place only in the classroom (e.g., what can be measured by achievement tests). The rest of the educational process is circumvented (in the extracurricular spaces) so that the amount of interaction between students' personalities and school officials is lessened considerably.

While the school believes that it is the parents' job to cultivate character and personality, the parents and the larger society treat the school as the space of character development (if they think about character development at all). As Winnicott argues, those students who are lucky enough to have an environment that facilitates the development of character and healthy personality, in aggregate, are the measure of the health and level of maturity of the society.

Democracies, according to Winnicott, test the psychological maturity of their members. As was noted in chapter 5, the public increasingly demands that its Being be managed by others is a sign, to Winnicott, of the immaturity of that society. There is a difference between technological efficiency that makes time for important decision-making processes and the efficiency that allows for the deferral of decision making indefinitely, perhaps making that capability appear as a nonessential feature of human life.

Consider Dewey's insight that democracy allows for the most far reaching and free space for experimentation of all political arrangements because it increases the level of choice a citizen is offered. Winnicott would agree, but would also note that with freedom comes a large amount of psychological strain. Alongside the democratic arrangement, according to Winnicott, one must consider the arrangement of the individual personality in society. This personality organization is made possible by the support the home receives from the society and the level of maturity of the caregivers of children in the home.

In other words, facilitating people in a democratic society by making it as open and free for experimentation as possible is not enough to ensure that the society develops to a satisfactory level of maturity. Democracy depends on a mature and psychologically stable individual whose personality has been allowed to develop with a view to the "whole" person; that is, that the integration of the personality is achieved.[20]

Winnicott describes in detail the signs of this integrated personality: an individual's ability to take responsibility for most of his or her feelings about his or her surroundings (whether negative or positive), to be depressed and emerge from this depression strengthened, and to elect leaders based on their personalities as they relate to issues of public welfare (Ronald Reagan would not count). Basically, the disposition would be summed up as one that has minimized the need for projection to a great degree.

Thus, for Winnicott, democracy is the most difficult of political arrangements for a nation-state to achieve because it requires mature and developed individuals who are able to be responsible for their feelings and ideas and to contextualize them properly within the larger ideals of the community, or what he calls the "Reality Principle." Simply "freeing" immature individuals is a dangerous proposition. Indeed, as Winnicott maintains, we ignore unconscious motivation at our collective peril, especially if we make democracy an arrangement that only allows for the allocation of our material needs, leaving the psychological elements of life to the private responsibility of the individual in a society that cannot deal with the unconscious.

The bias against looking into the unconscious or even managing it (expert discourse causes people to search for deviant behavior that should not be viewed as such) is strong. Unless an agency can produce scientific results or a pill to deal with emotional problems, policymakers cannot legislate a response to a widespread problematic behavior. However, what accounts for this behavior—which is no different from that displayed by radicals and nonradicals alike in the 1960s—being labeled deviant or as a public health problem? Why cannot the public see that acting out is normal for adolescents and that simply "knowing" things might demonstrate their cognitive knowledge about aspects of life, but that it does not communicate that they understand what to do with this knowledge or what it means emotionally for a person who contributes to a democratic community?[21] Furthermore, for those students alienated from the hidden curriculum of schooling because they refuse to participate in both learning and free time in "normative" ways, the school when not supplemented by other activities or parental understanding can exacerbate their hopelessness.

When they are forced into "compliance," students will react negatively, if not violently. As many commentators have forgotten to note, many students could be saved by violent video games, Marilyn Manson, and movies like *The Basketball Diaries.* Thus, while there is lots of interesting discussion of educational technologies and new teaching techniques that encourage student participation, there is little discussion of the *goal* of all these strategies or how they affect the way in which students (and adults) interact with one another. With no end-in-view, even if provisionary and subject to change, students (and faculty) spend more time concentrating on the objects and objectives of learning than on how to incorporate these strategies into a living community or publicity.[22]

As Dewey states in *The School and the Society and the Child and the Curriculum,* the "degenerate reminiscence" becomes the ultimate developmental and educational goal in schools and in society and the public ignores the antisocial tendencies inspired by the avoidance of a more personal or inspirational form of learning.[23] The degenerate reminiscence works well on the policy level because measuring intelligence and democratic health through facts makes citizens easy to manipulate and control. Giving them a sense of community through the encouragement of practical experience makes them reluctant to participate in fact-finding missions, much less standardized tests. Why is this?

This is because they can see that statistics, as they are presented to the public, inform nothing but their ready attention to paranoia and, as Joel Best points out, encourage the formation of "victim industries" and corresponding "wars on social problems." Best's research is important since he emphasizes that in the United States the war metaphor for social problems corresponds to their "randomness" and "patternlessness." He adds that this emphasis on a few incidents as the norm creates an atmosphere of hopelessness so that the public no longer thinks there is an answer to social problems—much like the Nietzschean claim that democracy applied to all of social life causes many to redress individual problems through bad conscience and ressentiment.[24] The war on youth culture, which is indirectly a war on youth, erases the boundaries between the generations, and the environment in which they develop becomes more and more controlling, leaving them very few options for creativity and imagination with reality.

I now turn to the type of environment envisioned by Winnicott that would constitute "good enough" care in order to trace the differences between past generations and present realities that work against youth cohesion or activity that is nonviolent, yet vital.

THE IMPORTANCE OF A HOLDING ENVIRONMENT

The obvious link that is missing between the adult and the child in society is a shared respect for the cultivation of practical experience, which gives children the knowledge that helps them understand why they should or should not do certain things or engage in certain behaviors. All childrearing and discipline cannot be simply a series of dos and don'ts without the "doing" attached to them. As Winnicott would argue, the child must test the morality of the parents and the society, and the society must "hold" firm in its position as this occurs.

This does not mean that the child is banned from trying anything, but that the adult must be there to manage the child's decision making and playing in order to foster the omnipotence necessary to mature development. On Winnicott's view, omnipotence is much like Dewey's confidence (discussed in the last chapter), but omnipotence is directly related to child development, not just cognitively, but emotionally.

One can see in this the same *integrity* that Dewey so valued in his philosophic and pedagogical works, an integrity of action and thought that assures the society that the child knows from practical experience how to conduct him- or herself in a community. If we want to "reclaim community" from those who make difference into an excuse for discrimination, then we need to make sure that practical experience is cultivated in this developmental space of adolescence.[25]

The child may not know that this practical experience is missing on a conscious level, but it is the one key type of experience that will give the child a sense of "omnipotence," the type of control "held" in a developmental environment. Furthermore, that youth feel continually frustrated by their environment should alert the society to the enormous amount of strain and responsibility that they feel under contemporary developmental arrangements.

Dewey had envisioned this holding environment as a laboratory, where practices, ideas, and emotions are tested without fear of punishment or consequences. It is of extreme importance to the development of children that they are held in this environment before being given adult responsibilities. If children are deprived of this "holding environment," they will turn to delinquency, but only after they have already presented a pattern of antisocial behavior.

Omnipotence is a subjective and creative coping mechanism that caregivers foster in children. It is a kind of creativity that is applied to reality, not mere academic speculation about radical theoretical inventions.[26] Specifically, omnipotence would be sensed by the child, in small ways, as he or she is introduced to the Reality Principle, that is, the fact that he or she lives in a society that cannot submit to all his or her individuated, subjective demands. Omnipotence is the result of children learning how to play creatively with reality in order to satisfy those subjective demands. A child with less opportunity for experiences of omnipotence tends to display antisocial characteristics, but both Dewey and Winnicott would agree that there will always be antisocial individuals and that they are necessary for showing the rest of the political community alternative means for living creatively.

The reverse of omnipotence is a sense of constant "futility." As Winnicott argues, the parent gives a baby everything he or she needs at the beginning and this is dependence, but gradually the infant assumes that these needs are met "magically" and it is necessary to the development of the child that he or she be slowly introduced to the idea that this is not magical at all, but the result of another anticipating his or her needs.

The opposite of magic is the Reality Principle. In an essay by Winnicott concerning couples living creatively, he describes the process, beginning with a description of the assumption of magic: "Not 'Ask and it shall be given,' so much as 'Reach out and it shall be there for you to have, to use, to waste.' This is the beginning. It must be lost in the process of the introduction of the actual world, of the Reality Principle, but in health we devise ways and means for recapturing the feeling of meaningfulness that comes from creative living. The symptom of uncreative living is the feeling that nothing means anything, of futility, I couldn't care less."[27]

As noted earlier, Winnicott does not use the term "deprivation" to signify lack of environmental aids such as food, shelter, education, or toys. He uses it to distinguish from interpretations of adolescent antisocial behavior that make the child's transgressions the result of a privation in the youth's life. That is, the antisocial behavior is not the result of the child's inner turmoil with minimal connection to the facilitating environment, but is the result of living in deprivation, of living in that environment. Children are being forcefully committed to idealizations created by society for them, ones that they cannot possibly live up to or understand, but desperately seek to effect. If they fail to "live creatively," it might help to ask whether they feel both a sense of "omnipotence" in relation to their environment and free enough to not be too terribly punished for possible transgressions. Furthermore, if the Reality Principle is simply applied to youth, through indoctrination rather than experimentation, then they are hard pressed to find creative ways on their own.

While children in American society committing "youth violence" have everything they could possibly need from their environment (indeed all the student shooters analyzed in this document are relatively well-off, white, suburban boys who want for nothing materially), they have been given an enormous amount of responsibility at the same time. They must all perform well in school (as if their lives were depending on it) because of the fierce competition fostered by achievement tests and college admission boards, and they must use "critical intelligence" to choose objects of cultural enjoyment that do not offend adult society. They virtually live for the adults in society and now, following publicized school shootings, they are carefully monitored to make sure they do so.

According to Winnicott's formulations, because they do not "know" on a cognitive level the deprivation they are experiencing, they believe it to be the result of each other's failings. They turn the hate and rage they feel about their lack of omnipotence and possibilities for creative play onto themselves as a generational category. This occurs, Winnicott is careful to note, not because of large-scale material inability to care for the youth, but because adults "hand over" responsibility to their children and let them down (in the case of adolescents) at the "critical moment" when they are on the verge of becoming adults. Youth violence is a response to this burden since "in violence there is an attempt to reactivate a firm holding, which in the history of the individual was lost at a stage of childhood dependence. Without such a firm holding a child is unable to discover impulse, and only impulse that is found and assimilated is available for self-control and socialization."[28]

Part of the problem with contemporary society is that parents in the United States are continually reassured, in cognitive and noncognitive ways, by public officials and experts that they have diminished responsibility for their children. This may account for the debates now taking place concerning truancy and skipping in high schools. As record numbers of students skip school, their parents claim to have no control over them by the time they reach a certain age.

This situation is the result of years of school officials taking up the management of youth attendance by instituting their own monitoring policies. Naturally, parents will wait for the school to alert them to the fact that their children are not in attendance and because the school has taken to punishing the students in lieu of transferring this responsibility to parents, the parents now claim to have no control (indeed they probably do not).

If parents claim they cannot control their kids, even when they are approaching adulthood, then the problem is not one that can be solved by physical discipline or bureaucratic containment; it is one of psychological control. Parents do not command their children's respect, nor do they have a transferential relation with them (neither do most teachers, administrators, or law officials). They have given over psychological control to the bureaucratic mechanisms that society has told them will make their lives function more efficiently. The control that they would gain through practical experience and the cultivation of a holding environment with their children is the same control that they give up when they agree to let bureaucratic agencies legislate all the minutia of their daily lives. Winnicott claims that the families who suffer the most under government intrusion into the home are those who are the most "usual," and that these families are the ones who have the best chance of producing a healthy individual with an integrated personality.

As a result of this increased dependency on extrafamilial agencies and government intervention, people begin to lose any sense of perception (of others around them, of their feelings, and of the consequences of their actions) because every detail of contemporary life becomes reified; no one knows why they do the things they do (and in what order) other than because it is law or they are told it makes things easier. And yet, paradoxically, when a child displays antisocial tendencies they are immediately interpreted as the fault of the home (which in a way, they are, but with the license given by the society), but the omissions in such cases are no different from those made in every other household in the United States where youth are deprived of practical experience and attention by their parents and the larger society.

This is a peculiarly democratic problem: We have taken the benefits of capitalist democracy (goods and material wealth) and ignored the psychological aspects that make democratic stability possible (personal integrity). Winnicott explicitly states that societies must accept this paradox and work with it, not come down on one side or the other and assume that matters of personality formation and subjectivity are being taken care of by technology or other caregivers.

It is at this point that children should be destroying their parents in fantasy by rebelling against them, but they would have to "know" them, would they not? Part of knowing how to do this (on the part of youth) is to perceive the differences between themselves and their parents as generations and as individuals undergoing different phases in life. With reference to citizenship, this is important because it means that the "mature" elements of society are handing over responsibility to the less mature, in fact, to those whose job, as adolescents, is to be immature and experiment creatively with a "potential space" provided for them by adults. This is especially true during adolescence, a period in which "youth will not sleep, and society's permanent task in relation to youth is to hold and to contain, avoiding both the false solution and that moral indignation which stems from jealousy of youthfulness."[29]

Parents and adults, being jealous of their children's youth (Winnicott wrote this in 1964), ignore the hidden message in youthful rebellion and retaliate with force that does not suit the attitude of youth. In addition, the solutions they conjure up to deal with *movements* of youth rebellion (whether antiwar demonstrations or school shootings) are not based on providing a worthy, yet mature adversary for kids to test their ideals against, but are based on making their own lives easier and alleviating their anxiety over the aging process.[30] How are the youth of today to see the differences between themselves and their parents when adult society takes "victimhood," a disposition previously reserved for youth, and turns it into a source of entertainment and self-improvement?

As Winnicott says, it is markedly different when adolescents are forced to become prematurely responsible because of adult lack,

> [h]owever, it is different when, as a matter of deliberate policy, the adults hand over responsibility; indeed, to do this can be a kind of letting your children down at a critical moment. In terms of the game, or the life-game, you abdicate just as they come to killing you. Is anyone happy? *Certainly not the adolescent, who now becomes the establishment.* Lost is all the imaginative activity and striving of immaturity. Rebellion no longer makes sense, and the adolescent who wins too early is caught in his own trap, must turn dictator, and must stand up waiting to be killed—to be killed not by a new generation of his own children, but by siblings. Naturally, he seeks to control them. Here is one of the many places where society ignores unconscious motivation at its peril.[31]

For Winnicott, if adolescents "turn dictator," it is because they are forced to compete with their own kind because they have all "become establishment," having graduated to adulthood before they have earned the right through rebellion and confrontation. Real fratricide replaces symbolic patricide.[32] As we saw chapter 4, the move from patricide to fratricide is fraught with difficulties, but necessary to the creation of the community.

One thinks of Norman O. Brown's *Love's Body,* in which the trials of the sons killing off the father leave them no choice but to band together in order to manage the kinship relations in society.[33] But it is only through first banding together that they come to know themselves as brothers (siblings worth trusting and cooperating with) who can overthrow the Law of the Father. When the Father is gone, there is no one there to overthrow since he has abdicated.

Now, do not get me wrong here. I am not advocating the return of the "father knows best" community, but only to point out that adolescents now have no one to fight against in authoritative positions, like their parents, or the generation of their parents. The role of the father in the development of the child is not predicated on it being male, but only that this figure has the phallus, or in contemporary discourse, the power—a power that requires the child to continually test with rebellion throughout the holding period. As we have seen, through the dissemination of the democratic sentiment (values adopted because they are rubber stamped by society, but not developed out of experience) and the gradual equalization of all values (boundaries between the adult and the child based on a personal responsibility that no longer exists), power has been slowly moving from the parent and the home (essentially the private sphere, even in fact, the individual) to the public sphere as it is represented by bureaucratic policies and technological efficiency.[34]

DISSOCIATION AND THE TRUE-FALSE SELF-DICHOTOMY

So what about these school shooters and their seemingly normal behavior prior to shootings fools society and brings it to the conclusion that this violence is "random" and at the same time common? For one thing, the media's amplification of the stories does not help and for another, the public is all too ready to receive this information.

Part of the reason for the shooters' normalcy is that they have created for themselves a "false self" that is basically a compliant public persona that allows them to get by at school, with parents and teachers, without much criticism. The false self is the persona that takes over once the child has become deprived and been foreclosed from adopting "secondary gains" to alleviate the pressure of conforming. Secondary gains are the very cultural artifacts and self-stylizations (these are creative ways of playing with reality!) of students that are currently under attack by the public for "triggering" shootings, such as "Goth" attire and paraphernalia or music like Marilyn Manson. When these secondary gains are banned by the society, the false self must protect and compensate for the true one, protecting it from harm by those around it.

Otto F. Kernberg summarizes the disposition of the false self as "a superficial, social oriented, basically inauthentic self (as opposed to the true self implying the integration of a person's conscious and unconscious internal world)" that is the result of contemporary socialization.

> [T]he existence of mutually dissociated or split-off ego states (related to non-integrated self-object units) represents one basic precondition for the establishment of the false self. The chameleon-like adaptability of some infantile characters, the overdependency on immediate interactions (regardless of the discontinuity between such interactions and other present or past experience) seen in the "as if" character, and the malignant identification of the narcissistic character with a pathologically condensed ideal self-ideal object formation all represent different formations of such a "false self."[35]

This would later be called Kip Kinkel's "mask" or Mitchell Johnson's "choir boy" persona by the media and public surrounding them. To date, their true selves remain a mystery, but Kernberg speculates as to how this self might be realized: "An authentic self can come about only when diverse self-images have been organized into an integrated self-concept, which relates, in turn, to integrated object-representations. Therefore, clinically speaking, the road to authenticity is the road to integration of mutually dissociated aspects of the self. There are many patients whose 'true self' does not lie hidden under repressive barriers, but exists only as a potential, fragmented structure."[36]

Where in the hidden curriculum of schooling (i.e., the hierarchically and normatively inspired values policed by the school) does the ability to form a true self lie? Now, following shootings, students have even fewer chances of finding creative alternatives to satisfy their need for authenticity, unless it falls within the limited range of options provided by experts who are totally out of touch and virtual strangers to the specificities of the individual in the process of forming a personality at the present time.

Two problems present themselves at this point. The shooters are all male and they are all thought to have been acting relatively "normally" prior to their deeds. Given the previous insight concerning the adolescent turned dictator, it is important to ask about the gendered and performative aspects of the shootings.

Central to Winnicott's psychoanalytic formulations concerning child development is its basis in infant-parent relationships. According to Winnicott, the most important fact about development is that children are all primarily dependent on women in the first (and most important) years of their lives. They will carry the knowledge of this dependency with them in their unconscious throughout their lives and it will influence the organization of society along gendered lines. In essays concerning the subjects of feminism and women in politics, Winnicott claims that the reason why it is so difficult for women to assume positions of power in public office is because the majority of people would have to revert to primary feelings of dependency if a woman were to assume power. Because people in society do not like to confront their unconscious, they balk at analyses that approach the contradictions unearthed there. But now, following the movements granting women and others more participatory rights in society, this position can be partially amended as caregivers can be men and not necessarily biological parents. The problem is how to deal with the dependence in a careful, nonjudgmental way and to remember that the paradox of omnipotence will erupt throughout the lifetime of any individual (old or young) and must not be resolved, but accepted.[37]

A CREATIVE PUBLIC SPHERE: THE PARADOX OF SUBJECTIVITY AND EDUCATION

Jacqueline Rose begins her book *War in the Nursery* by outlining the political stakes of a psychoanalytic debate that took place between Melanie Klein and Anna Freud.[38] She queries the particular crime against institutions that either of the two women may or may not be committing in their respective theoretical positions concerning child analysis.

According to Rose, while transgressing the laws of their fathers (Ernest Jones and Sigmund Freud), the two women analysts simultaneously relate something to us about their debt (and filiation) to those same paternal laws. Between the laws of the institution (psychoanalytic schools and their futures) concerning the analysis of children and the reality of the analytic scene, there emerges a tension that Rose equates with the tension one encounters while trying to achieve psychic "health." This is the tension between the child in the process of forming a subjectivity (and resisting certain aspects of reality that threaten to squelch this fragile self) and complying with societal standards, in order to demonstrate acceptance of this reality (the reproduction insisted on by formal education or what Joel Spring calls passing through "the sorting machine").

Ideally, the goal of analysis is to reduce the anxiety and disturbances associated with social norms and familial ties. But, Rose asks, is it not also the goal of analysis to achieve the health and independence (emotional autonomy) of the individual in the process of transference? Rose's task became finding out how Klein finds that independence while at the same time acknowledging a form of dependence. Indeed, Rose's reading of Klein (Winnicott's contemporary) is close—close enough to reveal that Klein's central thesis regarding children is that they do not go bad or criminal, but are, in fact, already that way in infancy. Klein's departure from Freudianism, according to Rose, is to claim that there cannot be liberation from superego functioning and that all the analyst can attempt to do is "tone it" down.

For example, in *Love, Hate and Reparation* Klein and Joan Riviere argue that games are a good way to vent "frustration" that stems from the love-hate relation that begins in separation (specifically, from the mother's breast).[39] For Klein, it seems that child analysis is necessary (in most cases) since learning to deal with anger and violence at an early age in constructive, nonviolent ways can help eliminate the pull of outward aggression later in life, or from introjecting it (as is common, but by no means exclusive to girls).

When experts discuss the "rage" that boys feel, as a public problem, they do not discuss it as the product of *relations* (with other people or objects that stand in for people) but as an organic urge specific to the individual, related to privations or disturbances having never been influenced by the environment, unless it is "predatory." Relations and relationships in the individual's life "should be understood in the strong sense of the term—as an interrelationship, in fact, involving not only the way the subject constitutes his objects, but also the way these objects *shape his actions.*"[40] And coincidentally, psychoanalysis, like some of philosophy, does not view the object as an alienating term (i.e., calling people objects should not be viewed as a bad thing) and in the Kleinian view, objects "actually *act* upon the subject—they persecute him, reassure him, etc."[41]

If we were to combine the insights from Winnicott with those of Klein, we should see that the relationship to objects, if "bad enough," could delve into or become a "persecution fantasy" and that rage is not contained to the individual, but is set in motion by the individual's relations with objects surrounding him or her. Furthermore, if we link this insight up with Winnicott's and Klein's imperative that destruction of objects is inevitable (because no one can please others forever) but that destruction, if healthy, remains at the level of fantasy, then taking away the tools to destroy in fantasy (youth culture, basically every aspect demonized following school shootings) leaves only real destruction as an option. Now, many shooters had these outlets for phantasmatic destruction of objects, but they were continually persecuted by other objects (perhaps out of paranoia) to such a degree that they could no longer remain in the fantasy space. Remember what Kinkel wrote in his diary: "When my hope is gone, people die."[42]

The two goals of fealty to and transgression against tradition are conflicting, but only when the subject is a *child*. As Rose outlines, the debate between Freud and Klein focused on whether children possessed a stable ego capable of undergoing analysis. Since children are often viewed, as Jo-Ann Wallace states, as "subjects-in-formation," the political stakes of psychoanalysis are thrown into relief when technique is debated.[43] This is because children are still in the process of developing emotionally and intellectually—thus, it becomes a question of which values and norms to affirm during the analyses of children, in order to protect the reproduction of certain symbolic formations. It is a question of which "cultural curriculum" in which to place the child and whose norms will produce the autonomous citizen: the family's or the school's? Currently, the debate rages on while neither side is decisive in its argumentation. The point here is that the school (in the strictest sense of the word—guidance, education, and pedagogy) and emotional autonomy are in many ways at odds with one another, especially in the current social climate where conformity is the goal of education.

In perusing the recent education journals, one finds that most students feel acute anxiety about the "usual" things: appearance and popularity. If this is true, then why are some kids being profiled for worrying about and toying with the "usual" things? The serial conformity of capitalist culture demands that students comply with dominant standards of dress, play, and thought, but it does not, as in previous times, allow for the existence of "marginality" in these same areas. Goth culture has been demonized by the right wing that, as Joel Best argues, focuses solely on the "pagan" aspects of the subculture, ignoring the belief systems attached to it and the religious aspects of its practices.[44]

But at the heart of this investigation into school violence lie the connected issues of dependence and control. Adolescents, on the brink of freedom, demand to control their own environment but have lost the ability to imagine a creative way to gain that control. Adults (parents and policymakers alike) have created a self-referential system of socialization in the public sector that turns the holding environment of youth into an emotional prison. They (the adults) can predict the behavior of students immediately and this makes childrearing and education efficient, but it does not foster the capacity to play with reality in inventive ways.

Students have, as Rauch underscores, a "limited horizon of meanings" like the trauma victims studied by psychoanalysts whose range of imagination is stunted by the repeated necessity of returning to the original injustice, never moving forward with emotional development. It stilts the emotional growth of students because they find the false self battling to find a vehicle for the more true one—the false self, as a projection constructed for the benefit of adults and other students, enables the deprived student to feign normalcy, but not for long. With no outlet for the true self, students turn the aggression and anger resulting from maintaining this frustrating position onto themselves (in the case of girls) or random others in the hated place (in the case of boys who shoot up schools or vandalize property).

These positions have cross-overs; as we saw in chapter 4, Cassie Bernall fought her parents over control of her true self and lost the battle in the end. Now, their story of her "unlikely martyrdom" passes as informative to parents who wish to control their kids in the same way. Even as the school shootings unfolded, every explanation for why focused on withholding the "secondary gains" that students might use as outlets for the true self or as vehicles for creativity and play, while, perhaps not conforming to the public's ideal of student behavior, were, nevertheless, not physically harmful.

NOTES

1. D. W. Winnicott, "Adolescent Immaturity," in *Home Is Where We Start From: Essays by a Psycho-Analyst* (New York: Norton, 1986), 166.

2. Sigmund Freud, *Collected Papers: Clinical Papers, Papers on Technique*, trans. Joan Riviere (1924; reprint, London: Hogarth, 1957).

3. Angelika Rauch, "Post-traumatic Hermeneutics: Melancholia in the Wake of Trauma," *Diacritics* 28, no. 4 (1998): 116. Primary narcissism refers to "this first narcissism—that of the child who takes itself as its love-object before choosing external objects. This kind of state is said to correspond to the child's belief in the omnipotence of its thoughts." See Jean Laplanche and J.-B. Pontalis, *The Language of Psycho-Analysis*, trans. Donald Nicholson Smith (New York: Norton, 1973), 337–38.

4. Rauch, "Post-traumatic Hermeneutics," 116.

5. For an analytic discussion of this, see Chantal Mouffe and Ernesto Laclau, *Hegemony and Socialist Strategy* (London: Verso, 1985).

6. Maxine Greene, *Dialectic of Freedom* (New York: Teacher's College Press, 1988).

7. Michel Foucault, *Discipline and Punish: The Birth of the Prison*, trans. Alan Sheridan (New York: Vintage, 1995).

8. See Peter McLaren, *Critical Pedagogy and Predatory Culture* (New York: Routledge, 1995); see also *Educational Theory* 50, no. 3 (Summer 2000): 279–418.

9. José Ortega y Gasset, *Man and Crisis*, trans. Mildred Adams (New York: Norton, 1958), 43.

10. Winnicott discusses "good enough" mothering as the appropriate type of childcare to raise healthy individuals and citizens capable of functioning in modern society. I would like to shift his argument apropos of American society's deemphasis on the mother. Instead of falling into the trap of discussing childrearing as the sole responsibility of one gender, or person, I would like to discuss what type of *environment* might provide "good enough" care.

11. Winnicott managed a hospital for orphaned children during both world wars in Great Britain. Many of his clinical observations would come from his experiences with war trauma and children, especially the notion of a holding environment and careful containment.

12. D. W. Winnicott, *Home Is Where We Start From: Essays by a Psycho-Analyst* (New York: Norton, 1986), 93.

13. D. W. Winnicott, *Deprivation and Delinquency* (New York: Tavistock, 1984), 212.

14. See chapter 3.

15. Winnicott would deplore the rampant psychologizing or demonizing of youth taking place today. He would view this public policy as harmful to "normal" (a term he always puts under erasure in his text) children who have a chance of finding creativity and inventive lives in reality without the benefit of psychiatric evaluation. Ideally, this would depend on their

subjective needs being met by those influencing their lives on a daily basis: the parents, teachers, and mentors around them who understand their needs and refuse to make moral judgments about their mediation of the Reality Principle. Indeed, he says the only morality that is important during development is "that which turns up in the child." This is very similar to the Deweyan notion mentioned in the last chapter that stresses that control and discipline will be organized into the system of the individual as the individual acts in the world; there is no need (excepting extreme cases) for children to be indoctrinated by caregivers. Examples of indoctrination range from "Just Say No" campaigns, to posting the Ten Commandments on school walls, to preaching nonviolence by pretending it does not exist, and to other such hypocritical educational strategies.

16. The quote is from the *Harper's Index* in the *Funny Times* (September 1999). In addition, CNN reported on a January 29, 2002, newscast that since 1992, the "record" year, 198 students have been killed at school.

17. Winnicott, *Home Is Where We Start From,* 45.

18. Winnicott, *Deprivation and Delinquency,* 114.

19. Lauren Berlant, *The Queen of America Goes to Washington City: Essays on Sex and Citizenship* (Durham, N.C.: Duke University Press, 1997).

20. This "wholeness" should not be confused with the educational movement that stresses the learning of the "whole child." Winnicott means something entirely different. He means the development of personality that is not linked to cognitive development. Winnicott would argue that a child's emotional development, when stilted by a deprivation, forecloses the possibility of intellectual development that is congruent with the educational standards of the society. It is not until the child is taken back to an experience of omnipotence that he or she can begin to feel secure enough to develop and deal with trauma. To remedy these problems, Winnicott made public a technique he used in private consultation with children called the "squiggle game," where the child and an adult (usually a therapist) take turns talking and drawing a picture together (with no objective in mind) in order to work out a trust relationship between the child and the adult (who represents reality, a place the child is in fear of because of the trauma he or she experienced sometime in the past). Play is the most important aspect of the game since the child who is depressed or undergoing a disturbance has lost the ability to play and have fantasies, locked in a world with his or her fears.

21. E. D. Hirsch Jr. adequately summarizes the position of those who believe that cognitive knowledge alone will increase democratic participation and strength. He argues that curriculum-based testing is the best way to ensure the "breadth of knowledge" necessary for citizens to participate in a democracy. Writing against those in favor of competency-based examinations, Hirsch claims that they single out students, unfairly ranking them with a view to excessive competition and do not promote further learning, but further failure.

However, Hirsch's argument concerning curriculum-based tests is faulty as well. He argues that emphasizing content of material on exams within disciplinary/subject domains will increase the amount of knowledge students possess. But he does not take into account that students are not going to be any more motivated to learn more content than they currently are learning specific, culturally biased logic, as in competency-based exams. Furthermore, his testing policy relies heavily on the influence of the home and of the school acting as a surrogate home to make sure that students learn the appropriate content. There are so many confounding elements in Hirsch's argument as to make it look as ridiculous as those in favor of competency-based tests. See E. D. Hirsch Jr., "The Tests We Need and Why We Don't Quite Have Them," *Education Week* 14, no. 21 (February 2, 2000).

22. So students can create websites and navigate the Internet, but they are still being trained, as if for a vocation, and are not learning and experiencing with a view to contributing to society in a congenial way. This is especially true when one considers that all the experiential learning via computers is through simulations, not with others in physical spaces (i.e., real time and space). Furthermore, the results of simulations are controlled, leaving little room for deviant responses that might in a dialogue setting be given partial credit and corrected or amended by another person.

23. John Dewey, *The School and the Society and the Child and the Curriculum*, ed. Philip W. Jackson (1900; reprint, Chicago: University of Chicago Press, 1990).

24. Joel Best, *Random Violence: How We Talk about New Crimes and New Victims* (Berkeley: University of California Press, 1999), 9–16.

25. Kathleen Knight-Abowitz, "Reclaiming Community," *Educational Theory* 49, no. 2 (1999): 143–59.

26. This kind of invention is only applied by educators for use as a cognitive developer. Following power shifts in scientific development internationally, American educators are encouraged to apply theoretical innovations in the classroom (e.g., *Sputnik*) and these have come to be labeled "new math" or "new science." The debate in education is played out between those who favor "back to the basics" learning or learning that emphasizes building blocks or practical math and science for pedestrian living, and those who favor theoretically based learning in the interests of a long-term goal (i.e. winning the space race). Creativity is often the impulse for adopting the theoretical approaches, but it is never a salient argument for emotional development or psychic health of citizens.

27. Winnicott, *Home Is Where We Start From*, 50.

28. Winnicott, *Deprivation and Delinquency*, 158.

29. Winnicott, *Deprivation and Delinquency*, 158.

30. Apparently, *Tuesdays with Morrie*, while a very popular book turned television movie (starring Jack Lemmon and Hank Azaria), has a central message that has been lost on the adult portion of this society. Morrie tells Mitch Albom, the main character and narrator, that it is easier to get older and that youth is too frustrating a period of life to remain attached to for long. See Mitch Albom, *Tuesdays with Morrie* (Rockland, Mass.: Wheeler, 1998); *Tuesdays with Morrie*, dir. Mich Jackson, ABC, 1999.

Today, adults are obsessed with equating themselves with the youth of society by dressing like them, altering their appearance through cosmetic surgery, and appropriating their culture (music, games, and attitudes). For example, the latest Walt Disney catalogue displays adults dressed up in Disney character costumes and trick-or-treating with their children. It is disturbing to see forty-year-old men and women wearing Winnie the Pooh and Ey'ore costumes and standing near their children, but an entire catalogue devoted to this equation of adults with children sponsored by one of the largest public stock corporations signifies that this occlusion of boundaries is not disturbing to stockholders. Perhaps the reason for this usurping of youth's ideals is that there are simply no rewards for being a mature adult in American society. People do not get medals for taking responsibility for their actions, but they do get huge settlements for suing their neighbors over minute disturbances.

31. Winnicott, *Home Is Where We Start From*, 161, emphasis mine.

32. Lt. Col. Dave Grossman's book *On Killing: The Psychological Cost of Learning to Kill in War and Society* (Boston: Little, Brown, 1995) became popular after the Jonesboro shoot-

ings because he framed his analysis of school violence from the perspective of the species. Arguing that humans do not easily kill other humans (a supposed rule of the species), he points out that video games simulate the psychological tactics used by the military to "enable" soldiers to kill. The effects of the video games is that they wear down the midbrain, enabling humans to find killing of those in their species desirable. It is the midbrain that acts as the "safety catch" for a nation. Curiously, Grossman never asks why they target members of their own generation instead of adults.

33. Norman O. Brown, *Love's Body* (1966; reprint, Berkeley: University of California Press, 1990).

34. Some theorists might point to this as the "implosion of sovereignty," an idea that comes from Michel Foucault and Jean Baudrillard. As sovereignty in societies moves from the nation-state to bureaucratic entities to individuals, will, political or otherwise, becomes the responsibility of the individual. In previous times (and the political theories that correspond to these times, such as those by Georg Hegel, Immanuel Kant, and Thomas Hobbes, basically the modern period), the state was responsible for certain acts on the part of its people (ensuring peace, stability, civil order, and eventually enfranchisement, education, economic concerns, and so on). In other words, it acted as the Big Other outlined by Slavoj Zizek in the introduction to this book. It took on certain limited responsibilities in exchange for the individual's allegiance, taxation, and so on. It rarely took responsibility for childrearing and development because that was the responsibility of adults in families.

As societies become more complex and nation-states take more responsibility for people's daily lives (i.e., you have to send your children to school and the state compels attendance to a certain age), there is a logical boundary confusion over responsibility. Now, schools have automatic phone services that call home to alert parents when their children have skipped school. This makes it more efficient for schools and parents to discipline children for truancy; however, it also creates the illusion for parents that the school is raising their children. It must be noted that this function is made necessary by the increasing pace at which people live their lives; most households have working parents who cannot account for their children at all times, and, yet, we as a society expect the state (in whatever form—the school, the police, and so on) to alert us to potential disasters so that we do not have to pay attention at all and we can be more productive. We fail to recognize, however, that this increased productivity breeds increased responsibility with less time to account for it.

35. Otto F. Kernberg, *Object Relations Theory and Clinical Psycho-Analysis* (New York: Aronson, 1976), 121.

36. Kernberg, *Object Relations Theory,* 121.

37. Winnicott, *Home Is Where We Start From,* 30.

38. Jacqueline Rose, *War in the Nursery* (London: Blackwell, 1993).

39. Melanie Klein and Joan Riviere, *Love, Hate and Reparation* (London: Hogarth, 1937).

40. Laplanche and Pontalis, *Language of Psycho-Analysis,* 278, emphasis mine.

41. Laplanche and Pontalis, *Language of Psycho-Analysis,* 278.

42. "The Killer at Thurston High," *Frontline,* videotape presentation, 1999.

43. Jo-Ann Wallace, "Technologies of the Child: Towards a Theory of the Child-Subject," *Textual Practice* 9, no. 2 (1995): 287.

44. Best, *Random Violence,* 175.

7

Heroism and Mastery
As Models of Reproductive
Anxiety in Education

([H]ow does a teacher make students "autonomous" without directing them?)

—Elizabeth Ellsworth, "Why Doesn't This Feel Empowering?"[1]

Elizabeth Ellsworth's parenthetical question confronts the role of the teacher in the educative process. Critical educators like Ellsworth are aware of the ethical problems associated with pedagogy and unlike most policymakers are not interested in reproducing an administrative hierarchy of power through their teaching practices. Policymakers, on the other hand, are very concerned with preserving this hierarchy. The predominant policy response to the school shootings examined here has been to develop mentoring or community policy programs to keep schools safe from guns and drugs. The individuals involved in these programs are said to serve as the role models who are so lacking in American public life. Indeed, Kathleen Heide, a forensic psychologist and author of the book *Young Killers,* argues that one of the "key ingredients" leading up to juvenile murder in this decade is the "crisis in leadership" and "lack of heroes" to guide students onto more peaceful paths of learning and expression in schools and in the surrounding community.[2] The hero would ostensibly provide a model of behavior that students could mimic that is nonviolent and community oriented.

Like most responses to the shootings, the resurrection of the hero in educational theory and policy works against the notion that education is an autonomous endeavor. It is a reaction-formation that feeds on a particular interpretation of the student (as blank, helpless, and the subject of banking education) and reasserts the more prominent and authoritarian role of the adult in the educative process. So in a sense, this hero longing is a retroactive move to bring back a form of Oedipal/patriarchal education. Reactionary thinking is never creative and usually falls back on "the good old ways" or dismisses the progressive changes that societies undergo in order to overthrow Oedipal politics (e.g., erasing and/or discrediting the real political advances made by the civil rights, gay rights, and women's movements).

This key factor, coupled with the charge that American society is increasingly violent, fuels the need for adults to play a central role in protecting students from witnessing violence. The culture of violence is to be contained by adult supervision (strict monitoring, the V-chip, net nannies, and so on) in schools and communities (e.g., Security Dads) in order to ensure the feeling of safety for each and every adult (and child). But these solutions do not adequately assess the problem of school violence. As was shown in the previous chapter, children lack a certain environment and simply resurrecting a few representative examples of heroism only takes us back to the 1950s and cannot address the larger failure of responsibility in American society.

If one takes more seriously than Barry Duff did concerning his own revelation that John Dewey equated his central philosophical and educational concept, experience, with a more tantalizing and recent concept of culture, then understanding and locating experience in contemporary society becomes an even more pressing concern, given that experience can no longer be viewed as an individuated process.[3] The perceived lines between the individual and the culture are blurred by television and print media to such an extent that, in order to navigate culture, people are coming to rely more and more on the advice, assistance, and expert knowledge of specialists. Our new hero is this specialist who makes sense out of the complexities of the cultural mélange.

This chapter outlines the notion of specialization as it manifests itself in certain educational theories, specifically those concerned with the problem of critical pedagogy and its rather tenuous relationship to politics. My aim is to locate an anxiety in these theories and to sketch out how this anxiety plays a central role in pedagogical theories that are unable to give up the position of expert. In fact, it is argued that these theories rewrite the notion of expertise through an unacknowledged form of heroism and mastery, something Dewey would rather have ascribed to students, not teachers.

This displacement of practical experience onto the imagined shoulders of experts in their fields presents a problem similar to the one that political theorist Bonnie Honig describes as the displacement of politics by theory. Though Honig's concern is much different in analyzing the ways in which certain liberal-democratic or communitarian theories of politics attempt to cover up injustice and further displace the political implications of it, the notion of expertise functions much the same way in the symbolic economy of the United States, even and especially within the university.

Here, the object doing the displacing is not political theory, but expertise, and the psychological identifications and investments that this notion proliferates in order to displace practical activity, which from the perspective of Deweyism, are decidedly political. These identifications and investments are bound up with notions of cognitive mastery, critical unmasking, social justice, and the role that the teacher as hero, expert, or master plays and makes within the identifications. Thus, to speak of specialization as a theory applied to culture (especially teacher education programs) today is also to speak of the category of expert as that conceptual container that displaces political activity; this means that learning is not—as these theories imply—about stimulating political action, but about ensuring its constant deferral.

I begin with a discussion of specialization and its relationship to politics as practical activity, that is, an activity that promotes and protects individual interests in the public and especially its institutions. Thus, my aim is to show that politics is very much concerned with practical activity, theoretical or otherwise, but that the practice of politics is anything but an enterprise so glamorous or ethical as to be thought of as resisting an obvious form of domination. Most pedagogies assume that they are confronting an alienating social process that is repeatedly performed by a specific conceptual and/or structural domination: capitalism, patriarchy, racism, and so on. The task of the pedagogue is then to unmask these processes by referring to the symptoms that these structures display and by pointing out their executing agents. The critical pedagogue is the one who makes sense out of these processes, showing how they work and then assuming the onerous task of directing students onto the path of enlightened knowledge. The pedagogue assumes the position of expert, specializing in a particular form of conceptual domination, further contributing to the division of labor and reproducing the discourse of the expert.

Specialization becomes increasingly important to a society in which the devaluation of practical activity is emphasized. It is assumed that in the interests of greater efficiency, special "thinkers" should be esteemed and placed in powerful positions that allow them to make decisions for the disembodied and disenfranchised masses. We constantly defer to the second-hand information of experts instead of trying to find practical ways of learning for ourselves. Experience in Dewey's sense becomes a rare event in the lives of many people as they begin to rely on the experiences and conclusions of these specialists in lieu of forming and testing their own hypotheses in tangible ways, or so the *critical argument* goes.

The critical argument assumes, as Linda Zerilli points out, that one can disabuse culture of its dependency on a certain type of cognitive knowledge by pointing out its lack of logic or coherence within its own referential spaces. Far from shaking the sedimented foundations of metaphysics, Zerilli notes that these critical strategies never succeed in unmasking their object of criticism, but instead reinforce its presence. Much like Thomas Keenan's argument that "we cannot slug it out with reality" in an open and confrontational manner, Zerilli claims that the reason that this confrontation is counterproductive is because it is also counterintuitive.[4] Taking Ludwig Wittgenstein under advisement, Zerilli claims that more often than is presumed, people do not act out of objective certainty (as in the discourse of the expert), but out of *subjective certainty.*[5]

Responding to feminism's anxieties over the category of "women," Zerilli rebukes the claim that people must cognitively know and conceptually define their object (in her case women) in order to describe their situadedness in politics. This is because the empirical subjects to which these categories refer do not act out of knowledge of their definitive power (or "lack" in some intellectual schematics: Lacanian theory), but rather act out of intuition and subjective certainty. They simply "do" without knowing how they might reproduce the orders of politics. This is because society does not operate with a view to reconfirming an objective reality, but an undisclosed working or bodily one. Thus, it is not a cognitive, but a noncognitive disposition that accounts for practices (some people might remember it is common sense).

In the remainder of this chapter, I will underscore the relationship between this noncognitive certainty and its dominant alternative, critical mastery or unmasking, by alluding to some of the debates within the pedagogical literature that have shaped the position in which educators now find themselves working. I do not just offer criticism, but begin by showing how Dewey and Roland Barthes might approach this very technical pedagogical problem in a different way and move on to the paradigm case of critical pedagogy, viewing this discourse as an exemplar of the reproductive anxiety promised in the chapter title. Critical pedagogy is not singled out because it is the only pedagogical theory that reluctantly occupies the position of expert, but it is the most debated and obvious example. Furthermore, my point in analyzing this genre of pedagogy is not to take issue with its authors or agents, but to discuss how the qualifying term "critical" is problematic given contemporary academic and political processes.

DEWEY AND BARTHES'S INSTRUMENTAL INDIVIDUALISM

From a more experimental and pedestrian perspective like Dewey's, science, as that enterprise that today reassures the masses of the objectivity of experts, does not (and should not) have to be an elitist enterprise. It, like any other method employed to form conclusions and judge the means to action, can be constructed by anyone to complete the most mundane task or grandiose project.

From a Deweyan perspective, the experience of this method may give greater confidence to those who are told they cannot "do." Many find they are able to "do" very well without the aid of established pedagogues and requisite certification programs (witness the accreditation of everything and everyone that is necessary for the right to work). This confidence can make them want to engage the rest of the world in a more meaningful way or it can make them want to destroy it, but the "why" that this emotion furnishes is as unimportant as the "why" of specialists and experts who never seem to have to supply justification for their motivations. Thus, for Dewey the point of democracy and science combined in a state is to make sure that one checks the other to avoid either getting the upper hand. Schools must nurture the free-thinking individuals necessary to experiment with politics like scientists, constantly checking their results against a noncognitive working hypothesis. On Dewey's view, schools must find an educational philosophy between reproduction and ineffective resistance to it by proposing learning strategies that stimulate active, textual participation by students.

As a bridged state between thinking and doing, an inherent bodily and cognitive event that begins and ends without a cognitive guide experience is more often and only allowed for in isolation from society. Experimental in its disposition, consummation of experience takes time in our society (for some more than others). It is more of a temporal act than a spatial one; as long as people can secure a relatively private place for it (either in the mental space of their minds or the physical space of their surroundings), they can enjoy it. It is also an event that is increasingly reserved for the privileged few under conditions of leisure provided by wealth and social mobility; alternatively, it is a practice entered into by those most alienated from the privileges of specialization: wealth, security, and an importance of knowing one's place. So in a sense, experience does have spatial boundaries within the social totality. Marked off by certain income indicators or by institutions that protect the freedom for experimentation with moneys provided by the corporate wolves howling outside their walls, some are able to know confidence or at least subjective certainty in a world that generates parallel levels of objective insecurity and diffidence.

University professors have the privilege of experimenting in their classrooms to greater and lesser degrees, depending on the level of academic freedom tolerated by the bureaucrats at their institutions. Think of Barthes's romantic and confident description of teaching in his essay "To the Seminar": "Is this site a real or imaginary one? Neither. An institution is treated in the utopian mode: I outline a space and call it: *seminar.*"[6] He compares his practice in the classroom to that of a hanging garden where, cut off from the "world of war" outside this room, he and the participants experiment with texts until they have exhausted and consumed their pleasurable possibilities. He writes, "A collectivity at peace in a world at war, our seminar is a suspended site; it is held each week, after a fashion, sustained by the world that surrounds it, but also resisting it, gently assuming the morality of a fissure within the totality which presses in on all sides (rather say: the seminar has its own morality)."[7]

In this depiction, one finds all the bravado of the utopian intellectual without the moralizing tendencies of the hero who is so caught up in forcing the seminar to confront the real world, the totality outside of it, that he forgets that the inspiration for acting comes from having the space marked off for experimentation. To refuse to be disciplined by the finality of responsibility and concerns outside its parameters—special or methodological concerns, revolutionary concerns, vanguard concerns, social justice, and inequality—is to be free in a nontraditional manner, that is, outside the political reproduction provided by academic discourse. "No," says this utopian to that other specialized teaching relationship, knowing that the capacity, the desiring relation that realizes itself in that other world of doing without thinking, comes from having had that space to breathe and think in a way not determined by final causes.

When Barthes says that the seminar has its own morality, he means a morality that develops within that space and is conditioned and developed in freedom from discipline, not a morality that is adopted by policy statements or found on the cover page of a syllabus, not a morality that is determined in advance of the proceedings of the seminar. The practice of teaching is thus an indeterminate one to be decided within that space, the seminar, not by the world outside it or in the mind of the vanguard intellectual who runs it.

Here in Barthes's text, at the intersection between "freedom from" and "freedom to" as outlined by educational philosopher Maxine Greene, is where the two modes of freedom are ambiguously situated in relation to one another. They deconstruct themselves here in the intuitive act that Barthes performs for us, not through a concept of rights given in advance. Barthes "knows" he can do this in a noncognitive way because he senses that he has a certain amount of Althusserian "relative autonomy." Indeed, the entire act that Barthes performs in his writing is made possible by his undisclosed recognition of his autonomy relative to the institution governing his practices. This is why tenure is important, while peer review is not.

Where does Barthes derive this attitude? What is the source of his ability to "treat an institution in a utopian mode"? This mode is like a spontaneous plan activated in response to the conditions imposed on thinking by institutions. Institutions rely on an entrenched idealism whose spirit has gradually given way to more permanent and enduring concerns, like security, stability, protection, and a corresponding growth in power. The *particular* vitality and action that inspired this idealism are forever inaccessible to those who operate within the institution when its origins are erased.

Michel de Certeau describes two dispositions that an individual can take in response to the rottenness of institutions:

> In truth, both our questions and the place where they are found precede us. The question at hand concerns either the utopia which, since the Reformation and the Aufklarung, has enacted the will to remake (rotten) institutions using fictions of "purity" as models, or the realism, the hidden figure of cynicism, which authorizes power by its ability to give recognition—or a noble adoptive filiation—to adherents who have already been convinced they are filth. In the first instance, the institution is the putrescence that must be reformed by recourse to more originary innocence, freedom and purity. In the second, rottenness is something originary that the institution makes it profitable to recognize, and at the same time covers up. The resultant modes of initiation and transmission differ from one another and place the subject in opposing positions in relation to power and knowledge.[8]

The utopian way emphasizes a pure agency that is necessary to reform institutions. Fueled by the idealistic accident called the Enlightenment, this disposition needs to believe in an imaginary innocence that can return in forms of freedom supplied by a rational individual. Yes, it says, the institution is rotten, but we can restore its innocence. The cynical way nurtures a masochistic relationship between individuals and the institution. Subtle forms of discipline and punishment confirm people's beliefs that they are not worthy of inhabiting the institution and should consider themselves lucky to never realize the violence and rot that precedes them. These two dispositions rely on an origin that has been erased; getting back to it or dispelling it is the way to reform an institution and only these two attitudes will generate strategies for critical recovery.[9] Barthes assumes neither of these positions. He is not reacting to an origin; rather, he is taking up the institution as is and looking for dislocations in it.

Furthermore, it is not a reaction-formation, which would presuppose that Barthes is taking the institution seriously enough to ask it for permission to treat it in a certain way; modes are always introduced, they are never expected. In some ways, they are new, yet in many ways they are old. Barthes, like a good Machiavellian, ambushes his reader with a novel attitude toward this entrenched idealism. He carves out and reterritorializes this utopian space for his own purposes. As he says, it is neither real nor imaginary, a combination of the two perhaps, but not reducible to either in any measurable way. The real and the ideal inform one another and fuse into an attitude so fraught with immediate meaning that action is absolutely imperative.

Dewey observes that this "psychological individual," whom we may compare to Barthes's intellectual,

> is engaging in an abstract idealism that is necessary to institutional reform. All abstractions arise for the sake of setting free some force which is not finding adequate expression; and they serve to set it free because they bring out some hitherto concealed unity, with reference to which it may function. In this particular case, the abstraction of the individual from any particular social status and work means that society is becoming conscious of its unity, of the necessity of defining the individual with reference to its unity, and is thus becoming consciously progressive.[10]

Lost in Barthes's utopianism, we forget that his introduction of a new mode is tactical and, in many senses, practical. In order to relate to the institution in a manner that is not depersonalized by the conditions that nourish its decaying idealism, one still has to realize their capacity for action. It will never be provided by a concept, a methodological paradigm, or a scientific conclusion, but only through the psychological individual who realizes that this capacity to pronounce something different is provided by an opening in the institution or social milieu itself and who is capable of introducing or pronouncing the new mode or form to that political space.

Were we to ignore the nuances of Barthes's language and read his text in a straightforward manner, we might come to the conclusion that he is mad or else living in an imaginary world. We would say that he has created a "safe place" psychologically speaking, where he, so weak and frail in relation to the strength of the world around him, can find respite from it.

By making such a response, we would be treating Barthes in exactly the same manner as our experts treat the individual in society who does not fall into one of their categories: as a deviant or pervert. We may call Barthes's ideas romantic and utopian to imply that they are not realistic, but if we can read what Barthes performs (he is truly an artist) through what Dewey explains, we would see that the real and ideal do fuse in this particular individual who experiences the changes in social reality and simply announces them to others.

It is not a pure agency or will that the individual doles out to and for others. It does not occur "de novo," as Dewey says over and over again in the *Lectures on the Psychological and Political Ethics,* but emerges from variations within society that produce different and not altogether new forms of social life. He writes, "The fallacy comes in when the historic reconstruction is conceived of as an essential split. The new social form is emphasized in its negative rather that in its positive relations to what preceded. Instead of the old made over through the instrumentality of the individual, it is regarded as a creation de novo from the individual's efforts and aspirations as an individual."[11]

In this passage, Dewey diagnoses the problems of institutions with a view to bringing forth the unacknowledged aspects of institutional reform; that is, individuals are usually viewed as agents within a structure (very illogical). If one is to have the agency necessary for reforming an institution, it is only because this agency is provided by that institution. Somewhere in between the individual and the institution an instrumentality arrives on the scene to make the reform necessary. This is the pragmatic moment when a compromise is forged between the individual and the embedded idealism of that institution. By contrast, philosophical instrumentalism, which abandons individual self-worth and investment in the social, is supplanted by a reformed instrumentalism tied to an individual who wishes to solve immediate, pressing problems with Dewey's view to an open and experimental future for that institution.

The capacity to have the courage to read a situation for its difference and to reveal it—simply because one must reveal—is a resigned form of heroism without the need for applause and vindication, whose only purpose is to introduce a form because practically speaking it would work and individually speaking it was desired. That others may or may not notice is really not the issue as it is for that other type of heroism, the heroism of the expert, which does not take its insights from the variable social world, but from reified interpretations of the existing order, sugarcoating them with promising, but empty words.

Dewey's and Barthes's technique is not reducible to the individual, but is provided by the instrumentality of the individual conditioned by a specific situation. Furthermore, it is possible that it is no longer confined to the egocentric space of heroism, but embraces the social act of instrumentalism. An individual is necessary for the instrumental act, but is not the key player in the move from "oppression" to "liberation." There is no need for a vanguard here because this act is not an expression of selflessness, but involves loss of self in the text laid out before the individual. There is no need to recover acknowledgment and recognition since the act was done out of sheer practical necessity. It should not be thought that this reading is meant to carve out a new hero in the figure of the teacher who makes practical judgments and thus frees up space for experimentation simply by reviving the discourse of philosophical instrumentalism. Only the hero who controls freedom through emancipatory verbiage needs to know in advance what students might do if they were permitted to experiment. Others are motivated by vital curiosity to view what is done, said, and thought with this bracketed freedom.

Finally, deauthorizing the individual of the act is of paramount importance to its success. Instead, the act is authorized by the interaction of the sociality and the instrumentality of the individual, who is now conceived of as a necessary myth gesturing the subject to act in accordance with desires set forth in the text. This gesture alone accounts for the subjective certainty of experience.

To read this through the teaching relationship, Barthes outlines three spaces that "supplement" one another in the classroom. Of importance here is the transferential relationship:

> Classically, it is established between the director (of the seminar) and its members. Even in this sense, however, this relation is not certain: I do not say what I know, *I set forth what I am doing;* I am not draped in the interminable discourse of absolute knowledge, I am not lurking in the terrifying silence of the Examiner (every teacher— and this is the vice of the system—is a potential examiner); I am neither a sacred (consecrated) object nor a buddy, only a manager, an operator, a regulator: the one who gives rules, protocols, not laws. My role (if I have one) is to clear the stage on which horizontal transferences will be established: what matters, in such a seminar (the site of its success) is not the relation of the members to the director but the relation of the members to each other.[12]

Clearly, this space is meant to be erotic if it is interpreted as transferential, since there will and should be desire circulating between the members of the seminar (the members should want to be there). It is also clear that the seminar is not a place where societal interaction is determined by the teacher or other obvious structural mechanisms like seating arrangements, but that the interaction provided by the "cleared stage" is provided by the teacher to the unwitting students. This move establishes the space where students can participate in experimentation that is not determined by anything other than the text.

Lately, however, as academic freedom has been threatened by forces outside the seminar, those jealous and warring factions of the world of bureaucratic responsibility, the confidence that Barthes so brilliantly displays when writing of his own pedagogical practice, retreat in favor of evaluation, testing, and methodological concerns. The utopian attitude is exchanged for the security or assurance of security provided by the bureaucrat who promises the individual institutional security for entrance into the seminar for evaluation and measurement. The morality of specialization now enters the seminar, rearranging and naming the priorities and moralities of the participants according to the imperatives of efficiency.

All students are interpellated into becoming what Paul Willis discovers in his study of junior high school boys in industrial England, "Er'oles" listening to what they are told, doing what they are told, and neither resisting (as the students did) nor becoming autonomous without direction.[13] This efficiency is imposed via strategies that combine certain aspects of technological savvy with the all too important task of crunching learning into established time slots designed to further validate a particular technology's efficiency premise. This operation is not quite a compromise formation, which would imply that participants might vaguely realize they are being duped or cheated out of something they probably deserve, yet are convinced otherwise through an established interpellation or promise. This type of social formation truly "goes without saying" and conforms more to the logic of the television sound byte or jump cut.

Manipulating the ideals of popular psychology (e.g., the mind is like a computer processing information), this bureaucratic bribery relies solely on inactivity and rhetorical compliance from its subjects. Instead of emphasizing the participant's experimental possibilities through doing without a scheduled meeting, this intervention, backed by government policy and state mandate, reproduces the need for expert advice and control. It tells students (and teachers) that they are incapable of doing anything without the insidious advice, special knowledge, technology, or orders of the expert.[14]

Many scholars have already noted this trend and have reacted with a concern conditioned by the ethical tradition imparted by Emmanuel Levinas and Jacques Derrida combined with the decisive yes-factor of pragmatism. Consider the resurgent analyses of "doing" or "experience" juxtaposed to critical pedagogy's recent attempt to salvage universal history; the most vital one has been the insight that we need to view politics and education as unfinished, disappointed, impossible, and interminable. This group of thinkers, largely unknown to each other (I assume), has the same subtext to their criticism: disappointment with pedagogies of (disoriented) dissent that does not bring deflated egos, but critical clarity to discussions of political practice. This research is the beginning of a renewed confidence that does not need to stop and check for permission from experts or assure itself that domination does indeed hold sway over schools.

For example, many actors and analysts often say that the worst sessions in their respective fields, the ones where failure imposes itself or closure ensues, are the most enlightening for future clarity. Gert J. J. Biesta describes this fundamental disposition of experimentalism as an emancipatory ignorance "that is neither naivete or skepticism. It is just an ignorance that does not claim to know how the future will be or will have to be. It is an ignorance that does not show the way, but only issues an invitation to set out on the journey."[15] This ignorance restores the initial confidence necessary to invite educators to disentangle themselves from a dependent relationship with expertise. It is an important step, since it reveals the uncertainty of a stable knowledge system. This makes experience the obvious next step in the educational processes, because to reveal is not to unmask or erase, but to permit.

Experience is not a process that society disavows because it is totally ignorant of its benefits, but because it is an embarrassing act that must remain hidden. To have an experience is to have to disavow it later socially, like a secret thought or precious treasure hidden away in some safe place. Experiencing implies that one constantly learns new insights and feels and thinks new and interesting variations of old insights as well. To assume that people do not already know something cognitively is to assume that they are stupid, inane, and incapable of contributing to the specialized needs of society. If they cannot find their niche almost immediately in life, they must have been developmentally retarded in some way by the surrounding culture that acts externally on them in disfiguring ways or they must be genetically inferior if they have failed to adapt to the processes of consumer and postindustrial society (as if consumerism were a natural activity and not a habitual one, hence a social one).

This is how the denigration of experience manifests itself in the historical present, but as is well known in philosophy, all concepts have a history and that determines and changes the way we interact with and view that concept in the present. To find that concept and its past, its workings and accomplishments of history, one must unearth and realize that concept in its relation to powerful interests and theoretical prejudices that may have worked in the service of ideas, norms, and processes.

A genealogical analysis of the concept of specialization appears in Dewey's *Experience and Nature* and implies that experience was forgotten somewhere in philosophy's ancient Greek past, with the separation of slaves and thinkers in that civilization. The foundation of the Athenian political community is made possible by the disavowal of a category of subjects: servile labor. Practical experience is reserved for the base members of society, those who provide the unacknowledged material foundations necessary for the commodious living that makes philosophy possible. Often, engagement with ancient thought is precluded by the very "fact" that ancient Greece practiced slavery, as if to reveal were to erase; but this sly denial of the past allows the knowledge of how the past informs the historical present in terms of thinking about the organization of political community as well as the thinking of alternative forms. According to Dewey,

> the Greek community was marked by a sharp separation of servile workers and free men of leisure, which meant a division between acquaintance with matters of fact and contemplative appreciation, between unintelligent practice and unpractical intelligence, between affairs of change and efficiency—or instrumentality—and the rest of enclosure—finality. Experience afforded therefore no model for a conception of experimental inquiry and of reflection efficacious in action.[16]

Plato's forms act as conceptual containers where politics (as a base, but noble stage one must pass through on the way to truth) might be displaced. Contemplation of forms, as otherworldly figures, allows for the construction of a republic that is unable to recognize its remainders and thus reinforces the importance of cognitive knowledge through the displacement of matter and experience onto a deviant or inferior other: the figure of the slave.

The figures of the teacher or specialist and the pedagogue or master in Greek culture are similar. Transference involves a series of displacements of political notions, which through the process of dialogue and desiring investment, are either acknowledged or continually deferred. If deferred indefinitely, they become the source of anger and frustration on the part of the student (witness Alcibiades in Plato's *Symposium*) or they are left out altogether and ignored. Greek society had no need for the recuperation of politics since it had philosophy. Unlike contemporary theory, Greek philosophy had already made its choice in favor of thought over and above action, and there was little cultural anxiety concerning this decision.[17] Dewey points out that the social stratification of Greek society alleviated the anxiety of public life, making theoretical leisure possible and preferable. By contrast, in modern society this theoretical stratification exists alongside a mass of imperfections, known as the public, at once driven to enlighten themselves through education and at the same time to equalize themselves in the realm of experience. Individual experiences are devalued while the will to enact them presents itself in symptomatic cultural formations.[18]

If the experience is traumatic, however, it is valuable and this is the only kind of experience that mass society tolerates openly (e.g., Jerry Springer). In this public form of recognition, the only type of experience that can be validated is an incomplete one with negative social and emotional consequences. As many social theorists have observed, trauma is an "unclaimed experience" that has no immediate meaning to the individual who suffers from it, but remains locked in its compulsive repetition. It may be described in Deweyan terms as a perpetual "undergoing" that never reaches up to reconnect with cognition in a relatively stable or reliable manner. While people may get pieces of the event back, they do not get enough to make sense out of it. Cathy Caruth writes: "Trauma, that is, does not simply serve as record of the past but precisely registers the force of an experience that is not yet fully owned."[19] Dewey would respond by adding that the experience was never consummated. Deemphasizing the "ownership" of experience and placing the significance of the experience in a future action or attitude toward living is more important to Dewey than whether or not an experience can be recuperated for use by an established doctrine, party, or political organization. Taking a cue from the Hegelian milestone hypothesis, Caruth implies that giving traumatic experiences a possessive identity will somehow incorporate them into a vital life.

The experience of trauma is a particularly brutal example of what psychologist Helen Morrison, responding to the murder of an eight-year-old girl by a fourteen-year-old boy in Jacksonville, Florida, calls "the abuse of conscience" that passes for socialization in our society. She stresses that, in our culture, "conscience is abused but not taught," implying that culture itself determines the sole (soul) of the individual.

Yet, her explanation does not get past the usual pop psychologist's response to events like Jacksonville because it implies that the problem lies with an abusive culture separate from individuals and groups within society that respond to, create, and experience that culture. It is unclear what generative principle or process is responsible for this abuse. It may be described as cyclical, assuming the form of a spiral of emotion with no beginning or ending, yet gathering up and incorporating more and more subjects into it and leaving many damaged in its wake, but this does not explain why it is abusive. Thus, the argument offered to us is the Nietzschean negative telos, the regressive idea that guides social practice that should be isolated and eliminated from its individual carriers within society. Ultimately, this social argument dwindles into a plea for more coercion and control over individuals through social policy. This is not a social response. The public is not asked to "do" anything but accept.

The determination of abuse presupposes an initial investment in and final disenchantment with ideals. It also assumes that the formation of conscience is a moral act that is realized in specific developmental phases carried out under the direction of experts. In other words, it brings the alienated (experiencing) individual back into the social sphere only through a planned regimen of social thought and action designed to ensure that the individual simply does not break the rules, without encouraging the necessary understanding and memory of the act that makes following those rules desirable to the individual. It instills exactly what Michel Foucault calls a regulatory or, specifically, a "philosophical ideal" that operates to regulate the bodies and souls of political subjects in the service of that idea.[20] Thus, there is no design to power that is conceived in advance; power works through its operations, its successful dos and don'ts, as it circumscribes and thereby regulates individuals. It is a specific form of social production, no less harmful or helpful than the production of commodities.

According to this model, experience is determined by the mode of production. Since the production of political, sexual, and cultural subjects is assumed under this mode, one can understand how certain experiences will reinforce dominant ideals in society. Society is always radically incomplete, as Ernesto Laclau and Chantal Mouffe argue in a Derridean vein, since it needs reinforcement of the ideal in all its varied forms.[21] This assumed incompleteness also accounts for the importance of certain virtu thinkers (Niccolò Machiavelli, Friedrich Nietzsche, and Dewey) according to Honig, because, as she argues, their political theories do not displace politics by closing down identity formation, but leave the process open (in fact, they demand an open situation or point one out where none is assumed to exist).

Several feminist scholars have recently insisted that experience, specifically women's experience, needs to be mediated in the classroom. This notion is not new, but its resurgence has been labeled problematic in terms of the poststructural turn in educational and political theory. Whereas advocates of critical pedagogy may argue that because poststructuralism has somehow failed to emancipate the poor and socially disadvantaged and protect them from Peter McLaren's powerful "kleptocrat," they nevertheless fail to understand that critical pedagogy has not salvaged anything for the poor either.[22] In fact, I will argue in the last section of this chapter that critical pedagogy conforms to the dominant model of specialization by reinforcing the notion of the expert through an unsubstantiated form of heroism. To accomplish this reading, I revisit the traumatic event, not in the interest of pouring more salt into it, but to understand how it works reproductively, analyzing the anxieties that fuel its operation.

Liberal and radical feminism argue that most of the concepts of philosophy, politics, and educational theory have been derived from and constituted by men's experiences throughout history, whereas women's experiences have been largely omitted as irrelevant, except when reproductively necessary. The bodies of these women were assumed and made invariable and given in the theories that scripted them (Machiavelli's "fortuna" is one such example, like Nietzsche's "truth"), just as were the bodies of women in these very philosophies and pedagogies condemned as sexist. Yet, it has been argued—and understandably so—that there is a serious lack of doing, of respect, and of encouragement for political praxis, or even of practice, since the end of the theory wars in the 1980s and the supposed victory of cultural studies in North American academic contexts.

A PARADIGM CASE OF REPRODUCTIVE ANXIETY

Ellsworth's commentaries on experience reveal to a considerable degree the way in which experience is devalued in our culture. Read as a "wounding event" in the heroic drama of critical pedagogy, Ellsworth's 1989 article has become something of a paradigm case in the history of the radical wing of the field of educational philosophy. This first direct "hit" on critical pedagogy's prominence was formulated out of her attempt to put into classroom practice the insights and theoretical presuppositions of the New Left canon in education.

Ellsworth explains that while trying to incorporate student experience into her classroom in the interest of cultivating respect for diversity, an unexpected situation arose: the class erupted into a quasi-Hobbesian state of nature. She explains in her article that because experience is always couched in terms of trauma and victimization (indicating that our culture, though not monolithic, but certainly hegemonic, has no other language to express experiential knowledge), the classroom erupts in a spewing forth of epithets and hatred.

In the rush to compete for victim status, students are nasty to one another and the entire exercise has the opposite of its intended cooperative effect. Instead of cultivating respect for diversity, students sense that they are at war with one another. Perhaps it is the pretension of equality in democratic classrooms that causes each member to have to vie for attention and set him- or herself apart from the rest. The status of the victim confers a certain kind of privilege on people in our society and this is what sets them onto the quest for what Thomas Hobbes calls "vain glory" (namely, "For they see their own wit at hand and other men's at a distance").[23] Their lack of trust in each other to conduct a respectful dialogue on the subject of diversity may be what accounts for their need to "one up" each other in such a public space.

Ellsworth's observations indicate that something is missing from the experiential process and that something is stifling it as well. How does the pedagogical process dealing with issues of social equality enact anything other than what Judith Butler describes as a censored discursive situation when she writes, "The question is not what it is I will be able to say, but what will constitute the domain of the sayable within which I begin to speak at all"?[24] Students come to the class knowing what is to be discussed and debated, and knowing that, in order to have their concerns and insights heard by the rest of the class, they must conform to a certain type of cognitive style and use the correct signifiers.

These words have different meanings for all participants in the room, but Ellsworth initially assumes that they mean the same thing to her as they do to her students. She assumes a sort of communicative rationality that is inherent in the theory of critical pedagogy, as she so rightly argues. Her conclusion is that experience is particular to the individual and for any one teacher to assume that direction is possible in a situation such as this is ridiculous because "there are things that I as a professor could never know about the experiences, oppressions, and understandings of the other participants in the class. This situation makes it impossible for any single voice in the classroom—including that of the professor—to assume the position of center or origin of knowledge or authority, of having privileged access to authentic experience or appropriate language."[25]

Ellsworth diagnoses the situation in a traditional manner by saying that the method she employed in the class to stimulate discussion (which was informed by a popular educational philosophy currently operating under the heading of "critical pedagogy") failed because many of the presuppositions of this pedagogical style actively work against cooperative exchange, lest they be mediated by that singular "foreman," the one who has access to all languages and experiences: the hero. She notes that this method assumes that at the end of deliberation in class there will be a concrete solution to the particular problem discussed.

This heroic aspect of rational thought operates under the assumption that if there is a large social problem it can (and must) be fixed by the correct social answer in a timely manner (how much more efficient can one get?). Only a certain type of agent can occupy this discursive position. This hero has access to an extrapolitical or linguistic (not subjective or intuitive) knowledge that can both diagnose the problem and propose solutions for it. Mimicking the discourse of the expert, this critical theory supports the idea that certain actors and ideas are incapable of posing questions and offering solutions to problems while others are not.

Having access to these extrapolitical categories and discursive forms ensures that certain agents can and will have a responsibility to those who cannot access this language and that they will translate it for them. Under this assumption, the teacher will assume the status of the hero and the job of teaching and its symbolic status in society will be preserved.

Ivan Illich writes that this process enforces the need for a client relationship between members of society, one that is premised on hierarchy and power differentials. He adds, "This suggests the possibility of a new Oedipus story—Oedipus the Teacher, who 'makes' his mother in order to engender children with her. The man addicted to being taught seeks his security in compulsive teaching. The woman who experiences her knowledge as the result of a process wants to reproduce it in others."[26]

This cultural vanguard, instead of clearing a space for students to work through their experiences and begin to pose their own, unique solutions (creatively play?), steps up to impose its own method for achieving social consciousness and justice that masquerades as an objective ideal or cogent regulatory norm, all in the interest of a floating signifier "emancipation." Illich, however, notes that pedagogical heroism plays on the weakness and alienation of others to secure its own position within the social all the while enslaving others to its supposed expert knowledge and access to reality. This critical theory always needs a "problem" to solve or, as Honig would say, "dissolve." Indeed, Honig's analysis of virtú theories points to the cognitive anxiety of well-meaning liberals and communitarians who would like to see politics as a neat space of rational deliberation once they applied their cleaning agents to the mess.

It is fitting that Ellsworth's course was constructed as a reaction-formation (perhaps a working through exercise) to a racial crisis at the University of Wisconsin. Wanting to work through some of the wounds that had surfaced during that semester at the university, when many students were offended (if not traumatized) by a decidedly racist presentation outside the Fiji fraternity house representing Pacific Islanders as primitives, Ellsworth devoted an entire seminar to cognitively working through issues that, to use Caruth's marker, "register" on another plane of intelligibility. This traumatic experience could not be worked over bureaucratically (as she mentions the university tried to do) or through rational deliberation in a class devoted to addressing the wound with the most genuinely derived of intentions.

It is understandable that educators want to work through these episodes, viewing them as an opportunity to engage political activism while remaining true to their theoretical station within the university. But these episodes are not problematic because they are rationally limited, needing more discussion and clarity, they are problematic because they actively work against the notion of objective certainty. (People can rationalize just about anything, such as the debates in economics and political science concerning rational choice theory—whose individual [unitary] actor maximizes self-interest, not communal interest, while acting the part of the "schizo."[27])

One would like to assume that people could just "get it right" if they had the correct knowledge and language to use in their everyday lives, supplied by critical educators who inform them of all the politically correct modes of behavior. But, as Ellsworth shows, even when it is textually grounded (perhaps, especially then), there is no guarantee that politics will be predictable, or even progressive. That is why most educators would rather displace politics theoretically and emotionally, forgoing the necessary work of attempting practical innovations in the classroom by letting the institution devise efficient ways around it. While critical pedagogy does not address this displacement of politics, it reacts to it in ways that reinforce its power.

One of the more marked characteristics of critical pedagogy's style is an obsession with finding political agency and distributing it to others. This obsession signifies a fear of paranoia of cognitive structures and frames of reference, particularly those marked by structural or institutional political analyses. In educational theory, these forms of knowing are placed under the heading of "reproduction theory." Usually marked by the master names Louis Althusser or Pierre Bourdieu, reproduction theories focus on the ways in which institutions shape and limit an individual's access to political agency. Indeed, institutional analysis generally assumes that the schools are self-contained units, referentially airtight, allowing no slippage between society and the exclusionary principles that formed (or rather, grounded) them. Thus, the concern about reproduction theory's capacity for castration is not unfounded. It is not, however, so grave an issue as to warrant wholesale rejection of reproduction theory. Indeed, Dewey would diagnose the situation by calling attention to the fact that this lack of trust among the members of the classroom and the incomplete or "thwarted" attempts to verbalize their so-called experiences tells us that part of the process of experience is actually missing or if it is there, it is ignored.

Perhaps the best way to understand the problems with reproduction theory is to admit that it is always a possible outcome of education, but that this possibility does not limit an individual's ability to act decisively. As long as people remain tied to the textual situation at hand and do not assume an "essential split" between their actions and the institutions they are treating, they are better able to effect social change. In education, specifically addressing the political factions of curriculum theory, reproduction should not be disavowed but rather understood. The individual is to be understood as a myth—albeit a necessary one—for reconstructing politics.

Barthes the structuralist has no problem outlining a space and admitting that "it is neither real nor imaginary," but that it is suspended with no guarantee of progress. Similarly, Zerilli has no problem giving up on objective certainty and asserting the more pedestrian subjective certainty. The place to begin reconstructing politics is literally in the classroom with the participants in it, not outside in the abstract thought of liberalism. By resurrecting and protecting the notion of academic freedom on the order that the students determine the textual imperatives (not the organizational or evaluative ones), experience is given a primary place in the educative processes. Permitting experimentation in the places already marked off for education, the classrooms, deemphasizes the importance of the expert who translates experience for students and reproduces the dependent relationship preferred by bureaucrats.

Social psychologist Philip Wexler's study of American intellectuals' anxious reactions to structuralism is relevant here. He notes that the reaction to reproduction theory (later to transform into resistance theory) in the critical literature, was not formulated as a logical or even theoretically informed reaction, but a normative one. Unlike Dewey's and Barthes's pragmatic response to institutional paradigms, these theorists balked at the chance to challenge the institution in a nonconfrontational manner and chose to react to it by displacing their anxiety onto a moral plane. Though Wexler does not diagnose the inability of resistance theory to engage its critical object in a theoretical or experimental fashion, he does diagnose the reaction historically:

> Willis . . . , in his small case study, from which the term "resistance" was appropriated, had argued that subcultural opposition among white working-class high school boys was an essential moment in the process of class reproduction in schooling. New sociologists were later urged, however, to champion the concept of resistance as a statement of their "optimism" and as a demonstration of their loyalty to the political goal of emancipation.[*sic*] The symbolic use of new sociology in a process of collective identity formation and professional legitimation among post-movement academic latecomers was underlined by the view that failure to echo the theme of resistance in education was not so much scientifically wrong as socially disloyal and politically incorrect.[28]

Similarly, Elizabeth Maddock-Dillon notes that the obsession with agency is pe-culiar to cultural studies in the United States, where it has found a comfortable stag-ing base within the university:

> [C]ultural studies in the United States at times concerns less the particulars of a politi-cal program such as socialism than a desire to have political agency as such. Such a claim embodies the sense [*sic*] that literary studies has become irrelevant, emasculated: cultural studies, then, would seem to restore the critic's ability to intervene in the "real" world of politics. However, the claim to political agency frequently is voiced without any specific political agenda attached: it is that the rhetoric of cultural studies in the United States often predicates "opposition" and "contestation" without an object.[29]

Maddock-Dillon then delves into an analysis of self-proclaimed "resisting intel-lectuals" who, adopting the position of advocacy for cultural studies in the univer-sity, slide the signifier "emancipation" out from under "reality" or "real politics" into the university's signifying chain. Her phrase for this operation, "the alternate col-lapsing and separating out of politics and textuality," describes the reproductive anx-iety of American (public/critical) intellectuals. This movement between the two dis-cursive fields of politics and the university is only made possible by the lack of a clear program (of formalism) in their call to resist institutional structures: "While they ar-gue for a resistance to existing institutional structures, the specific political stakes of this resistance is nowhere spelled out. As a result, some of the power of this emanci-patory language would seem to accrue to the academic as emancipated subject—as one who escapes his or her own 'suffocation' within the academy and thus secures his or her own political agency."[30]

Borrowing Maddock-Dillon's determination that this is anxiety, I would only add that while this anxiety does indeed constitute a "fear of formalism," it also effects a re-productive function that all at once disavows its reproductive activity while it ensures its survival within the institution. This anxiety's main objective is to ensure the re-production of its discourse through ineffective formalisms. Critical pedagogy is a for-mal theory in a decidedly nonformal guise. Wexler's claim that the resistance was "nor-mative" rings true for a theoretical program at once resisting the expertise of the bureaucrat and then reproducing it in its own way. The critical object, whether capi-talism or the social injustice it breeds, displaces the anxiety of the master onto the stu-dent and ensures that the object (and objectivity) remains intact. While it is thought that displacing the anxiety onto students might alienate them to such a degree that they would "do" something about it, this is not the case. The students are so entranced by the position of the master that they seek to occupy it and thus to reproduce it.

Here it is appropriate to bring out Thomas S. Popkewitz's argument (which I have left in the margins so as not to detract from the larger argument) and admit its rele-vance to understanding reproductive teaching and the false promises of heroic educa-tion and moral indoctrination. Popkewitz analyzes the careerist impulse that makes it tempting for a student to respond positively to heroism when he argues that repro-ductive education no longer needs to mold and form certain subject(ivities) and skills (as in industrialized times), but only needs to cultivate dispositions toward work and career (noncognitive aspirations!) that attract students to occupy a future role in the world of work. Instead of the goal being subject formation, the factor that counsels one to engage in reproductive teaching (i.e., contributions to a field of specialization of work), the goal becomes *"subjective destitution,"* which is a reproductive strategy that makes students fear an uncertain future and fosters their will to occupy whatever is proffered to them through indirect means by a limited economy claiming to be working at full capacity.[31] Forget practical experience: this is real life.

THE PARADOX OF SPECIALIZATION

When presented with the problem of specialization, educators have continually deferred politics by reproducing its processes (as have political scientists and theorists). This is because of an understandable anxiety that one experiences when faced with the unpleasant task of confronting the Other in the form of student particularities (not commonalities). Educators are simultaneously to produce their expert knowledge for students and bureaucrats (why else would anyone hire them?) and to disavow it to each other in their scholarly exchanges, which are formulated with the genuine intention of resisting the devitalizing tendencies of the institutions in which they work.[32]

The text is only engaged (and by the text I mean the problem at hand, the trauma confronted, or the institution one is trying to subvert or reform) when it is least effective to do so. Instead of remaining tied to the institution in a way that reform is possible, that is, that the education proposals respond to a particular textual form, educators often act outside the text by cognitively disconnecting from the institution and adopting the discourse of the hero or master who speaks in universalizing tones. An alternative to heroism is the example that Barthes provides in his essay "To the Seminar," where he outlines, but does not determine, a course of action to subvert the institutional policies that work against promoting experiences among students. The bureaucrat-voyeur who sneaks (well, does he or she "sneak" or simply ask to come?) into the classroom to measure the students against each other and the text ensures that the students develop a disposition favorable to work.

The crux of the matter is simply (and yet it is so difficult to put into practice) that of determining where and when authority arrives on the pedagogical scene in the form of a reproductive anxiety to ensure that students (and educators) remain isolated from the realm of experience. Resistance theories that do not accord students primacy in education (not as "center," "children," or zones of nonknowledge) are heroic, but ineffective. One can find a similar hero worshipped in the current policy proposals that emphasize the importance of heroes and leaders in the form of counselors, community police, and Security Dads who are not present in the school as an accessory to the students' desires, but as "protectors" of these unformulated, nebulous dreams. None of these policy reforms engage the text of the students themselves, but only find insidious ways to control them in order to alleviate the reformers' anxieties about students and their experiences. The students and the institution become the same thing under what I call contemporary surveillance strategies; it is not the school, administration, or function that is questioned, but the student body itself as if it were the school. So, the indictment against public schooling is also an implicit indictment against the student body, and consequently, future citizens of the United States.

NOTES

1. Elizabeth Ellsworth, "Why Doesn't This Feel Empowering? Working through the Repressive Myths of Critical Pedagogy," *Harvard Educational Review* 59, no. 3 (1989): 298.

2. Kathleen Heide, *Young Killers: The Challenge of Juvenile Homicide* (Thousand Oaks, Calif.: Sage, 1999), 5.

3. Barry E. Duff, "'Event' in Dewey's Philosophy," *Educational Theory* 40, no. 4 (1990): 463.

4. Thomas Keenan, *Fables of Responsibility* (Palo Alto, Calif.: Stanford University Press, 1997), 175–89.

5. Linda Zerilli, "Doing without Knowing," *Political Theory* 26, no. 4 (1998): 440.

6. Roland Barthes, *The Rustle of Language,* trans. Richard Howard (Berkeley: University of California Press, 1986), 341.

7. Barthes, *Rustle of Language,* 341.

8. Michel de Certeau, *Heterologies: Discourse on the Other,* trans. Brian Massumi (Minneapolis: University of Minnesota Press, 1986), 45.

9. Thomas S. Popkewitz diagnoses the reform strategies of recent educational theory from the viewpoint of the efforts of Dewey and Lev Vygotsky to form a "constructivist pedagogy" that sparks participation in schools. He writes, "The new pragmatic outlook of social movements entails a form of constructivism that is organized through a particular type of expert knowledge. . . . [I]nscribed in the diverse organizational strategies of systemic school reform is a constructivist structuring of the capabilities of the individual who participates and acts. The reform discourses, for example, are based on the concept of a teacher who is personally responsible for solving problems in a world that is personally unstable. The professional teacher is self-governing and [has a] greater local responsibility in implementing curriculum decisions—a normativity also found in the structuring of the new constructivist teacher, that, as discussed earlier, cites Dewey and Vygotsky as sources of its vision." See Thomas S. Popkewitz, "Dewey, Vygotsky and the Social Administration of the Individual: Constructivist Pedagogy As Systems of Ideas in Historical Spaces," *American Educational Research Journal* 35, no. 4 (1999): 553.

Popkewitz views the constructivist pedagogues as part of a larger continuum of educational control described by Foucault as regulators of individual's souls. I wish to distance my reading of Dewey from that offered by Popkewitz's new constructivists. My reading differs in several ways that I will note throughout the reading in the textual margins. Finally, Popkewitz's reading does not clearly demarcate the boundaries between reformists in schools and reformist theorists.

10. John Dewey, *Lectures on the Psychological and Political Ethics: 1898* (1898; reprint, New York: Hafner, 1976), 15.

11. Dewey, *Lectures on the Psychological and Political Ethics,* 17.

12. Barthes, *Rustle of Language,* 332–33, emphasis mine.

13. Paul Willis, *Learning to Labour* (Hampshire, UK: Gower, 1977).

14. Popkewitz reverses the locus of agency in his article, continuously citing "the teacher (and the students)" and in this way misrepresents Dewey's pragmatism. Dewey would never have made the teacher into the most important agent in the schooling process. Rather than the student, Popkewitz's reading of Dewey (with Vygotsky) hinges on a reading of Dewey as an Enlightenment thinker that privileges mastery. I would emphasize Dewey's truncated idealism that is undoubtedly informed by Enlightenment notions, but is very much disciplined by realist premises.

Dewey does not guarantee or "ensure" political participation as the necessary result of his educational reforms (neither does Barthes, for that matter), but this admission definitely signifies his willingness to dispense with the certainty Americans have come to rely on in the figure of the expert. The only impediment to Dewey's pragmatism is the reception it finds in the public sphere (i.e., the classroom), which is where the teacher's role comes into play, finally. The teacher is not there to impart knowledge (as in banking education) or to form students into a specific prototype, but to protect students' freedom to experiment and to guide them when they ask for help.

Furthermore, Dewey does not imply that this work is as easy as most Enlightenment thought would have us believe (i.e., just find the right communicative strategies, reason, languages, policing mechanisms, and so on). Dewey's philosophy implies a significant amount of dedication on the part of teachers and administrators within schools. It is not the quick fix with which educational policymakers are so obviously contented.

15. Gert J. J. Biesta, "You Say You Want a Revolution . . . Suggestions for the Impossible Future of Critical Pedagogy," *Educational Theory* 48, no. 4 (Fall 1998): 505.

16. John Dewey, *Experience and Nature* (1938; reprint, New York: Dover, 1952), 94.

17. With the exception of Alcibiades who says of Socrates: "He compels me to realize that I am still a mass of imperfections and yet persistently neglect my own true interests by engaging in public life. So against my real inclinations, I stop up my ears and take refuge in flight, as Odysseus did from the Sirens; otherwise I should sit here beside him until I was an old man." See Plato, *Symposium,* trans. Walter Hamilton (New York: Penguin, 1951), 101–2.

18. Well, stalking comes to mind as an expression of feeling "unrelated" to others. People want to have their own experiences, but they need others to recognize them or relate to them. This kind of cultural formation is a perverted form of reaching out in a bureaucratically organized society that makes light of the need for human contact and understanding. This analysis may recall Émile Durkheim's thoughts on anomie. The problem is that we cannot reach back to some mythologized form of community out of nostalgia. Communities are pragmatic; they serve the needs of people in a particular space and time, they are not eternal.

Mark Seltzer's discussion in *Bodies and Machines* (New York: Routledge, 1992) about the figure of the serial killer in relation to postindustrial society is informative here by linking the rise of interest in serial killing to life in a postindustrial world. I would also recommend Glenn Tinder, "Transcending Tragedy: The Idea of Civility," *American Political Science Review* 68, no. 2 (June 1974): 547–60. He argues that civility in democratic societies is less about a utopian vision of what might be than about a public coming to terms with the limitations of political action. Another more positive example of this cultural formation is the peaceful prayer groups analyzed in chapter 4. While I disagree with the ideological orientation of these groups, which seek to undermine a free public space by an appeal to Christian religiosity (because we should continue to support a form of secular humanism, but it needs to be reimagined. The lack of imagination on the Left to defend public spaces for all people is a serious shortcoming, especially for the public schools), they are a positive form of relatedness, and they show, symptomatically, that something is missing in schools that has nothing to do with instruction or competitiveness.

19. Cathy Caruth, ed., *Trauma: Explorations in Memory* (Baltimore, Md.: Johns Hopkins University Press, 1995), 151.

20. Michel Foucault, *The Birth of the Clinic: An Archeology of Medical Perception* (New York: Vintage, 1994), 13.

21. Ernesto Laclau and Chantal Mouffe, *Hegemony and Socialist Strategy: Towards a Radical Democratic Politics* (London: Verso, 1985), 112 .

22. Peter McLaren, *Critical Pedagogy and Predatory Culture* (New York: Routledge, 1995), 1–25.

23. Hobbes, *Leviathan,* 63.

24. Judith Butler, *Excitable Speech* (New York: Routledge, 1997), 133.

25. Ellsworth, "Why Doesn't This Feel Empowering?" 13.

26. Ivan Illich, *Deschooling Society* (New York: Harper and Row, 1970), 39.

27. Gilles Deleuze and Felix Guattari, *A Thousand Plateaus: Capitalism and Schizophrenia,* trans. Brian Massumi (Minneapolis: University of Minnesota Press, 1987).

28. Philip Wexler, *Social Analysis of Education: After the New Sociology* (Boston: Routledge and Kegan Paul, 1987), 41.

29. Elizabeth Maddock-Dillon, "Fear of Formalism: Kant, Twain and Cultural Studies in American Literature," *Diacritics* 27, no. 4 (Winter 1997): 50.

30. Maddock-Dillon, "Fear of Formalism," 48.

31. Judith Butler, *The Psychic Life of Power: Theories in Subjection* (Stanford: University of California Press, 1997), 167–98.

32. I am aware that education is one of the only disciplines that actively promotes engagement with the public. Educational experts are usually required to maintain a significant working relationship with schools in order to provide novel learning techniques and assessments. I do not take issue with this client relationship (the schools are the ones funding the researchers! Who has the power in that relationship?) on the basis of public engagement, but with the way in which mastery is reproduced. Educators should be encouraging the schools through their expert function to work against the evaluative process and to promote experimentation. A necessary step in this direction entails admitting that learning is never a neat process and that students are learning to question their competency every time they take a test.

Conclusion

Post-Columbine—Reflections on Youth Violence As a National Movement

The event "Columbine" crashed into our collective present on April 20, 1999, and, to add further aspects of incomprehensibility to the event, its authors chose Adolf Hitler's birthday to symbolize their rage at the students at Columbine High School in Littleton, Colorado. This event marked the trauma of school shootings in so serious a way that it took school violence outside the intelligible boundaries in which it had been previously been contained; furthermore, the choice of date identified the event with fascism.

As has been demonstrated throughout this book, the effects of the shooting events prior to Columbine were neutralized by the hermeneutic bandages provided by experts. Focusing on the specific themes raised by the means of violence, they exploited the obvious features (violent films, guns, and psychiatric disorder), ignoring the role that schools and society might play in provoking violence. The public was able to believe these explanations and managed to separate the experiences of those communities from ones that might take place closer to home. After Columbine, the school became the locus of intervention, but when the critical gaze turned inward it was not the school that was examined, it was the student body.

Post-Columbine, the wound was continually torn open by episodic witnessing rituals (such as See You At the Pole) throughout the country or scare campaigns promoted by the antigun lobby; these forms of collective renewal were largely confined to the special interest groups that sponsored them. The boldest example of this has been the campaign suggested by Senator Jesse Helms and subsequently written into the Juvenile Justice Bill to have the Ten Commandments posted in schools. The Family Research Council has extended this campaign, encouraging positive role models (lawmakers, teachers, and so on) to post them in their offices.

As was seen in chapter 4, students recruited into prayer circles following the shooting at West Paducah were not primarily concerned with witnessing the shooting events in an effort to prevent their occurrence in the future. Nor were they speaking out to "work through" their emotional implications, but rather to witness the presence of God in their lives to others. This witnessing is significantly different from the type that would take place following Columbine. Instead of witnessing as an exercise of persuasion (persuading students to bring God "back" into the schools, to feel his presence in their lives, and to serve as missionaries for the Christian cause), the post-Columbine testimonies mirrored the event, exploding the public's defenses. No longer able to get the necessary pathos of distance from school violence, the public began talking, incessantly.

By way of conclusion, I discuss the ways in which that "talking cure" has been allowed to take place, the environment in which it situates itself, and the forms of testimony that make it possible. Furthermore, I examine the reactionary response of the public to the event. While nonstop talking has characterized the posttraumatic stages of Columbine as means of healing, more aggressive forms of preventive medicine have been favored to deal with the threat of a repetition elsewhere. Within schools, any and all available means to contain student violence have been implemented without regard for the difficulty they may cause students and how they could possibly contribute to future violent episodes. Finally, I examine the shooting at Columbine High School as an *effect* of the hidden curriculum of schooling. This third, and perhaps most important concern, is to interpret the case results in order to provide an explanatory model for school violence that does not reduce the school to a dependent variable. By favoring epiphenomenal sources of motive such as predatory culture, violent masculinity, guns, video games, pornography, biology, and psychiatric illness, the "experts" have ignored the material evidence of the shootings. The fact is that shootings take place at school, against classmates, and in areas that are not beholden to the formal curriculum. Returning to the concerns in chapter 5, I show that the environment in which education takes place (by no means limited to the school site, but reflecting the school's absorption into the political environment that houses it) determines the ways in which student resistance takes place. That is, the Deweyan model of experience operating in society denies the reality of conflict and resistance in public life and this denial leads to Nietzschean ressentiment and bad conscience on the part of the public. Sigmund Freud provides the subtext between Friedrich Nietzsche and John Dewey, thereby demonstrating how "doing" is an effective displacement of emotional resistance to the hidden curriculum of schooling.

"Columbine" had an enormous impact on the way in which schools would respond to student violence. We call it "violence," decontextualizing it from its environment and the conflicts that bring it into being, but the fact remains that while critical scholars bemoan the lack of resistance by students to the hidden curriculum, the resistance is there, although it has not been interpreted. As was seen in part I, scholars view "curriculum agitado" as a reactionary response to the hidden curriculum of schooling and ignore it. Students are either conformist or fascist and are provided virtually no autonomy relative to these labels. Significant semiotic challenges during the 1980s discredited Marxist theorizing of the hidden curriculum because researchers could no longer find *contradictions* to analyze that were located at the school level. Resistance theory, which had announced the practical implications of these contradictions, could not stay analytically grounded and impotently grasped at normativity until its demise. What was and is needed is a new way of looking at the hidden curriculum, one that applies new concepts to a radically altered form of hidden curriculum.

CONTAINMENT

It is an undeniable privilege of every man to prove himself right in the thesis that the world is his enemy; for if he reiterates it frequently enough and makes it the background of his conduct he is bound eventually to be right.

—X, "The Sources of Soviet Conduct"[1]

Educational researchers frequently reference the events of the Cold War between the United States and the Soviet Union as determinants of curriculum development. For example, allusions to *Sputnik* as the watershed event in American education often bring with them accusations that the "space race" reoriented the curriculum to over-represent certain subject areas, such as math and science. Alongside this curricular change, a significant amount of shaming took place in which educators were criticized for dropping the ball during the competition between the two superpowers. The metaphors of the Cold War were very important rhetorical devices used to motivate and at times coerce educational scholars and practitioners into dropping their own educational standards in favor of those inspired by American foreign policy. This occurred even when such remarks were as unabashedly condescending as Ronald Reagan's proud assertion that teachers were "clerks for the empire."

Even though the Cold War is over, its policies still operate in the minds of American policymakers, especially those who have been called on to address the problem of school violence. In the aftermath of the Columbine shootings, the media debated which level of the government should intervene to assess and recommend policies to prevent further student violence. The predominant response was that the federal government should address the problem immediately. President Bill Clinton called on Attorney General Janet Reno to work out the prosecutorial options presented by the shooting (i.e., whether or not the case could try anyone and, if so, at the federal level). Congress put aside regular business to formulate a Juvenile Justice Bill that would effectively dismantle the juvenile justice systems operating at the state level. No longer content with panel sessions discussing student violence hosted by the first lady and Carolyn McCarthy (D-New York), the public invited the federal government to enact large-scale policies that would be designed to prevent further violence. Meanwhile, this focused attention obliged school administrators to take under advisement the policy initiatives recommended by the federal government. Part of this initiative demanded that schools look to exemplars of school security such as Boston public schools and those systems that had already adopted surveillance strategies.

Perhaps it is an effect of policy lag; that is, that foreign policy during the American reign as international hegemon operated at such an existential level that it became part of its national identity. This claim implies that the United States does not know itself, as such, without containing resistance to an opposition. The influences that formerly presented themselves as capitalist contradictions are now signified as systemic "glitches." Now that the war is over and capitalist logic operates as uncontested victor, there is nothing more to do, as Jean Baudrillard says, than perfect the model. Part of this model is the perfect citizen-consumer, disciplined and quieted by consumer comforts. This disposition is molded by the hidden curriculum of the schools. By way of historical example, this section demonstrates the peculiar logic of this containment strategy.

The policy of containment recommended by George Kennan in the spring of 1946 was received by the State Department as an appropriate response to rumored Soviet hostility toward the United States. Kennan's policy, this section suggests, is the appropriate trope for understanding the national security response to the Columbine shooting. Though not formally called "containment" by its promoters (if we could indeed identify them definitively), the security measures implied by the national response conform to Kennan's ideological policy toward the Soviet Union.

As Kennan states in that early, if not reactionary, letter "The Sources of Soviet Conduct," signed "X," the Soviet Union's expansive tendencies threatened to extend toward Europe and thus needed to be contained by a "long-term, patient but firm and vigilant containment of Russian expansive tendencies. . . . It is important to note, however, that such a policy has nothing to do with outward histrionics: with threats or blustering or superfluous gestures of outward toughness."[2] Indeed, as Kennan would later comment in his memoirs, the American response to his recommendation bore no resemblance to the original message sent by X. Instead, policymakers interpreted the message not as a diplomatic problem, but as a potential military problem. Rather than dealing with alleged Soviet expansion through diplomatic means (i.e., as an ideological battle), they chose to accelerate the problem by demonstrating what scholars call the tangible elements of power through which all the material indicators of a nation's strength relative to others (i.e., military and economic factors) are brought to bear in order to deter an aggressor. Kennan's point was that the situation with the Soviet Union was an ideological conflict between two competing views of economic production: capitalism and socialism. In Kennan's view, this was not a problem of might, but of right. This is demonstrated by his frequent use of terms such as "conduct of foreign policy," "diplomatic solutions," and "psychological elements of power." The phrases clearly indicate that the problem of Soviet hostility (toward the

United States and its allies) was not formulated by the Kremlin to signify its external policy objectives. Instead, Kennan is alluding to the Soviet strategy of diverting the national gaze from its own internal contradictions onto those of the United States; that is, Soviet hostility toward the United States rallied popular support around the Kremlin in order to avoid confronting failed domestic policies. In this way, the American response to the information provided by Kennan shows that the recipients of his message misinterpreted his recommendations and that this caused them to react, mirroring the Soviet position.

Now, my point in going through all of this historical intrigue is not to exonerate Kennan (he attempted this on his own in his *Memoirs*), but to point to the similarities between student hostility and school response. Instead of analyzing the hostility to see how and why it operates, schools, taking their cue from the federal government's initiatives, have unwittingly enacted a similar policy of containment that responds to student hostility with displays of physical force and equally "superfluous gestures of outward [hostility]," demonstrating to students that diplomacy is not an option. This amounts to a declaration of war on student populations, whose response will mirror that of the schools' hegemony over their conduct in schools, creating a vicious cycle. As schools reported immediately following Columbine, the number of students who thought threatening their school was appropriate rose dramatically. Is this the beginning of a mini cold war between students and schools? A national movement of youth resistance squelched by disciplinary power?

Instead of asking how and why a few cases of school shootings have invoked such an elemental terror in schools, administrators have reacted to the trauma in an unthinking, yet material manner. Thinking and doing are never integrated in these responses, but instead are radically separated. The question always asked when such tragedies occur is "What are the government, schools, and lawmakers going to *do* about this problem?" never "Why is this happening now, to whom, and in what setting?" They may ask "why?" as noted in chapter 3, but never with a view to understanding the events from the actor's position. Kennan wanted the United States to respond diplomatically because the problem, as he had assessed it, was located in the realm of ideology, a war of competing ideas, not yet pushed to the point of incomprehensibility that would necessitate increased armaments and the combative disposition summarily chosen in the following years.

Now, I want to take this analysis one step further and estimate the outcome of an attempted diplomatic resolution to that Soviet hostility, because Kennan did not argue that the United States should begin negotiating peace with the Soviet Union. He argued that the United States should pursue diplomatic ties in which it would forge alliances with those countries surrounding the Soviet Union in order to shut Marxism-Leninism out of the international system as a credible alternative to democratic capitalism (the very same solution that President George W. Bush now recommends as policy toward China). Kennan's policy would not have required diplomats to meet with the Soviets to work out their differences; his policy foreclosed communication with the resistors as a viable policy option. The excessive description of

Soviet hostilities and historical biases of Marxism-Leninism against capitalist countries like the United States given by Kennan in his letter make it quite clear that there
was no possibility for diplomatic resolution of the problem. In fact, the clear indication of his message is that the Soviets are unreliable sycophants, saying one thing then
doing another. Either policy, the one recommended by Kennan or the one actually
pursued by Paul Nitze's Department of Defense, conformed to a policy of containment similar to that which is practiced in the schools as a response to the "threat" of
violence posed by shootings: The object of the policies is to never trust or consult the
policy object directly, but to slowly and deliberately locate it and shut it down, forcing it to conform to the dominant ordering principle.

In schools whose communities and workers find overt security measures distaste-
ful or harsh, programs designed to target nonconformist student behavior are becoming popular. Marketed as the "humanitarian" alternative, conflict management
programs, in which monitoring and surveillance of behavior are a significant feature
of violence prevention, are designed to mediate problems between students whose
anger interferes with school functioning. Not only are students asked to conform to
the rigid disciplinary concerns of the school administration through conflict management programs, but they are also asked to snitch on one another. What is so insidious about this ideological alternative is that it is justified as protectionism with
the intention of looking after the welfare of those nonconformists. For their own
good, peer reporting is rewarded by school administrators. Students in the new
"leadership" programs report students whose behavior, dress, and extracurricular performance deviates from the (invisible) norm of the school. Most disturbing, however,
is the revelation that medicated students are routinely monitored to ensure that they
do not lapse in taking their antidepressants. This might not be so disturbing if studies were not reporting 25 percent of the student population on medicine for depression. Yet, as a school administrator claims, the situation is under control now that
the normal students are cooperating with the disciplinary apparatus. She credits the
system of peer reporting because it "gives us 130 pairs of eyes."[3]

Other forms of monitoring not popularly associated with security technology
are more easily adopted yet infringe on student rights. Policies like dress codes
prevent students from wearing clothing that could conceal weapons or demonstrate consumer preferences. Also, the banning of backpacks or the adoption of a
clear-backpacks-only policy limit student confidence and trust. These forms of
discipline are the most popular because they, unlike metal detectors and body
searches, do not resemble prison security procedures.

Yet, these forms of monitoring and control do slowly chip away at the confidence
students may have and the trust they feel for one another. Specifically, these disciplinary procedures act as subtle forms of fear-based indoctrination. It does not matter how indirectly offensive the procedures may be (certainly the Cold War was indirectly offensive, primarily defensive) because they still undermine the public trust
necessary to develop the skills students need to cultivate to live and participate in a
healthy democracy. Furthermore, these measures also exist outside of public schools

in places of business where employees are forced to carry clear purses as the assumption is they might steal the merchandise.

So, returning to the environmental concerns covered in chapter 6, it has been demonstrated that bad conscience and ressentiment, throughout the public sphere, dominate the responses to crime, tragedy, and violence. Instead of asking, in a serious way, how these measures might affect the development of students' democratic skills, they are enacted in the name of safety and protection. Security has become the only response to school violence, but it will never solve the problem. Meanwhile, students will grow up as if they were inmates in a prison, not citizens in a free society.

If there is indeed a widespread problem concerning rage and violence in the United States, then more people need to use critical intelligence when assessing these violent episodes. Critical intelligence possessed by experienced individuals, Dewey thinks, is the primary guarantee of responsible practice in the public sphere. Critical intelligence is always the problem that public policy cannot encourage; in fact, public policy has the opposite effect on citizens because it only causes them to look to government for solutions to community problems. Kip Kinkel was not angry at the government, the school officials, the teachers, or the homework assignments. He was angry at the entire environment of the school and anyone in it was targeted by his rage. The same goes for Eric Harris and Dylan Klebold, Michael Carneal, and Barry Loukaitis and Luke Woodham. They had tangible elements in common: video game use, gun collecting, psychiatric encounters, and being picked on at school. The most salient factor tying them together, however, is intangible. It is the complex anger they felt toward the schools they attended and everything in them.

While it may indeed be true that a combination of problems is at work in fueling the rage that these boys felt toward their school environment, it is also true that what sutures them in a much more convincing way is the fact that they are repressed by the social control at work in the schools. This social control is acute at the school site, but it is also at work everywhere else in the society. While Americans have no problem endorsing economic liberalism and are able to support freedom of trade (because they like the economic advantages), they fail to realize that the price they pay for that freedom is paid by the repression of political and social factors in the society.

John Stuart Mill fought to articulate a reasonable balance for this dialectic between the rights of the individual and the necessity of limited social control, but Dewey demonstrates that they are inextricably linked and that the major problem in American society is the refusal to see their interconnectedness. When the advantages of economic success (and excess) leak into the political and social spheres in such a way that they are finally perceived, and perhaps experienced by some, the society does not know how to handle the seeming chaos and reacts with containment strategies that limit the freedom of the individual. What is needed is an acknowledgment that these two spheres (the political and the economic) are not separate. We may separate them analytically and rhetorically, but we experience them together without the knowledge that this is the case. Test scores, I agree, are very important in the grand scheme of things for American democracy. I mean, where will we find ourselves if we cannot continue to draw on capital reserves and have our technological goods? The problem, Dewey would say, is that we do not know how to use the technological goods intelligently if we continue to repress the social aspects of them. It is a bad use of technological culture; it is a cop-out.

Twenty years ago, school failure was not called failure, and performance did not indicate that someone had not perfected or mastered the system to fall into a perfect career, it simply meant that someone performed at his or her individuated capacity (and there was something personally satisfying in this determination) and was directed to the career option that matched his or her skills. I do not say this to argue that people cannot "be anything" if they "dream," but only to say that the unrealistic expectations fostered by an economic policy that does not recognize how it affects social life is damaging to the political culture of a democracy. In fact, it is demoralizing. Everybody is submitting to an ideal that cannot be accommodated by the society. This idealization will haunt the public when it fails and it already has in the form of school shootings.

But I ask you to look at the reaction to the students' admitted failure and assess for yourself whether or not you think the direction of the schools is positive. After all, where in all of this excessive attention to human tragedy is there a response that questions the perpetrators' motivation on an individual level, that acknowledges that these are people who experience their environments in a negative way? Nowhere. Yes, the media discusses the students' abject status in the school, but this only serves to legitimate the scapegoating that will inevitably follow in the media. The questions are asked in terms of the individual, an entity that was never acknowledged in the schooling process prior to the tragic act. People want to know why the student could not just fit in, not what is going on at the school that is problematic. Those in power in the schools are able to condemn them with impunity and pretend as if their hands are clean. In fact, they become the new victims.

As the public school system falls apart because of the pressures from outside sources such as testing facilities, funding agencies, parental concern, and cultural balkanization, the long-favored movement for charter schooling and voucher systems looks much more pleasant to many parents. Instead of trying to reform the public schools in a genuine way and look at what individuals working within the schools can do to make them better, the public prefers to allow this citizen-building institution to fall apart.

Alongside this, students are treated as if they are at once an adult and a child. They are held responsible for their actions if they are violent, but they are banned from experimenting with the cultural artifacts that are said to have caused them to act irresponsibly in the first place. D. W. Winnicott's insights concerning adolescent immaturity might be better used to describe most adults in American society, but until these adults "hold" firm in values and pay attention to the effect on their children, they will continue to witness seemingly random episodes of violence by students and to claim that they do not know "why" it is happening.

NOTES

1. George Kennan, "The Sources of Soviet Conduct" (original author published as "X"), *Foreign Affairs* (1947): 852–68.

2. Kennan, "Sources of Soviet Conduct," 861.

3. Dan Goodgame, "A Week in the Life of a High School: What It's Really Like since Columbine," *Time*, 25 October 1999, 66–112, 75.

References

Abram, Jan. *The Language of Winnicott.* London: Aronson, 1996.

Acker, Kathy. *Blood and Guts in High School.* New York: Grove Weidenfeld, 1989.

Adler, Mortimer J. *Reforming Education.* New York: MacMillan, 1988.

Albom, Mitch. *Tuesdays with Morrie.* Rockland, Mass.: Wheeler, 1998.

Alford, C. Fred. *What Evil Means to Us.* Ithaca, N.Y.: Cornell University Press, 1997.

Althusser, Louis. *Lenin and Philosophy.* Trans. Ben Brewster. New York: New Left, 1971.

American Association of University Women. *Hostile Hallways: The AAUW Survey of Sexual Harassment in America's Schools.* Research Report no. 923012. Washington, D.C.: Harris/Scholastic Research, 1993.

Apple, Michael W. *Education and Power.* 2nd ed. New York: Routledge, 1995.

———. "The Hidden Curriculum and the Nature of Conflict." In *Curriculum Theorizing: The Reconceptualists.* Ed. William Pinar. Berkeley, Calif.: McCutchan, 1975.

Arendt, Hannah. *Crises of the Republic: Lying in Politics, Civil Disobedience on Violence, Thoughts on Politics, Revolution.* New York: Harcourt Brace Jovanovich, 1972.

———. *Eichmann in Jerusalem: A Report on the Banality of Evil.* New York: Penguin, 1963.

———. *The Human Condition.* Chicago: University of Chicago Press, 1958.

Aristotle. *The Nicomachean Ethics.* New York: Dover, 1998.

Astor, Ron Avi, Heather Ann Meyer, and William J. Behre. "Unowned Places and Times: Maps and Interviews about Violence in High Schools." *American Educational Research Journal* 36, no. 1 (1999): 30–42.

Bachman, Richard. "Rage." In *The Bachman Books: Four Early Novels by Stephen King.* New York: Plume, 1977.

Barnes, Crystal Amanda, and Debi Martin-Morris. "I Was Shot at School: Personal Narrative of a School Shooting Incident." *Teen Magazine* (September 1998): 1.

Barret-Kriegel, Blandine. "Regicide and Parricide." In *I, Pierre Riviere, Having Slaughtered My Mother, My Sister and My Brother . . : A Case of Parricide in the Nineteenth Century.* Ed. Michel Foucault. New York: Random House, 1975.

Barthes, Roland. *The Rustle of Language.* Trans. Richard Howard. Berkeley: University of California Press, 1986.

The Basketball Diaries. Dir. Scott Kalvert. Island Pictures and New Line Cinema, 1995.

Baudrillard, Jean. *America.* Trans. Chris Turner. 1986. Reprint, New York: Verso, 1988.

———. *Impossible Exchange.* Trans. Chris Turner. New York: Verso, 2001.

———. *The Perfect Crime.* Trans. Chris Turner. New York: Verso, 1996.

———. *Symbolic Exchange and Death.* Trans. Ian Hamilton Grant. London: Sage, 1993.

———. *The System of Objects.* Trans. James Benedict. 1968. Reprint, New York: Verso, 1986.

De Becker, Gavin. *The Gift of Fear: And Other Survival Signals That Protect Us from Violence.* Boston: Little, Brown, 1997.

Belkin, Lisa. "Parents Blaming Parents." *New York Times Magazine,* 31 October 1999, 67, 78.

Benedek, Elissa P., and Dewey G. Cornell, eds. *Juvenile Homicide.* Washington, D.C.: American Psychiatric Press, 1989.

Berlant, Lauren. *The Queen of America Goes to Washington City: Essays on Sex and Citizenship.* Durham, N.C.: Duke University Press, 1997.

Bernall, Misty. *She Said Yes: The Unlikely Martyrdom of Cassie Bernall.* Farmington, Penn.: Plough, 1999.

Best, Joel. *Random Violence: How We Talk about New Crimes and New Victims.* Berkeley: University of California Press, 1999.

Biesta, Gert J. J. "You Say You Want a Revolution . . . Suggestions for the Impossible Future of Critical Pedagogy." *Educational Theory* 48, no. 4 (Fall 1998): 505.

Blanchot, Maurice. *The Writing of the Disaster.* Trans. Ann Smock. Lincoln: University of Nebraska Press, 1995.

Block, Alan. *I'm Only Bleeding: Education As the Practice of Violence against Children.* New York: Peter Lang, 1997.

Bloom, Allan. *The Closing of the American Mind.* New York: Simon and Schuster, 1987.

Bourdieu, Pierre. *The Logic of Practice.* Trans. Richard Nice. Stanford, Calif.: Stanford University Press, 1976.

———. *Masculine Domination.* Trans. Richard Nice. Stanford, Calif.: Stanford University Press, 2000.

Brown, Norman O. *Love's Body.* 1966. Reprint, Berkeley: University of California Press, 1990.

Browning, Christopher R. *Ordinary Men: Reserve Police Battalion 101 and the Final Solution in Poland.* New York: HarperCollins, 1992.

Burke, Kenneth. *A Grammar of Motives.* Los Angeles: University of California Press, 1969.

Butler, Judith. *Excitable Speech.* New York: Routledge, 1997.

———. *The Psychic Life of Power: Theories in Subjection.* Stanford: University of California Press, 1997.

Capell, Jon. "Kinkel Arraigned on 58 Counts." *MSNBC News,* 5 August 1998, at www.msnbc.com/local/KMTR/14815.asp (accessed March 1, 2002).

Caruth, Cathy, ed. *Trauma: Explorations in Memory.* Baltimore, Md.: Johns Hopkins University Press, 1995.

de Certeau, Michel. *Heterologies: Discourse on the Other.* Trans. Brian Massumi. Minneapolis: University of Minnesota Press, 1986.

Cervantes. *Don Quixote.* Trans. W. Starkie. New York: Penguin Classics, 1964.

Cherryholmes, Cleo H. *Power and Criticism: Poststructural Investigations in Education.* New York: Teacher's College Press, 1993.

Clark, Doug. Director and Promotion Coordinator of the National Network of Youth Ministries. E-mail to the author, 12 April 1999.

"The Columbine Tapes." *Time,* 20 December 1999, 40–59

Connell, R. W. *The Men and the Boys.* Berkeley: University of California Press, 2000.

Connelly, William E. "Beyond Good and Evil: The Ethical Sensibility of Michel Foucault." *Political Theory* 21 (1993): 365–89.

Cushmann, Phillip. *Constructing the Self, Constructing America: A Cultural History of Psychotherapy.* Reading, Mass.: Addison-Wesley, 1995.

Deleuze, Gilles, and Felix Guattari. *Anti-Oedipus: Capitalism and Schizophrenia.* Trans. Robert Hurley, Mark Seem, and Helen R. Lane. Minneapolis: University of Minnesota Press, 1983.

———. *A Thousand Plateaus: Capitalism and Schizophrenia.* Trans. Brian Massumi. Minneapolis: University of Minnesota Press, 1987.

Dewey, John. *Art As Experience.* 1934. Reprint, New York: Capricorn, 1959.

———. *Essays in Experimental Logic.* New York: Dover, 1916.

———. *Experience and Nature.* 1938. Reprint, New York: Dover, 1952.

———. *Lectures on the Psychological and Political Ethics: 1898.* 1898. Reprint, New York: Hafner, 1976.

———. *The School and the Society and the Child and the Curriculum.* Ed. Philip W. Jackson. 1900. Reprint, Chicago: University of Chicago Press, 1990.

Doan, Janice, and Devon Hodges. *From Klein to Kristeva: Psychoanalytic Feminism and the Search for the "Good Enough" Mother.* Ann Arbor: University of Michigan Press, 1992.

Doll, William. *A Post-modern Perspective on Curriculum.* New York: Columbia University Press, 1991.

Duff, Barry E. "'Event' in Dewey's Philosophy." *Educational Theory* 40, no. 4 (Winter 1990): 463–70.

Educational Theory 50, no. 3 (Summer 2000): 279–418.

Ellsworth, Elizabeth. "Why Doesn't This Feel Empowering? Working through the Repressive Myths of Critical Pedagogy." *Harvard Educational Review* 59, no. 3 (1989): 297–342.

Erickson, Kai. "Notes on Trauma and Community." In *Trauma: Explorations in Memory.* Ed. Cathy Caruth. Baltimore, Md.: Johns Hopkins University Press, 1995.

Erikson, Erik H. *Childhood and Society.* New York: Norton, 1950.

———. *Identity: Youth and Crisis.* New York: Norton, 1968.

Ewing, Charles Patrick. *Kids Who Kill: Bad Seeds and Baby Butchers—the Shocking True Stories of Juvenile Murders.* New York: Avon, 1990.

Farr, James. "John Dewey and American Political Science." *American Journal of Political Science* 43, no. 2 (1999): 520–41.

Felman, Shoshana. "Education and Crisis, or the Vicissitudes of Teaching." In *Trauma: Explorations in Memory.* Ed. Cathy Caruth. Baltimore, Md.: Johns Hopkins University Press, 1995.

Fitch, Lawrence. "Competency to Stand Trial and Criminal Responsibility in Juvenile Court." In *Juvenile Homicide.* Ed. Elissa Benedek and Dewey Cornell. Washington, D.C.: American Psychiatric Press, 1989.

Flower-MacCannell, Juliet. *The Regime of the Brother.* New York: Routledge, 1993.

Fortgang, Erika. "How They Got the Guns." *Rolling Stone Magazine* 51 (June 10, 1999): 51–53.

Foucault, Michel. *The Birth of the Clinic: An Archeology of Medical Perception.* New York: Vintage, 1994.

———. *Discipline and Punish: The Birth of the Prison.* Trans. Alan Sheridan. New York: Vintage, 1995.

———. *The History of Sexuality.* 3 vols. Trans. Robert Hurley. New York: Vintage, 1980.

———. "Nietzsche, Genealogy, History." In *The Foucault Reader.* Ed. Paul Rabinow. 1971. Reprint, New York: Pantheon, 1984.

Fraser, James W. *Between Church and State: Religion and Public Education in a Multicultural America.* New York: St. Martin's, 1999.

Freire, Paulo. *Pedagogy of the Oppressed.* Trans. Myra Bergman Ramos. New York: Continuum, 1970.

Freud, Sigmund. *Civilization and Its Discontents.* Trans. James Strachey. New York: Norton, 1961.

———. *Collected Papers: Clinical Papers, Papers on Technique.* Trans. Joan Riviere. 1924. Reprint, London: Hogarth, 1957.

———. "Creative Writers and Day-Dreaming." In *The Freud Reader.* Ed. Peter Gay. 1907. Reprint, New York: Norton, 1989.

"From Adolescent Angst to School Shootings: Patterns in the Rage." *New York Times,* 14 July 1998, A1.

Fuss, Diana. *Essentially Speaking.* New York: Routledge, 1989.

Gallop, Jane, ed. *Pedagogy: The Question of Impersonation.* Bloomington: Indiana University Press, 1995.

———. *Reading Lacan.* Ithaca, N.Y.: Cornell University Press, 1985.

Garbarino, James. *Lost Boys: Why Our Sons Turn Violent and How We Can Save Them.* New York: Free Press, 1999.

Giroux, Henry. *Disturbing Pleasures.* New York: Routledge, 1994.

Giroux, Henry, and Roger I. Simon, eds. *Popular Culture, Schooling and Everyday Life.* New York: Bergin and Garvey, 1989.

Goffman, Erving. *Frame Analysis: An Essay on the Organization of Experience.* Boston: Northeastern University Press, 1974.

Goldhagen, Daniel. *Hitler's Willing Executioners: Ordinary Germans and the Holocaust.* New York: Knopf, 1996.

Goodgame, Dan. "A Week in the Life of a High School: What It's Really Like since Columbine." *Time,* 25 October 1999, 66–112.

Gore, Jennifer. *The Struggle for Pedagogies.* London: Routledge, 1993.

Gourevitch, Peter. "The Second Image Reversed: The International Sources of Domestic Politics." *International Organization* 32, no. 4 (1978): 881–911.

Greene, Maxine. *Dialectic of Freedom.* New York: Teacher's College Press, 1988.

Grossberg, Lawrence. "The In-Difference of Television." *Screen* 28, no. 2 (1987): 28–45.

Grossman, Lt. Col. Dave. *On Killing: The Psychological Cost of Learning to Kill in War and Society.* Boston: Little, Brown, 1995.

Grumet, Madeleine R. *Bitter Milk: Women and Teaching.* Amherst: University of Massachusetts Press, 1988.

Heide, Kathleen. *Young Killers: The Challenge of Juvenile Homicide.* Thousand Oaks, Calif.: Sage, 1999.

Hernandez, Max. "Winnicott's 'Fear of Breakdown.'" *Diacritics* 28, no. 4 (1998): 134–43.

Herrnstein-Smith, Barbara. *Belief and Resistance: Dynamics of Contemporary Intellectual Controversy.* Cambridge, Mass.: Harvard University Press, 1997.

Hickman, Larry A., ed. *Reading Dewey: Interpretations for a Postmodern Generation.* Bloomington: Indiana University Press, 1998.

Hirsch, E. D., Jr. "The Tests We Need and Why We Don't Quite Have Them." *Education Week* 14, no. 21 (February 2, 2000).

Hirschberg, Margaret. "The Real of Edye-Icon: Edye Smith, the Oklahoma City Bombing and the Mobilization of Ideologies." *Genders* 29 (1999): 1–14.

Hobbes, Thomas. *Leviathan.* 1652. Reprint, London: Everyman's Library, 1973.

Honig, Bonnie. *Political Theory and the Displacement of Politics.* Ithaca: Cornell University Press, 1993.

hooks, bell. *Killing Rage: Ending Racism.* New York: Henry Holt, 1995.

———. *Teaching to Transgress: Education As the Practice of Freedom.* New York: Routledge, 1994.

"How to Spot a Troubled Kid: Special Report on School Violence." *Time,* 31 May 1999, 32–58.

Illich, Ivan. *Deschooling Society.* New York: Harper and Row, 1970.

James, William. *Pragmatism and the Meaning of Truth.* Ed. A. J. Ayer. Cambridge, Mass.: Harvard University Press, 1975.

Johnson, Chalmers. *Blowback: The Costs and Consequences of American Empire.* New York: Owl, 2000.

Kant, Immanuel. *Perpetual Peace and Other Essays.* Trans. Ted Humphrey. 1784. Reprint, Indianapolis, Ind.: Hackett, 1983.

Keenan, Thomas. *Fables of Responsibility.* Palo Alto, Calif.: Stanford University Press, 1997.

Kellerman, Jonathan. *Savage Spawn: Reflections on Violent Children.* New York: Ballantine, 1999.

Kennan, George. "The Sources of Soviet Conduct" (original author published as "X"). *Foreign Affairs* (1947): 852–68.

Kent, Jamon. Springfield Superintendent of Schools, *School Violence Prevention.* Part 2. White House, 15 October 1998.

Kernberg. Otto F. *Object Relations Theory and Clinical Psycho-Analysis.* New York: Aronson, 1976.

"The Killer at Thurston High." *Frontline,* 18 January 2000.

Klein, Melanie. *The Psycho-Analysis of Children.* Trans. Alix Strachey. London: Hogarth, 1937.

Klein, Melanie, and Joan Riviere. *Love, Hate and Reparation.* London: Hogarth, 1937.

Kliebard, Herbert M. *The Struggle for the American Curriculum: 1893–1958.* 2nd ed. New York: Routledge, 1995.

Knight-Abowitz, Kathleen. "Reclaiming Community." *Educational Theory* 49, no. 2 (1999): 143–59.

Labi, Nadya. "The Hunter and the Choir Boy." *Time,* 6 April 1998, 2–3.

Laclau, Ernesto, ed. *New Reflections on the Revolution of Our Time.* London: Verso, 1990.

Laclau, Ernesto, and Chantal Mouffe. *Hegemony and Socialist Strategy: Towards a Radical Democratic Politics.* London: Verso, 1985.

Laplanche, Jean, and J.-B. Pontalis. *The Language of Psycho-Analysis.* Trans. Donald Nicholson-Smith. New York: Norton, 1973.

Lather, Patti. *Getting Smart: Feminist Research and Pedagogy with/in the Postmodern.* New York: Routledge, 1991.

Lesko, Nancy. *Act Your Age!: The Cultural Construction of Adolescence.* New York: Routledge and Falmer, 2001.

"Liberal Unfriendly Place: Jonesboro, Arkansas." At www.turnleft.com/places/jonesboro.html (accessed March 1, 2002).

Lifton, Robert Jay. *Nazi Doctors: Medical Killing and the Psychology of Genocide.* New York: Basic, 1986.

Maddock-Dillon, Elizabeth. "Fear of Formalism: Kant, Twain and Cultural Studies in American Literature." *Diacritics* 27, no. 4 (Winter 1997): 46–69.

Males, Mike A. *The Scapegoat Generation: America's War on Adolescents.* Monroe, Maine: Common Courage, 1996.

de Man, Paul. *The Resistance to Theory.* Minneapolis: University of Minnesota Press, 1993.

Martusewicz, Rebecca A., and William M. Reynolds, eds. *Inside Out: Contemporary Critical Perspectives in Education.* New York: St. Martin's, 1994.

Marx, Karl. *Capital.* 3 vols. 1867. Reprint, New York: International, 1992.

Mastrosimone, William. *Bang, Bang, You're Dead.* 1999, at www.bangbangyouredead.com (accessed April 8, 1999).

———. "Notes from the Playwright." 1999, at www.bangbangyouredead.com/authornotes. html (accessed April 8, 1999).

McLaren, Peter. *Critical Pedagogy and Predatory Culture.* New York: Routledge, 1995.

———. "Decentering Culture: Postmodernism, Resistance, and Critical Pedagogy." In *Current Perspectives on the Culture of Schools.* Ed. Nancy B. Wyner. Cambridge, Mass.: Brookline, 1991.

———. *Life in Schools: An Introduction to Critical Pedagogy in the Foundations of Education.* New York: Longman, 1989.

———. *Revolutionary Multiculturalism: Pedagogies of Dissent for the New Millennium.* Boulder, Colo.: Westview, 1997.

———. *Schooling As a Ritual Performance: Towards a Political Economy of Educational Symbols and Gestures.* New York: Routledge, 1986.

Melson, Robert F. *Revolution and Genocide.* Chicago: University of Chicago Press, 1993.

Michaels, Joseph. "Enuresis in Murderous Aggressive Children and Adolescents." *Archives of General Psychiatry* 94 (1961). Cited in Charles Patrick Ewing, *Kids Who Kill* (New York: Lexington, 1990), 10–11.

Milgram, Stanley. *Obedience to Authority: An Experimental View.* New York: Harper and Row, 1974.

Miller, Mark Crispin. *Boxed In: The Culture of T.V.* Evanston, Ill.: Northwestern University Press, 1988.

Mitchell, Emily. "O, Say, Can You Pray? A Grass-Roots Ritual by Young Christians Test Church and State Borders." *Time,* 28 September's 1998.

Mitchell, Juliet. "Trauma, Recognition, and the Place of Language." *Diacritics* 28, no. 4 (1998): 121–33.

Morrione, Deems D. "Sublime Monsters and Virtual Children." Ph.D. diss., Purdue University, 2002.

Mouffe, Chantal, and Ernesto Laclau. *Hegemony and Socialist Strategy.* London: Verso, 1985.

Nadel, Alan. *Containment Culture: American Narratives, Postmodernism, and the Atomic Age.* Durham, N.C.: Duke University Press, 1995.

National Institute of Justice. "Guns in America: National Survey on Private Ownership and Use of Firearms." May 1991, at www.ncjrs.org/txtfiles/165476.txt (accessed 7 February 2002).

National Network of Youth Ministries. "Network Covenant." 2 February 1999, at www.nnym.org (accessed March 1, 2002).

Nietzsche, Friedrich. *Beyond Good and Evil: Prelude to a Philosophy of the Future.* Trans. Walter Kaufmann. 1886. Reprint, New York: Vintage, 1966.

———. *Daybreak: Thoughts on the Prejudices of Morality.* Ed. Maudemarie Clark and Brian Leiter, and trans. R. J. Hollingdale. 1881. Reprint, New York: Cambridge University Press, 1997.

———. *The Gay Science.* Trans. Walter Kaufmann. 1882. Reprint, New York: Vintage, 1974.

———. *Human, All Too Human.* Trans. Marion Faber. 1878. Reprint, Lincoln: University of Nebraska Press, 1984.

———. *On the Advantage and Disadvantage of History for Life.* Trans. Peter Preuss. Indianapolis, Ind.: Hackett, 1980.

———. *On the Genealogy of Morals.* Trans. Walter Kaufmann and R. J. Hollingdale. 1887. Reprint, New York: Vintage, 1967.

———. *Thus Spoke Zarathustra.* Trans. Walter Kaufmann. 1883. Reprint, New York: Penguin, 1966.

Ortega y Gasset, José. *Man and Crisis.* Trans. Mildred Adams. New York: Norton, 1958.

———. *Man and People.* Trans. Willard R. Trask. New York: Norton, 1957.

Peirce, Charles Sanders. *Philosophical Writings.* New York: Dover, 1955.

Phillips, Adam. *The Beast in the Nursery: On Curiosity and Other Appetites.* New York: Vintage, 1998.

———. *On Kissing, Tickling and Being Bored: Psychoanalytic Essays on the Unexamined Life.* Cambridge, Mass.: Harvard University Press, 1993.

Phillips, Adam. *Winnicott.* Cambridge, Mass.: Harvard University Press, 1988.

Pinar, William F., ed. *Curriculum: Toward New Identities.* New York: Garland, 1998.

———. *Queer Theory in Education.* New York: Erlbaum, 1998.

Pinar, William F., William Reynolds, Patrick Slattery, and Peter Taubman. *Understanding Curriculum.* New York: Lang, 1995.

Pipher, Mary Bray. *Reviving Ophelia: Saving the Selves of Adolescent Girls.* New York: Putnam, 1994.

Plato. *Symposium.* Trans. Walter Hamilton. New York: Penguin, 1951.

Poe, Edgar Allen. "The Black Cat." In *Tales of Terror and Detection.* 1843. Reprint, New York: Dover, 1995.

Pollack, William. *Real Boys: Rescuing Our Sons from the Myths of Boyhood.* New York: Henry Holt, 1998.

Popkewitz, Thomas S. "Dewey, Vygotsky and the Social Administration of the Individual: Constructivist Pedagogy As Systems of Ideas in Historical Spaces." *American Educational Research Journal* 35, no. 4 (1999): 535–70.

Putnam, Robert D. *Bowling Alone: Civic Disengagement in America.* New York: Simon and Schuster, 1999.

Rauch, Angelika. "Post-traumatic Hermeneutics: Melancholia in the Wake of Trauma." *Diacritics* 28, no. 4 (1998): 111–20.

Readings, Bill. *The University in Ruins.* Cambridge, Mass.: Harvard University Press, 1995.

"Refugees Cheer Clintons in Macedonian Camp." *CNN,* 22 June 1999, at www.cnn.com/ WORLD/europe/9906/22/clinton.04/index.html (accessed March 1, 2002).

Ronell, Avital. *Crack Wars: Literature, Addiction, Mania.* Lincoln: University of Nebraska Press, 1990.

Rorty, Richard. *Contingency, Irony and Solidarity.* Cambridge: Cambridge University Press, 1989.

Rose, Jacqueline. *War in the Nursery.* London: Blackwell, 1993.

Rosenberg, Sharon, and Roger I. Simon. "Beyond the Logic of Emblematization: Remembering and Learning from the Montreal Massacre." *Educational Theory* 50, no. 2 (2000): 133–55.

Rosenblaum, Nancy L. "Compelled Association." In *Freedom of Association*. Ed. Amy Gutmann. Princeton, N.J.: Princeton University Press, 1998.

Rousseau, Jean Jacques. *Reveries of a Solitary Walker.* Trans. Peter France. London: Penguin, 1979.

———. *The Social Contract and Discourses.* Trans. G. D. H. Cold. London: Everyman, 1973.

Rubenstein, Diane S. "Chicks with Dicks: Transgendering the Presidency." Paper presented at the annual meeting of the Western Political Science Association, Los Angeles, California, March 1998.

———. *What's Left? The Ecole Normale Supérieure and the Right.* Madison: University of Wisconsin Press, 1990.

Saltman, Kenneth. *Collateral Damage.* Lanham, Md.: Rowman and Littlefield, 2000.

"School Safety and Youth Violence, Panel I." White House Conference on School Safety, Departments of Education and Justice, Washington, D.C., 15 October 1998.

"School Shooting Numbers Actually Down." *The Gottlieb-Tartaro Report* (Second Amendment Foundation) 40 (April 1998).

Seltzer, Mark. *Bodies and Machines.* New York: Routledge, 1992.

———. "Wound Culture: Trauma in the Pathological Public Sphere." *October* 80 (1997): 3–26.

Shapiro, Michael. *Violent Cartographies: Mapping Cultures of War.* Minneapolis: University of Minnesota Press, 1997.

Shklar, Judith. *American Citizenship: The Quest for Inclusion.* Cambridge, Mass.: Harvard University Press, 1991.

Silverman, Kaja. *Male Subjectivity at the Margins.* London: Routledge, 1992.

Slattery, Patrick. *Curriculum Development in the Postmodern Era.* New York: Garland, 1995.

Spivak, Gayatri Chakavorty. *Outside-In the Teaching Machine.* London: Routledge, 1993.

Spring, Joel. *Conflict of Interests: The Politics of American Education.* New York: Longman, 1988.

———. *The Sorting Machine: National Education Policy since 1945.* New York: McKay, 1976.

———. *The Sorting Machine Revisited: National Education Policy since 1945: Updated Edition.* New York: Longman, 1989.

———. *Wheels in the Head: Educational Philosophies of Authority, Freedom and Culture from Socrates to Paulo Freire.* New York: McGraw-Hill, 1994.

Sturken, Marita. "The Remembering of Forgetting: Recovered Memory and the Question of Experience." *Social Text* 57, no.16 (1998): 103–26.

Sullivan, Randall. "A Boy's Life: Kip Kinkel and the Springfield, Oregon Shooting, Part I." *Rolling Stone Magazine,* 17 September 1998, 76–85, 106–7.

———. "A Boy's Life: Part 2." *Rolling Stone Magazine,* 1 October 1998, 46–54, 72.

Sullivan, Shannon. "Democracy and the Individual: To What Extent Is Dewey's Reconstruction Nietzsche's Self-Overcoming?" *Philosophy Today* (Summer 1997): 299–312.

Swanson, Elissa. "Killers Start Sad and Crazy: Mental Illness and the Betrayal of Kipland Kinkel." *Oregon Law Review* 79, no. 4 (Winter 2000): 1081–1120.

Taylor, Charles. "To Follow a Rule . . ." In *Pierre Bourdieu: Critical Investigations.* Ed. Craig J. Calhoun, Edward Lipuma, and Moishe Postone. Chicago: University of Chicago Press, 1993.

"Teen Rage." *The Montel Williams Show.* 8 October 1998. Replayed 10 June 1999.

Theweleit, Klaus. *Male Fantasies.* 2 vols. Trans. Erica Carter and Chris Turner. Minneapolis: University of Minnesota Press, 1989.

Tinder, Glenn. "Transcending Tragedy: The Idea of Civility." *American Political Science Review* 68, no. 2 (June 1974): 547–60.

Trend, David. *The Crisis of Meaning in Culture and Education*. Minneapolis: University of Minnesota Press, 1995.

Tuesdays with Morrie. Dir. Mick Jackson. ABC, 1999.

Wallace, Chris. "Boy on the Brink." *20/20*, 9 February 2000.

Wallace, Jo-Ann. "Technologies of the Child: Towards a Theory of the Child Subject." *Textual Practice* 9, no. 2 (1995): 285–302.

Watkins, W. "Black Curriculum Orientations: A Preliminary Inquiry." *Harvard Educational Review* 63, no. 3 (1998): 321–38.

Wenner, Jann. "Guns and Violence." *Rolling Stone Magazine*, 10 June 1999, 45–49.

Wexler, Philip. *Becoming Somebody: Towards a Social Psychology of School*. London: Falmer, 1992.

———. *Social Analysis of Education: After the New Sociology*. Boston: Routledge and Kegan Paul, 1987.

Willis, Paul. *Learning to Labour*. Hampshire, UK: Gower, 1977.

Wilkinson, Peter, and Matt Hendrickson. "Humiliation and Revenge: The Story of Reb and VoDKa." *Rolling Stone Magazine*, 10 June 1999, 49–51.

Winnicott, D. W. *Deprivation and Delinquency*. New York: Tavistock, 1984.

———. *Home Is Where We Start From: Essays by a Psycho-Analyst*. New York: Norton, 1986.

———. *The Maturational Processes and the Facilitating Environment*. New York: International Universities Press, 1965.

———. *Playing and Reality*. New York: Basic, 1971.

———. *Psycho-Analytic Explorations*. Ed. Clare Winnicott, Ray Shepherd, and Madeleine Davis. Cambridge, Mass.: Harvard University Press, 1989.

———. *Thinking about Children*. Reading, Mass.: Addison-Wesley, 1996.

Zerilli, Linda. "Doing without Knowing." *Political Theory* 26, no. 4 (1998): 435–58.

Zizek, Slavoj. *The Plague of Fantasies*. London: Verso, 1997.

———. *The Sublime Object of Ideology*. London: Verso, 1989.

Index

adolescence, 20, 31–33, 71, 82–83, 87–88n17, 112; critical moment of, 155; discrimination during, 145–46; essence of, 113; fantasy and, 110–12, 145; "normal," 31–32; practical experience during, 154; psychopathology in, 31; rebellion during, 157; virtual space of, 110; Winnicott, D. W. on, 143, 146, 147–53, 154–55, 157, 196

adolescent(s): acting out, 152; behavior, 33; citizenship of, 156; in contemporary society, 20; development, 111–12; gun fetishism in, 36; hate/aggression in, 144; media portrayal of, 145; misrecognition of, 149; positive containment of, 145; reared in hostile environment, 112–13; relative autonomy of, 147; religion as rebellion by, 113; repression of, 143–44; role of father for, 157; as scapegoats, 32–34; socially constructed term of, 20; stereotyping of, 111; violence, 33; wanting freedom, 3

adult: anxiety, 76; fear of children, 33; reaction to school shootings, 22–23; role in educative process, 168; supervision of violence, 168

adult-child binary, 40

aggression, 60, 83
aggressivity, 6, 7
Albom, Mitch, 164n30
Alcibiades, 177, 187n17
Althusser, Louis, 36, 119, 147, 182
Althusserian theory, 23, 95, 172
American: citizenship, 14, 117, 118, 119–20; culture, 33, 55, 117, 118, 137, 138; democracy, 9, 120, 195–96; family, 103; society, 63, 139, 168
American Medical Association, 73
American Psychological Association, 82, 140n4
analysis, child, 159, 160, 161
ancient Greece, 177–78
animal torture, 31, 71–75, 87n4, 115n24
antidepressants, 194
antisocial behavior, 8, 71, 154–55
anxiety, 76, 168, 170, 180–85
Apple, Michael W., 3, 15n5, 37, 119, 140n7
Arendt, Hannah, 46
Art as Experience (Dewey), 130
atheism, 22–23, 95
at-risk students, 33, 42n28
Augustus, Frank, 36
authority figures, 2, 47
autonomy, 167, 175

About the Author

Julie A. Webber is assistant professor of politics and government at Illinois State University.